OXFORD READINGS IN PHILOSOPHY

THE PHILOSOPHY OF LIN

Other volumes are in preparation

THE PHILOSOPHY OF LINGUISTICS

EDITED BY

JERROLD J. KATZ

OXFORD UNIVERSITY PRESS
1985

Oxford University Press, Walton Street, Oxford, OX2 6DP

London New York Toronto
Delhi Bombay Calcutta Madras Karachi
Kuala Lumpur Singapore Hong Kong Tokoyo
Nairobi Dar es Salaam Cape Town
Melbourne Auckland

and associated companies in
Beirut Berlin Ibadan Mexico City Nicosia

Oxford is a trade mark of Oxford University Press

Published in the United States
by Oxford University Press, New York

Introduction and selection © Oxford University Press 1985

British Library Cataloguing in Publication Data
The Philosophy of Linguistics. —(Oxford
readings in philosophy)
1. Linguistics—Philosophy
I. Katz, Jerrold J.
410'.1   P121
ISBN 0-19-875070-6
ISBN 0-19-875065-X (pbk.)

Library of Congress Cataloging in Publication Data
Main entry under title:
The Philosophy of linguistics.
(Oxford readings in philosophy)
Bibliography: p.
Includes index.
1. Linguistics—Philosophy.   I. Katz, Jerrold J.
II. Series.
P121.P437   1985   410'.1   84-18933
ISBN 0-19-875070-6
ISBN 0-19-875065-X (pbk.)

Typeset by Joshua Associates, Oxford
Printed in Great Britain
at the University Press, Oxford
by David Stanford
Printer to the University

CONTENTS

INTRODUCTION

THERE have been two linguistic turns in twentieth-century philosophy. In the first and most celebrated, *language* became the central concern of philosophers who broke with nineteenth-century idealistic philosophy. In the second, *linguistics* became the central concern of philosophers who wished to put their thinking about language on a scientific basis. This book is an attempt to stimulate a third linguistic turn, one in which the *foundations of linguistics* becomes the central concern of philosophers who have tried to think about language from the perspective of the science of language.

This book is a reader in the philosophy of linguistics, which is conceived as a branch of philosophy parallel to the philosophy of mathematics, the philosophy of logic, and the philosophy of physics. The philosophy of linguistics has a potential importance for twentieth-century philosophy that those established branches of philosophical investigation lack. Its potential derives from the fact that it concerns the foundations of the science whose object of study, language, has been central to philosophy in this century.

There is no doubt about the centrality of language to twentieth-century philosophy. As Ryle once wrote:

The story of twentieth-century philosophy is very largely the story of [the linguistic] notion of sense or meaning. Meanings . . . are what Moore's analyses have been analyses of; meanings are what Russell's logical atoms were atoms of; meanings, in one sense but not in another, were what Russell's 'incomplete symbols' were bereft of; meanings are what logical considerations prohibit to the antinomy-generating forms of words on which Frege and Russell had tried to found arithmetic; meanings are what the members of the Vienna Circle proffered a litmus paper for; meanings are what the *Tractatus*, with certain qualifications, denies to the would-be propositions both of Formal Logic and of philosophy; and yet meanings are just what, in different ways, philosophy and logic are *ex officio* about.[1]

---

[1] G. Ryle, 'Introduction', in *The Revolution in Philosophy*, Macmillan & Co. Ltd., London, 1960, p. 8.

In perhaps the most influential book in twentieth-century philosophy, the *Tractatus Logico-Philosophicus*, Wittgenstein wrote:

> Most questions and propositions of the philosophers result from the fact that we do not understand the logic of our language. . . . All philosophy is 'Critique of language' . . .[2]

The most influential schools of thought in this century—logical empiricism, ordinary language philosophy, and Wittgenstein's two philosophies—tried to interpret traditional philosophical questions linguistically and to give, according to their particular conception of language, linguistic solutions or dissolutions. Even today one finds a prominent philosopher like Dummett asserting that

> . . . philosophy has, as its first if not its only task, the analysis of meanings, . . . the theory of meaning . . . is the foundation of all philosophy, and not epistemology as Descartes misled us into believing.[3]

Not every contemporary Anglo–American philosopher would agree with Dummett's claim, but all would agree that the salient characteristic of twentieth-century philosophy has been its emphasis on language.

The linguistic philosophers of the first linguistic turn paid no attention to scientific linguistics (though they sometimes pointed to old-fashioned grammar to prove that the study of the grammatical syntax of natural languages is not philosophically promising). Each version of linguistic philosophy—logical empiricism, ordinary language philosophy, and Wittgenstein's philosophies—pursued a philosophical or logistic approach to language. Each diagnosed philosophical problems as due to confusion about language, in some sense a consequence of philosophers going beyond the limits of language. Their constructive task was to delineate the limits of language. In the *Tractatus Logico-Philosophicus*, Wittgenstein praised Russell for showing 'that the apparent logical form of the proposition need not be its real form' and undertook to show that when the real form of philosophical propositions is revealed most of them turn out to be 'not false, but senseless'.[4] Moore sought to develop ways to get behind the superficial grammatical similarity of sentences like 'Tame tigers exist' and 'Tame tigers growl' on the basis of a semantic analysis.[5] Carnap sought to construct a logical syntax to make up for the alleged failure of grammatical syntax to

[2] L. Wittgenstein, *Tractatus Logico-Philosophicus*, Routledge & Kegan Paul Ltd., London, 1922, p. 63.

[3] M. Dummett, *Frege: Philosophy of Language*, Duckworth, London, 1973, p. 669.

[4] L. Wittgenstein, op. cit., p. 63.

[5] G. E. Moore, 'Is Existence a Predicate?', in *Logic and Language*, Second Series, ed. A. G. N. Flew, Basil Blackwell, Oxford, 1955, pp. 82–93.

expose sentences like 'Caesar is a prime number' as pseudo-statements.[6] Ryle sought to explain 'systematically misleading expressions' and 'category mistakes' and exhibit them as the source of metaphysical views like Cartesian dualism.[7] In the *Philosophical Investigations*, Wittgenstein also wanted to show that philosophical propositions are not false but senseless, although being senseless was now a matter of using words eccentrically rather than at variance with an ideal calculus.[8] But these linguistic philosophers paid no serious attention to how the scientific study of language might specify the limits of the meaningful.

In the early fifties, the second linguistic turn was undertaken, by philosophers who felt the need to inform their thinking about language by what the science of language had to say. Quine was the first Anglo-American philosopher to investigate what the science of language says about language. In 'The Problem of Meaning in Linguistics',[9] and in subsequent papers such as 'Two Dogmas of Empiricism',[10] he examined current linguistics and applied the linguistic theories he found to philosophical issues. Quine thereby set an example of how linguistics could be used in philosophy.

The second linguistic turn got underway when linguistic philosophers, following Quine's example, discovered a philosophically more interesting form of linguistics than Quine had access to and when philosophically minded linguists, principally Chomsky, began to develop the philosophical applications of some of their linguistic ideas. Fodor and Katz argued that philosophical attempts to separate sense from nonsense and reveal the logical structure in natural language suffered from defects that only sophistication in linguistics could overcome.[11] Carnap and other logical empiricists tried to do the job by constructing elaborate systems of formal syntax and semantics, but they constructed them without regard for, and therefore without relevance to, natural language. Carnap and the logical empiricists assumed that the then current theories of grammatical syntax were the last word on the grammar of natural

[6] R. Carnap, 'The Elimination of Metaphysics through the Logical Analysis of Language', in *Logical Positivism*, ed. A. J. Ayer, The Free Press, Glencoe, 1959, pp. 60–81.

[7] G. Ryle, *The Concept of Mind*, Barnes & Noble, New York, 1949; 'Systematically Misleading Expressions', in *Logic and Language*, First Series, ed. A. G. N. Flew, Basil Blackwell, Oxford, 1955, pp. 11–36.

[8] L. Wittgenstein, *Philosophical Investigations*, Basil Blackwell, Oxford, 1953.

[9] W. V. O. Quine, *From a Logical Point of View*, Harper & Row, Publishers, 1953, pp. 47–64.

[10] Ibid., pp. 20–46.

[11] J. A. Fodor and J. J. Katz, 'What's Wrong with the Philosophy of Language?', *Inquiry*, Volume 8, 1962, pp. 197–237.

language. But they gave no reason to believe that, in a more developed form, grammatical syntax would still be unable to expose pseudo-sentences and reveal logical structure. On the other hand, Ryle and other ordinary language philosophers were admirably faithful to the facts of natural language use, but they failed to give attention to the construction of theories that could substantiate philosophical significant structure. Ryle attributed the oddity of the sentence 'She came home in a carriage and in tears' to a category mistake, but it might instead be a stylistic *faux pas*. Without a theory that explains the kinds of deviance found in connection with natural language, no final decision in such cases is possible. Fodor and Katz claimed that attention to the most advanced work linguistics would preserve the logical empiricist's concern with theory and formalization as well as the ordinary language philosopher's fidelity to the facts of natural language use, while at the same time compensating for the defects of both approaches.

The principal factor in convincing philosophers of the relevance of linguistics to philosophy was Chomsky's application of his linguistic research to philosophical questions. In the early stages of the second linguistic turn, two features of Chomsky's work played a major role. One feature was the new theory of grammatical syntax which resulted from the combined work of Harris and Chomsky: the theory of generative transformational grammar made famous in philosophy with the publication in 1957 of Chomsky's *Syntactic Structures*.[12] The new theory was radically different from and went well beyond anything that Carnap had in mind when he advocated supplementing theories of grammatical syntax with theories of logical syntax. The other feature was Chomsky's formulation of linguistic theory as a nativist theory of language learning and his use of the theory to revive the rationalist theory of innate ideas.

Philosophers quickly noticed the relevance and importance of Chomsky's work. Two early examples: before his death in 1960, J. L. Austin had planned to use Chomsky's *Syntactic Structures* in his 'Saturday morning' discussion group; four years after the publication of Chomsky's 'Explanatory Models in Linguistics', which put forth his nativist formulation of linguistic theory, the American Philosophical Association held a symposium in which Chomsky debated his nativism with Goodman and Putnam.[13] In subsequent years, there were a number

[12] N. Chomsky, *Syntactic Structures*, Mouton & Co., 's-Gravenhage, 1957.
[13] N. Chomsky, H. Putnam, and N. Goodman, 'Symposium on Innate Ideas', *Boston Studies in the Philosophy of Science*, Volume III, The Humanities Press, New York, 1968, pp. 81-107. Reprinted in *The Philosophy of Language*, ed. J. R. Searle, Oxford University Press, Oxford, 1971, pp. 121-44.

of examples showing that attention to work in linguistics could shed a good deal of light on philosophically significant aspects of language. It will be useful to discuss a few such examples.

The theory of transformational grammar has led to a way of capturing something very close to the philosopher's distinction between the apparent or superficial grammatical structure of sentences and their real or deep logical structure.[14] Transformational grammar represents the structure of a sentence at different levels, with a phonetic level representing its surface structure and phonological, syntactic, and semantic levels representing its underlying structure. This form of multiple representation enables the transformational grammarian to reveal the real logical differences between sentences that are superficially similar in their surface structure. A time-honoured example is the pair of sentences 'John is easy to please' and 'John is eager to please'.[15] Even though their surface structure masks their logical differences, we can, of course, tell that 'John' is the object of the verb 'please' in the first sentence, but its subject in the second. Transformational theory provides a systematic formalization of such intuitively determined facts. In a transformational grammar of English, the two sentences would be derived from quite different structures, the first containing a clause of the form 'NP-pleases-John' and the second containing a corresponding clause of the form 'John-pleases-NP'.[16] Similarly, hidden differences in semantic structure, such as between 'John is a suspended judge' and 'Louie is a suspected criminal' (the first implies that John was a judge while the second does not imply that Louie was a criminal), can be explained in terms of the representations of these sentences at the semantic level where their meaning is described as a function of the meanings of 'suspend' and 'suspect' as well as the other words in them. Thus, generative transformational grammar opens the way for studying logical form as part of sentence grammar.[17]

[14] These developments are presented in J. J. Katz and P. Postal, *An Integrated Theory of Linguistic Descriptions*, MIT Press, Cambridge, Mass., 1964, and N. Chomsky, *Aspects of the Theory of Syntax*, MIT Press, Cambridge, Mass., 1965.

[15] These examples continue to be of theoretical interest. See N. Chomsky, 'On WH-Movement', in *Formal Syntax*, eds. P. W. Culicover, T. Wasow, and A. Akmajian, Academic Press, New York, 1977, pp. 102–11.

[16] N. Chomsky, 'Current Issues in Linguistic Theory', Mouton & Co., The Hague, 1964, pp. 34–50.

[17] Wittgenstein had doubts about the possibility of penetrating the grammatical disguise in which language clothes logical form even at the time he wrote the *Tractatus* (see p. 63). These doubts are surely one of the things behind his abandonment of the *Tractatus* view for the view in the *Philosophical Investigations*.

Another example of the contribution that linguistics has made to our understanding of philosophical issues is Chomsky's revival of the rationalist position on innate knowledge. Two aspects of Chomsky's linguistics were relevant. One was the interpretation of grammars as theories of an ideal speaker's knowledge of the language; the other was the interpretation of the theory of grammars, linguistic theory, as a theory of an ideal language learner's initial knowledge of language.[18] Language acquisition was pictured as a process in which innate knowledge of the universals of language gives rise, under appropriate exposure to utterances of a particular language, to acquired knowledge of its structure. Chomsky argued for the necessity of rich innate knowledge on the grounds that the phonetic form of utterances provides the language learner with information that is too impoverished for acquisition to take place on the basis of environmental input alone. Chomsky argued further that, in order to explain the speed and uniformity of children's acquisition of language, it is necessary to hypothesize that the innate knowledge of the child includes grammars for all human languages, a simplicity metric for ordering these grammars, and a device for testing the simplest grammars against the evidence from the language to which the child is exposed.[19]

Chomsky's revival of the rationalist position on innate knowledge has led to a number of philosophically fruitful debates. We have already mentioned the debate with Goodman and Putnam over nativism. Another debate arose over the related issue of whether the principles of a generative grammar can, in any appropriate sense, be taken as knowledge. Chomsky's rationalism depends on so construing them, but it has not been clear to many philosophers that his is a legitimate construal. The principles are highly abstract generative rules which one has no explicit awareness of until one is introduced to the subject of generative grammar. Since, according to Chomsky, those rules constitute the knowledge on which one's use of language rests, and since one does not have conscious knowledge of such abstract rules, Chomsky must claim that one knows them tacitly or unconsciously. Philosophers have been reluctant to accept Chomsky's claim.[20] The principles in

---

[18] *Aspects of the Theory of Syntax*, pp. 3–15.

[19] N. Chomsky, *Language and Mind*, Harcourt, Brace, & World, Inc., New York, 1968, pp. 18–59.

[20] There has been a good deal of discussion on these complexities. See *Aspects of the Theory of Syntax*, pp. 3–15; G. Harman, 'Psychological Aspects of the Theory of Syntax', *The Journal of Philosophy*, Volume LXIV, 1967, pp. 75–87; N. Chomsky, 'Linguistics and Philosophy', in *Language and Philosophy*, ed. S. Hook, New York University Press, New York, 1969, pp. 51–94; G. Harman, 'Linguistic Competence and Empiricism', in *Language and Philosophy*, pp. 143–

question seem to be neither *knowledge how* nor *knowledge that*. How, moreover, can such tacit principles be distinguished from the principles underlying the maintenance of balance in bicycle riding, to which no one is inclined to grant epistemic status? Furthermore, on what basis can we decide whether the speakers of a language use the principles of some particular grammar when, first, the speakers themselves have no conscious awareness of using them, and second, there are indefinitely many other sets of principles that could be used to produce the same speech?

A still further example of the relevance of Chomskian linguistics to philosophy is the challenge its methodology poses to extensionalist views of language and logic that have been erected on Quine's criticism of meaning and analyticity.[21] Quine based his criticism on the methodology of the school of American structuralist linguistics. This school was based on Bloomfield's view that grammars are theories of speech sounds, nothing more. According to the methodology developed on this view, the linguist's job is to discover and classify distributional regularities in speech with the use of substitution criteria. For example, two speech sounds are counted as members of the same phoneme class in case substitution of one for the other does not change one word into another, e.g. 'bin' into 'pin'. Quine found the Bloomfieldian view of grammars congenially anti-mentalistic and its associated methodology useful in providing a test for the clarity of linguistic concepts generally.[22] As Quine himself put it, 'substitution criteria . . . have in one form or

51; N. Chomsky, 'Comments on Harman's Reply' in *Language and Philosophy*, pp. 152-9; T. Nagel, 'Linguistics and Epistemology', in *Language and Philosophy*, pp. 171-82; R. Schwartz, 'On Knowing a Grammar', in *Language and Philosophy*, pp. 183-90; S. Stich, 'What Every Speaker Knows', *The Philosophical Review*, Volume LXXX, 1971, pp. 476-96; J. A. Fodor, 'The Appeal to Tacit Knowledge in Psychological Explanation', *The Journal of Philosophy*, Volume LXV, 1968, pp. 627-40; C. Graves *et al.*, 'Tacit Knowledge', *The Journal of Philosophy*, Volume LXX, 1973, pp. 318-30; N. Chomsky, *Reflections on Language*, Pantheon Books, New York, 1975; and much more.

[21] *From a Logical Point of View*, pp. 20–46. Quine's indeterminacy thesis can be shown to depend on the arguments against analyticity and synonymy in this earlier work; see J. J. Katz, *Language and Other Abstract Objects*, Rowman & Littlefield, Totowa, 1981, pp. 151-3.

[22] Quine's anti-mentalism is quite explicit in these early essays. See *From a Logical Point of View*, pp. 47-8. I should note here that Quine, of course, considers various non-linguistic ways of clarifying concepts in his argument that notions like meaning, analyticity, and synonymy are essentially unclear. He considers ordinary definition, explication, abbreviation, and Carnapian meaning postulates. Since I agree with Quine that none of these is any help, I am limiting consideration in the text to ways of clarifying concepts using technical machinery from

another played central roles' in phonology and syntax,[23] and 'For the synonymy problem of semantics such an approach seems more obvious still'.[24] Quine concluded that the impossibility of using substitution criteria non-circularly in application to analyticity and synonymy demonstrates that the concepts of intensional semantics are essentially unclear.[25]

The Chomskian revolution replaced the methodology of substitution criteria with a methodology of theory construction in both the area of syntax and phonology.[26] A concept is deemed sufficiently clear if it can be formalized and used to state the rules of a theory that describes the facts of a language or if it can be defined on the basis of the formal rules of such theories. A concept like 'noun' is thus legitimized in generative rules like NP → (Det) N (S) which express the composition of a phrase, and a concept like 'well-formed sentence of L' is legitimized on the basis of a definition like 'string having a derivation in an optimal grammar of L'.[27] The success of this theory construction approach to the clarification of syntactic and phonological concepts shows that the use of a substitution criteria approach in semantics can no longer be considered 'obvious'. Indeed, the bare possibility of clarifying semantic concepts like analyticity and synonymy in the same way that syntactic and phonological concepts are undermines Quine's criticism.[28]

The final example I wish to give of how the second linguistic turn

---

linguistics. Quine assumes, I shall argue erroneously, that substitution criteria are the only technical machinery from linguistics that needs to be considered in the argument. He must be supposing that substitution criteria are the only machinery available in linguistics for such clarification, since his argument against meaning, analyticity, and synonymy requires that every possible way of clarifying concepts in linguistics be considered.

[23] *From a Logical Point of View*, p. 56.
[24] Ibid.
[25] Ibid., pp. 32-7.
[26] N. Chomsky, 'Introduction', in *The Logical Structure of Linguistic Theory*, Plenum Press, New York, 1975. See also N. Chomsky, 'Current Issues in Linguistic Theory', pp. 28-50; M. Halle, *The Sound Pattern of Russian*, Mouton & Co., The Hague, 1959; N. Chomsky and M. Halle, *The Sound Pattern of English*, Harper & Row, New York, 1968.
[27] *Syntactic Structures*, pp. 13-17.
[28] The demonstration of circularity in the attempt to clarify semantic concepts proves nothing without the assumption that substitution criteria are the proper way to clarify concepts in linguistics. Without this assumption, the circularity need be nothing more than a consequence of the inadequacy of the methodology of substitution, a symptom of this methodology being applied beyond its limits. This, moreover, seems to be so. If instead of requiring that semantic identity

has shed light on philosophically important aspects of language is the development of semantic theories of natural language in relation to linguistics. Broadly, there have been two different approaches to clarifying and explaining semantic concepts, and they reflect the theory-of-meaning vs. theory-of-reference ambiguity in the way 'semantic' is used in philosophy and logic. On the theory-of-meaning side, there have been two ways of constructing theoretical definitions of semantic concepts. One models them directly on theoretical definitions of syntactic and phonological concepts. A system of formal representations of sense structure is constructed in analogy to systems of formal representations of syntactic structure and phonological structure; synonymy is then defined, in analogy to sameness of syntactic structure and sameness of phonological structure, as identity of representation within the system.[29] The other way of constructing theoretical definitions of semantic concepts exploits syntax and phonology to provide representational apparatus for expressions in natural language but uses Carnapian meaning postulates to state semantic facts.[30] Meaning postulates are analogues of logical postulates, used to state logical relations that hold among the so-called "extra-logical" vocabulary of a language. Given a suitable set of meaning postulates, such as $(x)(S_x \equiv SB_x \& F_x)$ to represent the synonymy of 'sister' and 'female sibling', synonymy can be generally defined as Carnapian L-equivalence with respect to this set. The usefulness of transformational syntax and phonology lies in providing representations of predicates that discriminate constructional ambiguities such as with the predicate in 'They are flying planes'.

On the theory-of-reference side, there is the model-theoretic approach to explicating the extensional structure of natural language based principally on the work of Richard Montague but developed in connection with linguistics by Barbara Hall–Partee and other linguists and philosophers.[31] This approach also exploits an idea of Carnap's,

be clarified by substitution criteria, we were to require that mathematical and logical identity be clarified by them, we would encounter the same circularity and be faced with having to reject mathematical and logical identity.

[29] J. J. Katz, *Semantic Theory*, Harper & Row, New York, 1972, and J. J. Katz, *Propositional Structure and Illocutionary Force*, T. Y. Crowell, New York, 1977.
[30] J. D. Fodor, *Semantics: Theories of Meaning in Generative Grammar*, T. Y. Crowell, New York, 1977, pp. 152–55; J. D. Fodor, J. A. Fodor, and M. Garrett, 'The Psychological Unreality of Semantic Representations', *Linguistic Inquiry*, Volume VI, pp. 515–31.
[31] R. Montague, *Formal Philosophy: Selected Papers of Richard Montague*, ed. R. H. Thomason, Yale University Press, New Haven, 1974.

namely, his state-description treatment of semantics, but it redirects Carnap's line of thought away from the referential structure of possible artificial languages toward describing the referential structure of actual natural languages. Carnap's principle of tolerance is abandoned in favour of the constraints on description imposed by linguistic methodology.[32]

The examples just given suffice to give some idea of the significance of the second linguistic turn. In doing so, the examples at the same time motivate what I have called the third linguistic turn, a focus of attention on the foundation of linguistics itself. Since it has had an important impact on linguistic philosophy, linguistics naturally becomes an object of philosophical interest. But there are practical and theoretical reasons beyond simple curiosity for undertaking a philosophical examination of the foundations of linguistics.

One practical reason is that, since the beginning of the second linguistic turn, there has been an enormous proliferation of theories in linguistics. When philosophers first looked at generative linguistics for ideas that they could apply in philosophy, there was only one theory of grammar to consider, the theory in *Syntactic Structures*. Now there are many. Chomsky himself is responsible for several different theories, and other linguists have produced a variety of theories different from any of Chomsky's. The Chomskian tradition contains, besides the *Syntactic Structures* theory, the standard theory from *An Integrated Theory of Linguistic Descriptions* and *Aspects of the Theory of Syntax,* the extended standard theory,[33] the revised extended standard theory,[34] and government and binding theory;[35] the other traditions contain the various forms of generative semantics,[36] Bresnan's realistic grammar,[37]

[32] The most recent example of their approach is J. Barwise and J. Perry, *Situations and Attitudes*, MIT Press, Cambridge, 1983.

[33] N. Chomsky, *Studies on Semantics in Generative Grammar*, Mouton & Co., The Hague, 1972.

[34] N. Chomsky, *Reflections on Language*, Pantheon Books, New York, 1975.

[35] N. Chomsky, *Lectures on Government and Binding*, Foris Publications, Dordrecht, 1981.

[36] There is a large literature containing very many versions of the theory. The best single paper I know of is P. Postal, 'The Best Theory', in *Goals of Linguistic Theory*, ed. S. Peters, Prentice–Hall, Inc., Englewood Cliffs, 1972, pp. 131–70.

[37] J. Bresnan, 'A Realistic Transformational Grammar', in *Linguistic Theory and Psychological Reality*, eds. M. Halle, J. Bresnan, and G. Miller, MIT Press, Cambridge, Mass., 1978, pp. 1–59.

Montague grammar,[38] Johnson and Postal's arc-pair grammar,[39] and Gazdar's abstract phrase structure grammar,[40] to mention only the most prominent cases. The philosopher who now wishes to make use of linguistics faces a bewildering complexity. With so many theories available in linguistics, philosophers unfamiliar with the issues either have to let their desire to apply linguistics to philosophy go unrealized or risk having happen to their applications of linguistics what happened to Quine's application of substitution criteria.

One navigational aid would be a robust philosophy of linguistics. It would provide an ongoing examination of theoretical developments in linguistics, classifying the theories that emerge, highlighting the philosophically important differences between them, and putting them in a form that is more accessible to philosophers generally. Specialists in the philosophy of linguistics would present the philosophically significant issues between alternative theories of linguistic structure in the way that philosophers of logic have presented the philosophically significant issues between alternative logics.

Alongside such a practical reason for a systematic examination of the foundations of linguistics, there are strong theoretical reasons. Philosophy of linguistics can have the same theoretical value in attempting to answer epistemological and metaphysical questions as established specializations such as philosophy of mathematics and philosophy of logic. Consider one of the most important questions in metaphysics, the question of what kinds of objects there are. The philosophy of mathematics and logic have approached the question by asking whether numbers, sets, properties, relations, and propositions are physical objects, as nominalists claim, psychological objects, as conceptualists claim, or abstract objects, as realists claim. The same way of approaching ontology is possible in linguistics. We can ask whether sentences and languages are physical, psychological, or abstract objects.

The philosophy of linguistics can play an indispensable role in answering the general ontological question. The realist position, for example, is correct if there is at least one domain of abstract objects. This is because realism claims only that there are abstract objects. Hence, if linguistic objects are abstract, realism is correct, even if the objects in mathematics, logic, and all other domains are not abstract.

[38] *Formal Philosophy*.

[39] D. E. Johnson, and P. Postal, *Arc-Pair Grammar*, Princeton University Press, Princeton, 1980.

[40] G. Gazdar, 'Phrase Structure Grammar', in *The Nature of Syntactic Representation*, eds. G. K. Pullum and P. Jacobson, Reidel, Dordrecht, 1981, pp. 131–86.

At a minimum, the general ontological question cannot be resolved until the status of linguistic objects is determined.

The importance of the philosophy of linguistics for ontology can also be illustrated in connection with developments in the second linguistic turn. As we saw above, the theory of generative transformational grammar recasts the problem of specifying the logical form of sentences as that of constructing a semantic level of grammatical analysis. This is true of almost all the serious theories of grammar developed in linguistics over the last 20 years. They have each hypothesized that sentences of natural languages have, as part of their grammatical structure, a logical structure, i.e. a level of grammatical structure that is the basis for the applicability of the laws of logic to them. Thus, there is wide agreement that the role of sentences in logical argument is determined by a system of logical features instrinsic to their grammatical structure and that this system can be formally described at an appropriate level of grammars.

There is at the same time much disagreement about what aspects of sentence structure are relevant to logical argument and what grammatical features should count as bona fide logical features.[41] Although such diversity raises a number of critical issues, it does not affect the connection between the domains of linguistics and logic, since all the rival theories of logical structure in natural language identify some set of grammatical structures in sentences as the basis for applying laws of logic to them. Hence, on the best theorizing in linguistics, logic and language overlap in the area of semantics. Accordingly, it makes no sense on these theories to ascribe one ontological status to logic and another to linguistics. Imagine construing logic realistically, as Frege did, and at the same time construing linguistics nominalistically in the manner of a linguist like Bloomfield or philosophers like Quine and Goodman.[42] What could be said about their common semantics? Given

---

[41] Some of these theories of grammar say that the logically relevant structures of sentences are the semantically interpreted deep structures (see the works referenced in n. 14); others say that they are semantically interpreted deep structure/surface structure pairs (see the work referenced in n. 33); and still others say that they are semantically interpreted surface structures (see the work referenced in n. 34). On another dimension of difference, some theories take semantic interpretation to be a representation of sense in something like Frege's notion of *sinn*. These theories identify logical form with sense or meaning. Other theories, following Quine, take semantic interpretation to represent something like quantificational structure (see the works referenced in nn. 35 and 37). Still others take it to represent possible word structures, weaker than senses in discriminating propositions but stronger than quantificational structure (see the work referenced in n. 38).

[42] G. Frege, *The Basic Laws of Arithmetic*, trans. and ed. by M. Furth,

a broad commitment to a conception of the domains of logic and linguistics on which there is a common area of semantic structure, at once both logical and grammatical, the ontological questions for logic and linguistics are connected.

Inquiries in the philosophy of linguistics might focus on a wide range of issues, but the one which must be the central focus of the philosophy of linguistics is the ontological question we have just been discussing. This question is of overriding importance both from a philosophical and a linguistic standpoint. I will try now to indicate the considerations that give it its prominence in philosophy and linguistics.

As we observed in discussing the motivation for the third linguistic turn, the general ontological issue can depend on the particular issue of whether sentences and languages are abstract objects. This in itself would make the question of the ontological status of sentences and languages important at any time in the history of philosophy. But today, in the wake of the first linguistic turn, this question takes on a special importance. For the attempt to solve or dissolve the ontological problem via language was one of the principal forces behind the first linguistic turn. Carnap claimed that *'the whole controversy about universals* rests on the misleading use of universal words. All pseudo-questions of this kind disappear if the formal instead of the material mode of speech is used.'[43] Wittgenstein clearly had Platonic realism in mind as much as mentalism in his attack on the calculus model of language, and the doctrine of family resemblance is specifically an alternative to the realist's doctrine of universals. Given the influence of the first linguistic turn on twentieth-century philosophy, it seems specially important to take the opportunity to re-examine the onto-logical problem from the viewpoint of the philosophy of linguistics.

The question of the ontological status of sentences and languages is equally important for linguistics. Twentieth-century Anglo-American linguistics has been shaped almost entirely by two major scientific revolutions, and in both, the fundamental issue was the ontological status of the objects that grammars are theories of. The outcome of each revolution was primarily to replace one conception of the ontology of grammars with another.

The first revolution was Bloomfield's revolt against the mentalist tradition of nineteenth-century linguistics. Inspired by the desire to

University of California Press, Berkeley, 1967, pp. 1–25. N. Goodman and W. V. Quine, 'Steps Toward a Constructive Nominalism', *The Journal of Symbolic Logic*, Vol. 12, pp. 105–22.

[43] R. Carnap, *The Logical Syntax of Language*, Routledge & Kegan Paul, Ltd., London, 1937, p. 311.

make linguistics a genuine science and taking his view of science from the neopositivism of his day, Bloomfield mounted an extensive argument against the conceptualist view of grammars as theories of a mental reality. As an alternative, he offered a nominalist view on which the reality of language consists in the physical sounds produced in speech. Bloomfield writes:

Non-linguists (unless they happen to be physicalists) constantly forget that a speaker is making noise, and credit him, instead, with the possession of impalpable 'ideas'. It remains for the linguists to show, in detail, that the speaker has no 'ideas' and that the noise is sufficient.[44]

Bloomfield's nominalist view of linguistics dominated Anglo-American linguistics until the early sixties. At that time, the second of the two scientific revolutions, the Chomskian revolution, took place. Chomsky mounted an argument against Bloomfield's nominalistic view of languages and its taxonomic conception of grammars, replacing them by his own conceptualistic view and a generative conception of grammars. On that view, the reality of language consists in the psychological states of their speakers. Chomsky writes:

Linguistic theory is concerned primarily with an ideal speaker-listener, in a completely homogeneous speech-community, who knows its language perfectly and is unaffected by such grammatically irrelevant conditions as memory limitations, distractions, shifts of attention and interest, and errors . . . in the application of his knowledge of the language to actual performance. . . . Hence, in the technical sense, linguistic theory is mentalistic, since it is concerned with discovering a mental reality underlying actual behavior.[45]

Since the early sixties, Chomsky's conceptualism has provided the framework for research in generative transformational grammar and has dominated modern linguistics to the present.

It is not surprising that the ontological issue has had such historical importance when one realizes that all the major questions in the foundations of linguistics depend on how the issue is resolved. What kind of science one takes linguistics to be—whether it is put with empirical sciences like psychology or with non-empirical sciences like mathematics and logic—depends on how one resolves the ontological issue. Similarly, what the nature of grammatical argumentation is, how we are to understand the claim that a statement about sentences or a

---

[44] L. Bloomfield, 'Language or Ideas?', *Language*, Volume 12, pp. 89-95.
[45] *Aspects of the Theory of Syntax*, p. 3.

language is true, what a grammatical fact is, how such facts are known, and what the essence of language is, are all questions to which we will give different answers depending on whether we are nominalists, conceptualists, or realists.

The interest of the ontological issue in linguistics is increased by the fact that there is now a number of linguists and philosophers who are trying to formulate a realist view of language and argue that it should replace the conceptualist views that are presently accepted widely.[46] By making the realist position in linguistics more than a logical possibility, these linguists and philosophers have raised the question of whether linguistics might take the next step from conceptualism to realism. Furthermore, in doing so, they have made certain linguistic and philosophical consequences more than mere logical possibilities.

As we have seen in the historical development from Bloomfield to Chomsky, there has been a correlation between the ontological position that linguists accept and the methodology and kind of grammar they propose. A different ontology might thus open up a new approach to the study of language. The formulation of a realist position for linguistics gives linguists some reason to think that new insights about grammatical structure may be forthcoming.[47] On the philosophical side, a serious formulation and defence of a realist view of linguistics would contribute to both the problem of universals and our understanding of the anti-metaphysical impetus behind the first linguistic turn and much subsequent philosophy in this century.

Because of the significance of the ontological issue for philosophy, the foundations of linguistics, and linguistics itself, I have centred the present collection of essays in the philosophy of linguistics on that

[46] Montague himself regarded linguistics as a branch of mathematics and a number of linguists and philosophers working within the Montague framework also take this point of view. Esa Itkonen and John Ringen have argued that linguistics is not an empirical science but an intuitional science (e.g. E. Itkonen, 'The Concept of Linguistic Intuition', in *A Festschrift for the Native Speaker*, ed. F. Coulmas, Mouton & Co., The Hague, 1981, pp. 127–40, and J. Ringen, 'Linguistic Facts: a Study of the Empirical Scientific Status of Transformational Generative Grammars', in *Testing Linguistic Hypotheses*, eds. D. Cohen and J. R. Wirth, Halsted Press, New York, 1975, pp. 1–41. Katz has argued in *Language and Other Abstract Objects* for linguistics to be taken as a branch of mathematics, for it to be an intuitional science, and for its truths to be about abstract objects. Langendoen and Postal argue that these objects have the same vastness as sets, D. T. Langendoen and P. Postal, *The Vastness of Language*, Basil Blackwell, Oxford, 1984.

[47] In *The Vastness of Language*, Langendoen and Postal argue that conjunction in natural language cannot be handled subject to *any* size constraint on the number of sentential structures conjoined and that this rules out the possibility of constructing grammars as generative devices.

issue. All the essays concern some important aspect of the question of what ontological status languages have, though, of course, each concerns much else as well. The essays are divided into three groups, one concerning the nominalist view of language, one concerning the conceptualist view, and one concerning the realist view. The essays are, with one exception,[48] drawn from the literature on the foundations of linguistics that has been accumulating over the years. Although the overall literature lacks clear focus and systematicity, it contains many valuable philosophical studies of the foundations of linguistics. I have tried to supply a clear focus and to select for systematicity, a choice which has led to excluding a number of interesting topics in the literature as well as many valuable contributions to topics that are included here.

My aim in compiling this reader is to introduce philosophers to the philosophy of linguistics, by giving some indication both of the intellectual richness of the literature that is available even at this early stage and of the philosophical potential of the philosophy of linguistics itself. I hope to launch the philosophy of linguistics as an independent branch of philosophy alongside other specialized branches like the philosophy of mathematics and the philosophy of physics. I hope also to provide philosophers with a new perspective from which to view the two linguistic turns that have so greatly shaped philosophy in this century. I think that neither of these linguistic turns will look the same when viewed from this new perspective.

[48] That exception is Soames's paper which appears for the first time in this volume.

A. NOMINALIST FOUNDATIONS

1

LANGUAGE OR IDEAS?

L. BLOOMFIELD
University of Chicago

[The logicians of the Vienna Circle have independently reached the conclusion of *physicalism*: any scientifically meaningful statement reports a movement in space and time. This confirms the conclusion of A. P. Weiss and other American workers: the universe of science is a physical universe. This conclusion implies that statements about 'ideas' are to be translated into statements about speech-forms.]

SOME years ago I had the honour of addressing the Linguistic Society of America and one of the sister societies upon a prescribed subject 'Linguistics as a science'.[1] The views which I was bound to express were shared by so few people that it seemed natural to state them in the form of prediction rather than of dogma. Linguistics as actually practised employs only such terms as are translatable into the language of physical and biological science; in this linguistics differs from nearly all other discussion of human affairs. Within the next generations mankind will learn that only such terms are usable in any science. The terminology in which at present we try to speak of human affairs— the terminology of 'consciousness', 'mind', 'perception', 'ideas', and so on—in sum, the terminology of mentalism and animism—will be discarded, much as we have discarded Ptolemaic astronomy, and will be replaced in minor part by physiological terms and in major part by terms of linguistics.

This prediction was based not only upon what seem to me to be the striking features of linguistic methodology, but in far greater measure upon the doctrine of non-animistic students of human behaviour, especially upon the conclusions of our late colleague, Albert Paul Weiss.

From *Language*, vol. 12 (1936), pp. 89–95. By permission of The Linguistic Society of America.

[1] *Studies in Philology*, 27 (1930), 553. The summary which follows above is stated so as to bring out the accord with the Viennese conclusions (see below).

A prophecy of this sort, no matter how deep the conviction from which it springs, is so pitifully subject to individual prejudices and errors that even more than most statements it needs to be confirmed or refuted. Within the last years a group of philosophers and logicians, known as the Vienna Circle, has arrived at the same conclusion concerning language.[2] Subjecting various branches of science to logical scrutiny, Rudolf Carnap and Otto Neurath have found that all scientifically meaningful statements are translatable into physical terms—that is, into statements about movements which can be observed and described in co-ordinates of space and time. Statements that are not made in these terms are either scientifically meaningless or else make sense only if they are translated into statements about language. The former, entirely meaningless type may be illustrated by the sentence: *The world is known to me only through my perceptions.* This statement is scientifically meaningless, for it directs us to no observation at any place or time; it predicts nothing.[3] The second type may be exemplified by the sentence: *Redness is a concept.* This makes sense only if it is translated into a statement about language, namely: *In the English language the word redness is a noun.*[4]

[2] R. Carnap, 'Überwindung der Metaphysik,' *Erkenntnis*, 2 (1931), 219; also in a French translation, which I have not seen, *La science et la métaphysique*, Paris, 1934 (= *Actualités scientifiques*, vol. 172); 'Die physikalische Sprache,' *Erkenntnis* 2 (1931), 432; also in an English translation, which I have not seen, *The Unity of Science*, London, 1934 (= *Psyche miniatures*, General series, No. 63); 'Psychologie in physikalischer Sprache,' *Erkenntnis*, 3 (1932), 107; 'Les concepts psychologiques,' *Revue de synthèse*, 10 (1935), 45; *Logische Syntax der Sprache*, Vienna, 1934 (= Schriften zur wissenschaftlichen Weltauffassung, 8); *Philosophy and Logical Syntax*, London, 1935 (= *Psyche miniatures*, General series, No. 70). O. Neurath, 'Physikalismus,' *Scientia*, 50 (1931), 297; 'Physicalism', *The Monist*, 41 (1931), 618; 'Soziologie und Physikalismus,' *Erkenntnis*, 2 (1931), 393; *Einheitswissenschaft und Psychologie*, Vienna, 1933 (= *Einheitswissenschaft*, Heft 1); *Le développement du cercle de Vienne*, Paris, 1935 (= *Actualités scientifiques*, vol. 290).

[3] This example is modelled on Carnap's examples in *Philosophy and Logical Syntax*, 16 ff.; for a thoroughgoing analysis see Weiss's article on solipsism, *Psychological Review*, 38 (1931), 474.

[4] Compare Carnap, 62, who uses *thing-word* for *noun*. The term *noun* (or *thing-word*), of course,—though Carnap does not mention this—must then be defined, for English grammar, and the term *word* for language in general, as technical terms of linguistics; this definition, moreover, must be made in terms of the postulates, undefined basic terms, and earlier definitions of linguistics— not by definitions of meaning and not in metaphysical terms. Thus, a *word* is the smallest meaningful unit that can be spoken alone. In English, a *noun* is a word which enters centrally into endocentric phrases with preceding adjective modifiers, serves as an actor with a finite verb, as the goal of a verb or preposition, and as a prediate complement, appears always in one of two sub-classes, singular and

The path by which Carnap and Neurath reach this conclusion is thorny. It is the path of 'pure' formal logic, with abstraction from all empirical content. Carnap employs mentalistic terms and has to struggle with them; both Carnap and Neurath use linguistic terms without reference to their empiric background. These defects keep our authors from attaining to the mathematical elegance and cogency, the surgical precision, or the vast human scope of Weiss's *Theoretical Basis*. Yet their thornier path follows the same direction. A summary of their argument, given in non-mentalistic terms, could serve directly as a formal résumé of the steps by which Max F. Meyer or A. P. Weiss reach the same goal.[5]

Carnap and Neurath agree, then, with the American students in saying that mentalistic phraseology, in so far as it is not nonsensical, is only a troublesome duplication of linguistic phraseology. The most important feature of this agreement is the circumstance that Carnap and Neurath have done their work in complete independence of their American predecessors. They mention American work a very few times, and then in such manner as to guarantee their lack of familiarity with it. It is safe to say that we have here a highly significant confirmation; the Vienna authors, working independently and with a different method, have reached the same conclusion, stating it in terms which need not even be 'translated' to show the equivalence.[6]

plural, and joins with the suffix [-*ez*, -*z*, -*s*] to form an adjective. Carnap, so far as I have found, nowhere mentions the fact that the discourse of logic presupposes descriptive linguistics and uses the technical terms of this empirical science. The complex linguistic background of logical and mathematical statement is generally ignored by philosophers and logicians; an informal outline of it will be found in *Philosophy of Science*, 2 (1935), 499; more formally in my *Language*, New York, 1933, chs. 2–16.

[5] Max F. Meyer, *The Psychology of the Other One*, 2nd edn., Columbia, Missouri, 1922. Albert Paul Weiss, *A Theoretical Basis of Human Behaviour*, 2nd edn., Columbus, 1929.

[6] In *Der logische Aufbau der Welt* (Berlin, 1928) 81, Carnap mentions Watson and, of all people, Dewey, as behaviourists; in *Erkenntnis* 3 (1932), 124, he mentions a German translation (1930) of Watson's *Behaviourism*. Neurath, *Einheitswissenschaft*, 20, analyzes a paragraph of this German translation and finds that Watson's use of the terms *good* and *bad* violates the rule of physicalism; from this, Neurath seems to draw the conclusion that Watson and all other American students fail to satisfy the demand of physicalism. As a matter of fact, Watson has in the original text (New York, 1924, p. 41) the words 'good' and 'bad' in quotation marks plainly as citations from everyday speech. Moreover, without prejudice to Watson's merits as an investigator and as a popularizer, his *Behaviourism* has the familiar faults of popularization and cannot be seriously used as Neurath uses it. In order to compare the Vienna students' physicalism with serious American work, one must study the latter as well as the former.

One cannot read modern writings without meeting [the realization that science can speak only in physical terms] again and again expressed by students who, to all appearance, have reached it independently. The early papers of Pavlov show dramatically how a group of physiologists is forced to accept this discipline.[7] In England, Lancelot Hogben demonstrates keenly and brilliantly how biology forces it upon us.[8] For physical science it is a working rule, but even when physicists look beyond this, some of them arrive at our conclusion. Thus, P. W. Bridgman, in spite of a perfunctory and otiose profession of mentalism, and in spite of much animistic verbiage which could be easily translated away—Bridgman always says 'concept' when he means simply 'word' or 'technical term'—formulates and applies an 'operational' rule for all definitions in physics, to the effect that terms which do not speak of operations are meaningless.[9] Doubtless also there is more than one isolated instance, such as the medical dissertation of H. Ahlenstiel, *Der Begriff psychisch und die Auffassungen vom Wessen der Wissenschaft*.[10] All these students, however, like their predecessors, the

Yet Neurath's point is not without interest. In correcting the passage from Watson, he can find only an ethnological translation for the words *good* and *bad*; meanwhile Weiss, *Theoretical Basis*, 102 ff., 446 ff. has given a strictly physical translation of these words in terms of the *variability of a system*.

Neurath proposes (*Einheitswissenschaft* 17) to designate his group as *Behavioristiker* and their discipline as *Behaviouristik*, in contrast with the American *behaviourists (Behaviouristen)* and *behaviourism (Behaviourismus)*. The distinction is illusory, since it is based upon lapses from exactitude, real or apparent, such as are to be found also in the writings of the Vienna circle. We shall do well not to insist upon such deviations, but rather to concentrate upon the necessary and sufficient rule: Every scientific statement is made in physical terms. The most perfect formulation of this, so far as I know, and the best exemplification, are to be found in Weiss's Theoretical Basis. As to the name *behaviourism* (which Weiss disliked), it is in many ways objectionable and has been adopted by writers who fail, not only in the way of lapses, but in actual operation, to fulfil the essential demand (Carnap, *Erkenntnis*, 3 125, 'unechter Behaviourismus'). *Physicalism* is a much better word. We should stress our agreement as to the essential point and join in defending it from misinterpretation. Note, for instance, the striking accord between Neurath's 'zweites Menschlein' (*Einheitswissenschaft*, 16) and Weiss's early essay, 'The mind and the man within', *Psychological Review*, 26 (1919), 327.

[7] I. P. Pavlov, *Conditioned Reflexes*, translated by G. V. Anrep, Oxford, 1927.

[8] L. Hogben, *The Nature of Living Matter*, London, 1930.

[9] P. W. Bridgman, *The Logic of Modern Physics*, New York, 1932; profession of mentalism (x); operational principle (5); application (28, an excellent example, whose very wording agrees with Carnap); 56 (an important point); 94; 130; 139; 153; 166; 203.

[10] Printed summary on a leaflet, Kiel, 1921; the original dissertation is typewritten only, and I have not seen it.

'materialists' of the eighteenth and nineteenth centuries, are left with the problem: How do ideas arise from mere matter?[11] The students of the Vienna group, alone, it would seem, agree with their American colleagues in viewing this as a pseudo-problem, because such terms as 'idea' are merely misnomers for linguistic events.

The testing of this hypothesis of *physicalism* will be a task of the next generations, and linguists will have to perform an important part of the work. Non-linguists (unless they happen to be physicalists) constantly forget that a speaker is making noise, and credit him, instead, with the possession of impalpable 'ideas'. It remains for linguists to show, in detail, that the speaker has no 'ideas', and that the noise is sufficient—for the speaker's words act with a trigger-effect upon the nervous systems of his speech-fellows. Linguists, then, will have to read the description of the universe, as men have written it, and wherever they come upon the mention of an 'idea' (or any synonym, such as 'concept', 'notion', or the like), they will have to replace this mention by terms relating to language. If the description so revised is better than the old—simpler and fruitful of sounder and easier prediction— then the hypothesis will have been confirmed and mankind will accept it as we accept the Copernican astronomy.

We may illustrate this by a simple instance of a typical sort. Here is a passage from a most admirable treatise on the foundations of scientific method.[12]

The geometrical ideas of line and plane involve absolute sameness in all their elements and absolute continuity. Every element of a straight line can in conception be made to fit every other element, and this however it be turned about its terminal points. . . . Further, every element of a straight line or plane, however often divided up, is in conception, when magnified up, still an element of straight line or plane.

The geometrical ideas correspond to absolute sameness and continuity, but do we experience anything like these in our perceptions? . . .

The fact remains, that however great care we take in the preparation of a plane surface, either a microscope or other means can be found of sufficient power to show that it is not a plane surface. It is precisely the same with a straight line; however accurate it appears at first to be, exact methods of investigation invariably show it to be widely removed

---

[11] Here we must include the doctrine predominant among Russian scholars. For example, R. Shor's article on Linguistics in the Encyclopedia (*Bol'shaja*) *sovetskaja entsiklopedija*), 64, p. 392, Moscow, 1931) represents not 'materialism' in any strict sense, but rather the normal nineteenth-century dualism.

[12] Karl Pearson, *The Grammar of Science*[3], 1 (London, 1911), 197.

from the conceptual straight line of geometry. . . . *Our experience gives us no reason to suppose that with any amount of care we could obtain a perceptual straight line or plane, the elements of which would on indefinite magnification satisfy the condition of ultimate sameness involved in the geometrical definitions.* We are thus forced to conclude that the geometrical definitions are the results of processes which may be started, but the limits of which can never be reached in perception; they are pure conceptions having no correspondence with any possible perceptual experience.

The terms 'perceptual' and 'conceptual' derive from the following consideration: 'My universe consists necessarily and exclusively of my experiences.' This, the solipsistic axiom, tells us nothing about anything *within* the universe; whatever its value for other activities, it has no bearing on science. Hence for 'perceptual' we shall say *actual*, and for 'conceptual' we shall say *verbal*.

Pearson speaks here of three things: (1) actual ('perceptual') objects, (2) speech-forms, namely geometrical definitions, and (3) 'ideas' or 'concepts', such as 'the concept of a straight line'. It is our hypothesis that (3) is merely a traditional but useless and confusing way of talking about (2); that we find in our universe (that is: require in our discourse) only (1) actual objects and (2) speech-forms which serve as conventional responses to certain features that are common to a class of objects.

Suppose that we know nothing of geometry. We have a great many little spots all over the floor, including two red ones, some distance apart, which we will call A and B; and we have a great many rods or strips of metal, of various shapes. We take these rods of metal and lay first one then another so as to cover both of the red spots A and B. We soon find that the metal rods are of two kinds. Some of them, when we lay them as to cover A and B, cover always the same other spots, no matter how we lay them or which rod we use. We call these rods 'straight'. Of the remaining rods this is not true; one and the same rod can be laid in various ways as to cover spots A and B; it will cover now some of the black spots and now others. Any two rods of this second class can be laid so as to cover different spots, always including A and B.

The geometrician gives us a succinct statement of this. Given a set of things called 'points', we define classes of these. The classes called 'straight lines' are classes such that on any two points there is one and only one straight line.

Now, it is probable that if we make the spots very small and place them very close together and examine the placing of the rods with a microscope, no rod will ever satisfy the geometric definition of 'straight'.

Also, this definition does not mention the width, thickness, weight, temperature, colour, and so on, of the rods, although every rod presents features of this sort. In these respects the term 'straight' resembles all other speech-forms; it is in such forms that we discourse and co-operate.

Now let us re-word the statement in non-mentalistic terms:

The geometrical definition of line and plane say that lines and planes are absolutely alike in all their elements and absolutely continuous. They say that every element of a straight line can be made to fit every other element, and this however it be turned about its terminal points. . . . Further, every element of a straight line or plane, however often divided up, is still, according to the geometrical definition, an element of straight line or plane.

The geometrical definitions imply absolute sameness and continuity, but we find no objects with these characteristics. . . .

The fact remains, that however great care we take in the preparation of a plane surface, either a microscope or other means can be found of sufficient power to show that it is not a plane surface. It is precisely the same with a straight line; however accurate a straight edge appears at first to be, exact methods of investigation invariably show it to be far from satisfying the geometric definition. . . . Our measurements give us no reason to suppose that with any amount of care we shall ever obtain a straight-edged or plane-surfaced object which will under careful observation satisfy the geometric definitions. We are thus forced to conclude that the geometrical definitions are simple verbal descriptions which roughly describe classes of objects but do not exactly describe any given object. In this the geometrical terms are like all other speech-forms.

It is our hypothesis that the terms 'concept', 'idea', and so on add nothing to this. We suppose that the person who says 'I was having an idea of a straight line' is telling us: 'I uttered out loud or produced by inner speech movements the words *straight line*, and at the same time I made some obscure visceral reactions with which I habitually accompany the sight or feel of a straight edge or the utterance or hearing of the word *straight*.' Of all this, only the verbal action is constant from person to person. If we are right, then the term 'idea' is simply a traditional obscure synonym for 'speech-form', and it will appear that what we now call 'mental' events are in part private and unimportant events of physiology and in part social events (responses which in their turn act as stimuli upon other persons or upon the responder himself), namely acts of speech. If this is true, then linguistics in the future will deal with much wider problems than today.

2

DISTRIBUTIONAL STRUCTURE
Z. HARRIS

1. DOES LANGUAGE HAVE A DISTRIBUTIONAL STRUCTURE?

FOR THE purposes of the present discussion, the term structure will be used in the following non-rigorous sense: a set of phonemes or a set of data is structured in respect to some feature, to some extent that we can form in terms of that feature some organized system of statements which describes the members of the set and their interrelations (at least up to some limit of complexity). In this sense, language can be structured in respect to various independent features. And whether it is structured (to more than a trivial extent) in respect to, say, regular historical change, social intercourse, meaning or distribution—or to what extent it is structured in any of these respects—is a matter decidable by investigation. Here we will discuss how each language can be described in terms of a distributional structure, i.e. in terms of the occurrence of parts (ultimately sounds) relative to other parts, and how this description is complete without intrusion of other features such as history or meaning. It goes without saying that other studies of language—historical, psychological, etc.—are also possible, both in relation to distributional structure and independently of it.

The distribution of an element will be understood as the sum of all its environments. An environment of an element A is an existing array of its co-occurrents, i.e. the other elements, each in a particular position, with which A occurs to yield an utterance. A's co-occurrents in a particular position are called its selection for that position.

1.1 *Possibilities of Structure for the Distributional Facts*

To see that there can be a distributional structure we note the following: First, the parts of a language do not occur arbitrarily relative to each

From *Word* 10, No. 2-3 (1954), pp. 775-793 and notes. By permission of the Executive Committee, *Word*.

other: each element occurs in certain positions relative to certain other elements. The perennial man in the street believes that when he speaks he freely puts together whatever elements have the meanings he intends; but he does so only by choosing members of those classes that regularly occur together, and in the order in which these classes occur.

Second, the restricted distribution of classes persists for all their occurrences; the restrictions are not disregarded arbitrarily, e.g. for semantic needs. Some logicians, for example, have considered that an exact distributional description of natural languages is impossible because of their inherent vagueness. This is not quite the case. All elements in a language can be grouped into classes whose relative occurrence can be stated exactly. However, for the occurrence of a particular member of one class relative to a particular member of another class it would be necessary to speak in terms of probability, based on the frequency of that occurrence in a sample.

Third, it is possible to state the occurrence of any element relative to any other element, to the degree of exactness indicated above, so that distributional statements can cover all the material of a language, without requiring support from other types of information. At various times it has been thought that one could only state the normative rules of grammar (e.g. because colloquial departures from these were irregular), or the rules for a standard dialect but not for 'substandard' speech or slang; or that distributional statements had to be amplified by historical deviation (e.g. because the earlier form of the language was somehow more regular). However, in all dialects studied it has been possible to find elements having regularities of occurrence; and while historical derivation can be studied both independently and in relation to the distribution of elements,[1] it is always also possible to state the relative occurrence of elements without reference to their history (i.e. 'descriptively').

Fourth, the restrictions on relative occurrence of each element are described most simply by a network of interrelated statements, certain of them being put in terms of the results of certain others, rather than by a simple measurement of the total restriction on each element

[1] The investigation of historical regularity without direct regard to descriptive (synchronic) structure was the major achievement of the linguists of the late eighteen hundreds. There are incipient studies of historical-descriptive inter-relations, as in H. M. Hoenigswald, 'Sound Change and Linguistic Structure', *Lg.* 22 (1946), 138–43; cf. A. G. Juilland, 'A Bibliography of Diachronic Phonemics', *Word* 9 (1953), 198–208. The independent study of descriptive structure was clarified largely by Ferdinand de Saussure's *Cours de linguistique générale*, the Prague Circle in its *Travaux du Cercle linguistique de Prague*, Edward Sapir in various writings, and Leonard Bloomfield's *Language*.

separately. Some engineers and mathematicians (as also phoneticians
and experimental psychologists) who have become interested in language
have sought a direct formulation of the total restrictions on occurrence
for each element, say for each sound.[2] This would yield an expression
for how the occurrences of each element depart from equiprobability,
and so would give a complete description of the occurrences of elements
in the language. Now it is of course possible to enumerate the relative
occurrences of a finite set of elements in finitely long utterances; but
direct enumeration is of little interest because it yields no simple description of the overall occurrences of elements, and because it does not
order the restrictions in such a way that the larger restrictions get
stated before the smaller ones. In contrast with this, it is possible to
describe the occurrence of each element indirectly, by successive groupings into sets, in such a way that the total statements about the groupings of elements into sets and the relative occurrence of the sets are
fewer and simpler than the total statements about the relative occurrence of each element directly.

We obtain then an ordered set of statements in terms of certain
constructs—the sets at successive levels. Since the ordering of statements can be arranged so that the earlier ones will deal with the more
inclusive sets, we can stop the process of setting up these statements
at any convenient point, and accept the unfinished list of statements
as an approximation to the distributional facts—knowing that the
subsequent statements will only make subsidiary corrections to the
earlier statements. (This is not the case for the direct enumeration of
restrictions, where the restrictions to be enumerated after a given point
may be greater than those enumerated before.)

In view of this we may say that there is not only a body of facts
about the relative occurrence of elements in a language, but also a
structure of relative occurrence (i.e. of distribution). Hence the investigation of a language entails not only the empirical discovery of what are
its irreducible elements and their realtive occurrence, but also the
mathematical search for a simple set of ordered statements that will
express the empirical facts.[3] It may turn out that several systems of
statements are equally adequate, for example several phonemic solutions
for a particular language (or only, say, for the long vowels of a language).
It may also be that different systems are simpler under different

[2] These approaches are discussed by Martin Joos, 'Description of Language
Design', *Journal of the Acoustical Society of America*, 22 (1950), 702–8, and
W. F. Twaddell, ibid. 24 (1952), 607–11.

[3] For a discussion of simplicity in this connection, see an unpublished article
by Noam Chomsky, 'Some Comments on Simplicity and the Form of Grammars'.

conditions. For example, one system may be adequate in terms of successive segments of sound (with at most stress and tone abstracted), while another system may be simpler if we admit the analysis of the sounds into simultaneous components of varying lengths. Or one system of stating distribution in respect to near neighbours (the usual environment for phonemic solutions) may be simple by itself, but if we are to imbed it in other statements about further neighbours we may find that when we choose a modified system the statements covering the imbedding are simpler (i.e. a different phonemic solution may be more convenient for use in statements about morphemes). If the distributional structure is to be used as part of a description of speech, of linguistic behaviour, then we will of course accept only such structures as retain a passably simple relation to the phonetic features. But for some other purpose, such as transmission or systemic analysis, phonetic complexity may be no serious objection. In any case, there is no harm in all this non-uniqueness,[4] since each system can be mapped on to the others, so long as any special conditions are explicit and measurable.

Various questions are raised by the fact that there can be more than one (non-trivial) structural statement for a given language. Can we say whether a particular item of structural analysis contributes to the simplicity of the system? It may be possible to do this: for example, if a given analysis involves a particular classification of elements (say, verbs), we may try some variation on this classification (say, by subdivision into transitive and intransitive—distributionally defined) and see whether the resulting analysis is simpler or not. Can we say what is invariant under all the possible distributional structures for a given body of data? For example, for all the phonemic solutions in a given language, there remains constant the minimal network of phonemically distinct utterance-pairs in terms of which we can distinguish every phonemically distinct utterance.

The various structural systems considered here all have this in common, that they list items and their occurrences. There is at least one other type of structural statement which is essentially distributional but couched in different terms. This is the style which describes one linguistic form as being derived by some process (operation) from another. The item style says: Form A includes elements $e+f$ while form B includes elements $e+g$; and thus it describes all forms as combinations of elements. The process style says: Form A is derived from B by

[4] Y. R. Chao, 'The Non-Uniqueness of Phonemic Solutions of Phonetic Systems', *Bulletin of the Institute of History and Philology, Academia Sinica*, 4 (1934), 363–98. Cf. the two solutions of Annamese phonemes in M. B. Emeneau, *Studies in Vietnamese (Annamese) Grammar*, 9–22.

changing *f* into *g*; and thus it describes most forms as derived from certain base forms. The combinational or item style, which has a more algebraic form, is more parsimonious and representative for much of linguistic data. The process style, which is more similar to historical statements, is useful in certain situations, especially in compact morphophonemics.[5] Both styles are based solely on the relative occurrence of parts, and are therefore distributional.

1.2 *Reality of the Structure*

Some question has been raised as to the reality of this structure. Does it really exist, or is it just a mathematical creation of the investigator's? Skirting the philosophical difficulties of this problem, we should in any case realize that there are two quite different questions here.

One: does the structure really exist in the language? The answer is yes, as much as any scientific structure really obtains in the data which it describes: the scientific structure states a network of relations, and these relations really hold in the data investigated.[6]

Two: does the structure really exist in the speakers? Here we are faced with a question of fact, which is not directly or fully investigated in the process of determining the distributional structure. Clearly, certain behaviours of the speakers indicate perception along the lines of the distributional structure: for example, the fact that while people imitate non-linguistic or foreign-language sounds, they 'repeat' utterances of their own language[7] (i.e. they reproduce the utterance by substituting, for the sounds they heard, the particular corresponding variants which they habitually pronounce; hence the heard sounds are perceived as members of correspondence sets). There are also evidences of perception of sounds in terms of their morphophonemic memberships.[8]

---

[5] This kind of formulation is best expressed in the work of Sapir and Newman; cf. reviews of *Selected Writings of Edward Sapir* (ed. by D. Mandelbaum) in *Language*, 27 (1951), 289–92 (Paper XXXIII of this volume); and of Stanley Newman, *Yokuts Language of California* in *International Journal of American Linguistics*, 10 (1944), 196–211 (Paper XII of this volume).

[6] An opposition has sometimes been claimed between real facts and mathematical manipulation of structure. This claim ignores the fact that science is (among other things) a process of indicating much data by few general statements, and that mathematical methods are often useful in achieving this. Mathematical and other methods of arranging data are not a game but essential parts of the activity of science.

[7] As pointed out by Kurt Goldstein, *Language and Language Disturbances*, 71, p. 103.

[8] e.g. in Edward Sapir, 'La réalité psychologique des phonèmes', *Journal de Psychologie Normale et Pathologique*, 30 (1933), 247–65 (translated in David

A reasonable expectation is that the distributional structure should exist in the speakers in the sense of reflecting their speaking habits.[9] Indeed, responses along the lines of distributional structure can be found in experimental psychology work.[10] However, different speakers differ in the details of distributional perception. One speaker may associate the stem of *nation* with that of *native*, while another may not: should the morpheme analysis be different for the two idiolects (individual dialects)? Even if we take the speaking habits to be some kind of social summation over the behaviours (and habits) of all the individuals, we may not find it possible to discover all these habits except by investigating the very speech events which we had hoped to correlate with the (independently discovered) habits.

If, as Hockett proposes, we measure the habits by the new utterances which had not been used in the structural description, we have indeed a possible and sensible measure; and this applies both to real productivity (the use of elements in environments in which they had not occurred before), and also to arbitrarily unused data (utterances which may have occurred before but which had not been used in deriving the distributional structure). However, even when our structure can predict new utterances, we do not know that it always reflects a previously existing neural association in the speakers (different from the associations which do not, at a given time, produce new utterances). For example, before the word *analyticity* came to be used (in modern logic) our data on English may have contained *analytic, synthetic, periodic, periodicity, simplicity*, etc. On this basis we would have made some statement about the distributional relation of -*ic* to -*ity*, and the new formation of *analyticity* may have conformed to this statement. But this means only that the pattern or the habit existed in the speakers at the time of the new formation, not necessarily before: the 'habit'—the readiness to combine these elements productively—may have developed only when the need arose, by association of words that were partially similar as to composition and environment.

For the position of the speakers is after all similar to that of the linguist. They have heard (and used) a great many utterances among which they perceive partial similarities: parts which occur in various combinations with each other. They produce new combinations of these along the lines of the ones they have heard. The formation of

Mandelbaum, ed., *Selected Writings of Edward Sapir*, 46–60). (See Paper XXXIII of this volume).

[9] C. F. Hockett, review of *Recherches structurales* in *International Journal of American Linguistics*, 18 (1952), 98.
[10] As pointed out to the writer by A. W. Holt.

new utterances in the language is therefore based on the distributional relations—as changeably perceived by the speakers—among the parts of the previously heard utterances.[11]

Concerning any habit, i.e. any predisposition to form new combinations along particular distributional lines rather than others, we know about its existence in the speakers only if we have some outside evidence (such as association tests), or if new formations of the type in question have been formed by these speakers. The frequency of slips, new formations, etc., is enough to make us feel that the bulk of the major structural features are indeed reflected in speaking habits—habits which are presumably based, like the linguist's analysis, on the distributional facts. Aside from this, all we know about any particular language habit is the probability that new formations will be along certain distributional lines rather than others, and this is no more than testing the success of our distributional structure in predicting new data or formations. The particular distributional structure which best predicts new formations will be of greatest interest from many (not all) points of view; but this is not the same as saying that all of that structure exists in the speakers at any particular time prior to the new formations.[12]

2. DISTRIBUTION AND MEANING

2.1 *Is there a Parallel 'Meaning Structure'?*

While the distinction between descriptive (synchronic) structure and historical change is by now well known, the distinction between distributional structure and meaning is not yet always clear. Meaning is not a unique property of language, but a general characteristic of human

[11] This applies to the grammatical innovation involved in new formations; the selection of morphemes within a class is determined, not only by these 'grammatical' associations but also semantically. Cf. the first paragraph of 1.1 above.

[12] Here we have discussed whether the distributional structure exists in the speakers as a parallel system of habits of speaking and of productivity. This is quite different from the dubious suggestion made at various times that the categories of language determine the speakers' categories of perception, a suggestion which may be a bit of occupational imperialism for linguistics, and which is not seriously testable as long as we have so little knowledge about people's categories of perception. Cf. for the suggestion, Benjamin L. Whorf, 'The Relation of Habitual Thought and Behavior to Languages', *Language, Culture and Personality (Sapir Memorial Volume)* (ed. by A. I. Hallowell, L. Spier, and S. Newman), 75–93; 'Languages and Logic', *The Technology Review* (1941), 43–6; and against it, Eric H. Lenneberg, 'Cognition in Ethnolinguistics', *Lg.* 29 (1953), 463–71; Lewis S. Feuer, 'Sociological Aspects of the Relation between Language and Philosophy', *Philosophy of Science*, 20 (1953), 85–100.

activity. It is true that language has a special relation to meaning, both in the sense of the classification of aspects of experience, and in the sense of communication. But the relation is not simple. For example, we can compare the structures of languages with the structure of the physical world (e.g. the kind of phenomena that are expressed by differentiation and integration in calculus), or with what we know about the structure of human response (e.g. association, transference). In either case, it would be clear that the structure of one language or another does not conform in many respects to the structure of physical nature or of human response—i.e. to the structure of objective experience from which we presumably draw our meanings. And if we consider the individual aspects of experience, the way a person's store of meanings grows and changes through the years while his language remains fairly constant, or the way a person can have an idea or a feeling which he cannot readily express in the language available to him, we see that the structure of language does not necessarily conform to the structure of subjective experience, of the subjective world of meanings.[13]

All this is not to say that there is not a great interconnection between language and meaning, in whatever sense it may be possible to use this word. But it is not a one-to-one relation between morphological structure and anything else. There is not even a one-to-one relation between the vocabulary and any independent classification of meaning: We cannot say that each morpheme or word has a single or central meaning, or even that it has a continuous or coherent range of meanings. Accidents of sound change, homonymity, borrowing, forgotten metaphors, and the like can give diverse meanings to a number of phonemic occurrences which we have to consider as occurrences of the same morpheme. Aside from this, if we consider the suggestion of Kurt Goldstein[14] that there are two separate uses and meanings of language—the concrete (e.g. by certain brain-injured patients) and the abstract—it would follow that the same grammatical structure and much the same vocabulary can carry quite different types of speaking activity.

The correlation between language and meaning is much greater when we consider connected discourse. To the extent that formal (distributional) structure can be discovered in discourse, it correlates in some

---

[13] In E. G. Schachtel's 'On Memory and Childhood Amnesia', *Psychiatry*, 10 (1947), 1–26 it is suggested that the experiences of infancy are not recallable in later life because the selection of aspects of experience and the classification of experience embodied in language, which fixes experience for recall, differs from the way events and observations are experienced (and categorized) by the infant.

[14] *Human Nature in the Light of Psychopathology: the William James Lectures for 1938-39*, ch. 3.

way with the substance of what is being said; this is especially evident in stylized scientific discourse (e.g. reports on experimental work) and above all in the formal discourses (proofs) of mathematics and logic. However, this is not the same thing as saying that the distributional structure of language (phonology, morphology, and at most a small amount of discourse structure) conforms in some one-to-one way with some independently discoverable structure of meaning. If one wishes to speak of language as existing in some sense on two planes—of form and of meaning—we can at least say that the structures of the two are not identical, though they will be found similar in various respects.

2.2 Are Morphemes determined by Meaning?

Since there is no independently known structure of meanings which exactly parallels linguistic structure, we cannot mix distributional investigations with occasional assists from meaning whenever the going is hard. For example, if the morphemic composition of a word is not easily determined, we cannot decide the matter by seeing what are the component meanings of the word and assigning one morpheme to each: Do *persist, person* contain one morpheme each or two? In terms of meaning it would be difficult to decide, and the decision would not necessarily fit into any resulting structure. In terms of distribution we have *consist, resist, pertain, contain, retain*, etc. (related in phonemic composition and in sentence environment), but no such set for *person*; hence we take *persist* as two morphemes, *person* as one.

Although rough indications of meaning are often used heuristically to guess at the morphemes of a word or utterance, the decision as to morphemic composition is always based on a check of what sections of that word or utterance are substitutable in a structured (patterned) way in that environment; as roughly indicated in the example above.

Where the meanings (in most cases, the translations) are not immediately suggestive, the analysis is laboriously distributional without any heuristic aids to test. For example in the Cherokee verb prefixes, we find scores of forms[15], e.g. /agwalənə̀ʔəgi/ 'I started', /sdəgadhénoha/ 'I and another are searching for you', /sdəgadhénohəgi/ 'I searched for you two'. These have obviously personal reference, but it is impossible

---

[15] The following analysis can be fully understood only if one checks through the actual lists of Cherokee forms. The few forms cited here are taken from William D. Reyburn, 'Cherokee Verb Morphology II', *International Journal of American Linguistics*, 19 (1953), 259-73. For the analysis, see the charts and comments in Reyburn's work and in Z. S. Harris, 'Cherokee Skeletal Grammar', and 'Cherokee Grammatical Word Lists and Utterances', in the Franz Boas Collection of the American Philosophical Society Library.

to separate out a small set of phonemic segments which will mean 'I' or 'I as subject', 'I as object', etc. It is nevertheless possible to discover the morphemes distributionally. First we identify the words by their distributional relation to the rest of the sentence. We find that certain words with many different stems and a few different prefixes have certain types of environment in common. For example /zinəgali'a/ 'I am cleaning' and /agiyoseha/ 'I am hungry' occur in certain environments in which /uniyoseha/ 'they are hungry' does not occur. We take a set of words each with different stems but which have the same environment in the sense referred to above. We will assume that the sameness in this feature of the environment correlates with some morphemic part that is the same in all these words (and is obviously not the stem).[16] This means that the different prefixes of these words contain alternants of the same morpheme; and we try to state a morphophonemic relation between /z/, /(a)g/, etc., giving the environing conditions (in phonemic rather than morphemic terms if possible) in which each alternant occurs: we write the morpheme {z} and translate it 'I'. Another set, containing e.g. /ozinəgali?a/ 'I and others are cleaning', /ogiyoseha/ 'I and others are hungry', would thus be analysed (in the same manner, but with the aid of {z}) as containing two morphemes, {o} 'others' and {z} 'I'. If we now turn to the set containing /osdinəgali?a/ 'I and another are cleaning', /oginiyoseha/ 'I and another are hungry', etc., our morphophonemic knowledge about {z} enables us to separate out /d/, /n/ etc. as alternants of some third morpheme {n}, with undetermined meaning. In /iginiyoseha/ 'you and I are hungry' our known morphophonemics enables us to analyze the prefix as an alternant of {z} plus an alternant of this same {n}, where it seems to have the meaning 'you'. However, in /hinəgali?a/ 'you (sg.) are cleaning' we are unable to fit the /h/ into the morphophonemic regularities of {n}, and thus set up a new morpheme {h} 'you'; and in /sdinəgali?a/ 'you two are cleaning' we can satisfy the morphophonemic regularities by saying that there are two morphemes: the /s/ alternant of {h} plus the /d/ alternant of {n}.

In this way we can divide each prefix into a unique combination of morphophonemic alternants of the following morphemes: {z} 'I', {h} 'you (sg)', {a} 'third person sg.', {i} 'plural' (always including 'you', at least due to absence of {o}), {o} roughly 'person(s) excluding you', {n} roughly 'another person, you as first choice'. These morphemes were obtained as solutions to the environmental regularities of the prefixed

---

[16] This assumption is based on the fact that each morpheme has a different distribution (2.36), so that same feature of environment points to the same morpheme.

phonemes. The translations offered above are an attempt to assign a single meaning to each on the basis of the meanings of all those words in which it occurs. If we write the prefixes morphophonemically, then the meanings of some of the occurring combinations are: {ozn} (phonemically /ods/ etc.) 'I and he', {oz} 'I and they', {zn} 'I and you (sg.)', {iz} 'I, you, and they', {h} 'you (sg.)', {hn} 'you two', {in} 'you (pl.)'. From this we can try to extract (as above) a single meaning contribution which {n} or {o} or {i} bring to each combination in which they are included. But it was not the isolation of these complicated central meanings (if that is always non-trivially possible) that led us to recognize {n} etc. as morphemes. We do not even know that these central meanings exist for the speakers: the speakers may be subjectively using two homonymous {n} morphemes, or they may be using these prefix combinations as fixed whole entities with only a vague impression of the phonemic and morphophonemic regularities.[17]

So far, we have not touched the great majority of verb forms, those which have objects together with the subjects. By using the morphophonemic relations established previously, we are able to extract the morphemes above from some of these new combinations, and small extensions of the morphophonemics reveal these morphemes in yet other combinations. Then we analyse the prefix in /gəiha/ 'I am killing you' as {z} + {n}, and in /sgwúsədohda/ 'you covered me' as {h} + {z}; and certain order statements about the two prefix components indicate the subject–object relation. The remaining phonemes of some of these prefixes can be grouped by rather simple morphophonemics into a few additional morphemes like {g} 'animate object'; and so we finally obtain a morphemic analysis of all the prefixes. This analysis does not necessarily correlate with any meaning units we may have in mind about person and number. For example, it gives the same morphemes {znn} for the prefix in /sdəgadhénoha/ 'I and another are searching for you (whether sg. or dual but not plural)' and in /sdəgadhénohəgi/ 'I searched for you two'. Even if we find different phonemes with different meanings, e.g. /izə-gow'diha/ 'I and he see you (pl.)' and /izəy-olighi/ 'I and they know you (sg.)' the analysis may say that these are alternants of the same morphemic composition {izn}; in that case both meanings can be obtained from each form.

The methods indicated so sketchily above suggest how the morphemic composition of a word or utterance can be determined by the occurrence of each phoneme sequence relative to others: e.g. *per,*

[17] Since new formations of these combinations do not appear, we cannot apply the productivity tests of 2.1 to discover the speakers' morphemic recognition.

con relative to *sist, tain*; or /z/, /gi/, /o/, etc. relative to various features of environment which are common to /z/ and /gi/ as against /o/. The final decision as to morphemic analysis always depends on this relative occurrence of phoneme sequences, since the grammar then proceeds to state compactly the relative occurrence of the morphemes. That is, we set up as morphemes those phonemic sequences (or features) such that all utterances are compactly statable relative occurrences of them.

The chief difficulty with this is that it provides us only with a criterion that tells us whether a given phoneme sequence is a morpheme or not; more exactly, whether a particular segmentation of an utterance (once we propose it) divides it into morphemic segments. It does not provide us with a procedure which will directly yield a morphemic segmentation of an utterance. There is available, however, a procedure which yields most if not all of the morphemic segmentations of an utterance. In outline it is as follows: given any test utterance, associate many utterances whose first phoneme is the same as that of the test utterance; and note how many different phonemes follow the first in these utterances. Then consider utterances whose first two phonemes are the same as the first two of the test utterance, and note how many different phonemes follow the first two in these. And so on. If after the first *n* phonemes the number of different phonemes which follow the *n*th (in the associated utterances) is greater than the number after the first *n*−1 phonemes or the first *n*+1, then we place a tentative morpheme boundary after the *n*th. Various operations are needed to correct and check the correctness of each result; but together with the final test of patterned relative occurrence, this yields the morphemes of a language without any reference to meaning or informant response.

2.3 *Meaning as a Function of Distribution*

Distribution suffices to determine the phonemes and morphemes, and to state a grammar in terms of them. However, both (*a*) in determining the elements and (*b*) in stating the relations between them, it turns out that the distributional structure does not give ideal coverage. It must either leave many details unsaid, or else become extremely complicated. For example: (*a*) Morphemes are determined on the basis of a patterned independence (replaceability in utterances) in respect to other morphemes (or phoneme sequences); but not all morphemes have the same degree of independence: compare *hood* (*boyhood*) with *ness* (*bigness*). (*b*) The grammatical statements group morphemes into classes, and then say that certain sequences of these classes occur; but not every member of the one class occurs (in any actual body of data) with every member of the other: not every adjective occurs with every noun. Finally we may mention one other respect in which distribution fails to cover all the facts about speech occurrence: (c) We can state distributional regularities only within narrow domains—for phonology usually the immediately neighbouring phonemes, for morphology usually the sentence or some part of the sentence.

At all these points where simple distributional regularities are no longer discoverable, people often revert to the position of our man in the street (§ 1.1) and say that here the only determinant is meaning: (a) *hood* has a meaning which ties it to certain few nouns; (b) with a given noun, e.g. *doctor*, there will be used those adjectives that make sense with it; (c) beyond the sentence there are no significant formal restrictions on what one says, and sentences are strung along purely according to meaning. Now meaning is of course a determinant in these and in other choices that we make when we speak. But as we make these choices we build a stock of utterances each of which is a particular combination of particular elements. And this stock of combinations of elements becomes a factor in the way later choices are made (in the sense indicated in the last two paragraphs of § 1.2); for language is not merely a bag of words but a tool with particular properties which have been fashioned in the course of its use. The linguist's work is precisely to discover these properties, whether for descriptive analysis or for the synthesis of quasi-linguistic systems. As Leonard Bloomfield pointed out, it frequently happens that when we do not rest with the explanation that something is due to meaning, we discover that it has a formal regularity or 'explanation'. It may still be 'due to meaning' in one sense, but it accords with a distributional regularity.

If we investigate in this light the areas where there are no simple distributional regularities, we will often find interesting distributional relations, relations which tell us something about the occurrence of elements and which correlate with some aspect of meaning. In certain important cases it will even prove possible to state certain aspects of meaning as functions of measurable distributional relations.

(a) There are different degrees of independence (§ 3.3). We find complete dependence in the various phonemes of one morpheme, or in the various parts of a discontinuous morpheme (including grammatical agreement). In *hood* we have sufficient independence to make it a separate morpheme, but it is limited to very few predecessors. In *ness* there is more independence. The degree of independence of a morpheme is a distributional measure of the number of different morphemes with which it occurs, and of the degree to which they are spread out over various classes or subclasses. The various members of a distributional class or subclass have some element of meaning in common, which is stronger the more distributional characteristics the class has. The major classes have the kind of common meanings that are associated, say, with the words 'noun' or 'adjective'.

(b) The fact that, for example, not every adjective occurs with every noun can be used as a measure of meaning difference. For it is not merely that different members of the one class have different selections of members of the other class with which they are actually found. More than that: if we consider words or morphemes A and B to be more different in meaning than A and C, then we will often find that the distributions of A and B are more different than the distributions of A and C. In other words, difference of meaning correlates with difference of distribution.

If we consider *oculist* and *eye-doctor*[18] we find that, as our corpus of actually occurring utterances grows, these two occur in almost the same environments, except for such sentences as *An oculist is just an eye-doctor under a fancier name*, or *I told him Burns was an oculist, but since he didn't know the professional titles, he didn't realize that he could go to him to have his eyes examined*. If we ask informants for any words that may occupy the same place as *oculist* in sentences like the above (i.e. have these same environments), we will not in general obtain *eye-doctor*; but in almost any other sentence we would. In contrast, there are many sentence environments in which *oculist* occurs but *lawyer* does not: e.g. *I've had my eyes examined by the same oculist for twenty years*, or *Oculists often have their prescription blanks printed for them by opticians*. It is not a question of whether the above sentence with *lawyer* substituted is true or not; it might be true in some situation. It is rather a question of the relative frequency of such environments with *oculist* and with *lawyer*, or of whether we will obtain *lawyer* here if we ask an informant to substitute any word he wishes for *oculist* (not asking what words have the same meaning). These and similar tests all measure the probability of particular environments occurring with particular elements, i.e. they measure the selections of each element.

It is impossible to obtain more than a rough approximation of the relatively common selection of a given word (with almost no indication of its rarer selection). But it is possible to measure how similar are the

---

[18] This particular pair was suggested to me by Y. Bar-Hillel, who, however, considers that distributional correlates of meaning differences cannot be established.

selection approximations of any two words (within various sets of data). If for two elements A and B we obtain almost the same list of particular environments (selection), except that the environment of A always contains some X which never occurs in the environment of B, we say that A and B are (complementary) alternants of each other: e.g. *knife* and *knive-*. If A and B have identical environments throughout (in terms of our data tests) we say that they are free variants: e.g. perhaps for /ekənamiks/ and /iykəanamiks/ *economics*. If the environments of A are always different in some regular way from the environments of B, we state some relation between A and B depending on this regular type of difference: e.g. *ain't* and *am not* have frequent differences of a certain type in their environments (*ain't goin'* but *am not going*) which we would call dialectal. If A and B have almost identical environments except chiefly for sentences which contain both, we say they are synonyms: *oculist* and *eye-doctor*. If A and B have some environments in common and some not (e.g. *oculist* and *lawyer*) we say that they have different meanings, the amount of meaning difference corresponding roughly to the amount of difference in their environments. (This latter amount would depend on the numerical relation of different to same environments, with more weighting being given to differences of selectional subclasses.) If A and B never have the same environment, we say that they are members of two different grammatical classes (this aside from homonymity and from any stated position where both these classes can occur).

While much more has to be said in order to establish constructional methods for such a classification as above, these remarks may suffice to show how it is possible to use the detailed distributional facts about each morpheme. Though we cannot list all the co-occurrents (selection) of a particular morpheme, or define its meaning fully on the basis of these, we can measure roughly the difference in selection between elements, say something about their difference in meaning, and also (above and § 4.1) derive certain structural information.

(*c*) If we investigate the relative occurrence of any part of one sentence in respect to any part of the neighbouring sentences in the same discourse, we will find that there are certain regularities (§ 3.5 end). The sequence of sentences is not entirely arbitrary; there are even certain elements (e.g. pronouns) whose occurrence (and meaning) is specifically related to the grammatically restricted occurrence of certain other morphemes in the neighbouring sentences (§ 4.1, first paragraph). Such regularities (and meanings) will not extend from one discourse to another (except to another related in some relevant way to the first, e.g. successive lectures of a series). A consecutive (or seriate) discourse of one or more persons is thus the fullest environmental unit for distributional investigation.[19]

3. DISTRIBUTIONAL ANALYSIS

We now review briefly the basic analysis applicable to distributional facts.

3.1 *Element*

The first distributional fact is that it is possible to divide (to segment) any flow of speech into parts, in such a way that we can find some regularities in the occurrence of one part relative to others in the flow of speech. These parts are the discrete elements which have a certain distribution (set of relative locations) in the flow of speech; and each bit of speech is a particular combination of elements. The first operation is purely segmenting, arbitrary if need be. The first step of segmenting has to be independent of any particular distributional criterion, since we cannot speak of distributional relations until we have not only segments but also a similarity grouping of them (§ 3.2). After the first segmenting of utterances, each segment is unique and has a unique environment (completely different from every other one); after the segments have been compared, and 'similar' ones grouped together, we find that various of these similarity groupings have partially similar and partially different environments. Hence we can speak about the distributional relations of these similarity groupings.

If we wish to be able, in the later operations (§ 3.3–4), to obtain elements (or classes of elements) whose distributions will have maximum regularity, we have to divide not only the time flow into successive portions, but also any single time segment (or succession of time segments) into simultaneous components (of one segment length, e.g. a tone, or longer, e.g. a pitch-stress contour). After we have set up the phonetically more obvious segmentations and simultaneities, and have studied their distribution, we may find that more regular distributions can be obtained if we change our original segmentation of elements,

---

[19] It should be clear that only after we discover what kinds of distributional regularities there are among successive elements or sections in discourses can we attempt any organized semantic interpretation (of sentences, clauses or other intervals). In mathematics and the constructed 'languages' of logic, certain conditions are imposed on what sentences can appear in succession in their connected discourses (proofs): each sentence (line in a proof) has to be a theorem or else derived from a preceding sentence in a particular way. This situation does not hold for natural languages, where the truth-value of logic is not kept constant through successive sentences, and where the types of succession are more varied.

even to ones that are phonetically less obvious, and even if some of our adjusted elements become components which extend over various numbers of other elements.

3.2 *Similarity*

Another essential distributional fact is that some elements are similar to others in terms of certain tests; or are similar in the sense that if we group these similar elements into sets ('similarity groupings'), the distribution of all members of a set (in respect to other sets) will be the same as far as we can discover. This reduces ultimately to the similarity of sound segments under repetition, or in the pair test: x_1 is similar to x_2 but not to y_1 if, when one native speaker repeats x_1z, x_2z, y_1z, . . ., a second speaker can guess correctly whether x_1z as against y_1z is being said, but not whether x_1z as against x_2z is being said. We call x_1 and x_2 free variants of each other (or members of a similarity grouping). Note that the pair test involves discrimination of sound but not of meaning.

3.3 *Dependence (Serial)*

To obtain a least set of elements sufficient for description we join any elements which are completely dependent: if A is a set of similar elements (a similarity grouping) and so is B, and (in a particular type of environment) only AB occurs (not necessarily contiguously), never A or B alone, then we set up AB as a single element (a single set of similar elements).

Thereafter we don't have any two elements which are completely dependent upon each other in occurrence. But our elements have various degrees of dependence: for each element we can say that any utterance (or shorter domain) which contains it will also contain such and such other classes. For example, morpheme A may occur always close to (i.e. within a statable distance from) any one of a few or many B_1, B_2, . . . If the sequence B_1A occurs in environments X, it may be that B_1 by itself also occurs in X (e.g. *kingdom* and *king*), or that B_1 does not (e.g. *kingly* and *king*). The B_1 with which A occurs may all have the same types of environment when they occur without A (e.g. all predecessors of *dom* are nouns), or some may have one type and some another (e.g. *ish* occurs with both nouns and adjectives). These are a few of the various degrees and types of occurrence-dependence which an element can have to the elements that occur in the same utterances as it does.

3.4 *Substitutability (Parallel)*

It will in general appear that various elements have identical types of occurrence-dependence. We group A and B into a substitution set whenever A and B each have the same (or partially same) environments X (X being at first elements, later substitution sets of elements) within a statable domain of the flow of speech. This enables us to speak of the occurrence-dependence of a whole set of elements in respect to other such sets of elements. Some of the types of partial sameness of environment were listed in § 2.3(*b*).

The elements of distributional structure are usually obtained by the operations of § 3.1, § 3.2, and the first paragraph of § 3.3. The distributional relations are usually combinations of § 3.3 and § 3.4. For example, *hood* occurs after few morphemes N_1, N_2, . . . of a certain substitution set ('nouns'), *ish* after many of them, *s* and its alternants after all or almost all of them. $N_i + hood$ or $N_i + s$ occur in the same large environments in which N_i occur alone. But $N_i + ish$ occur in different environments than N_i alone; however *ish* also occurs after many members of another substitution set, A_1, A_2, . . . ('adjectives'), and both $N_i + ish$ and $A_i + ish$ occur in the larger environments of A_i alone.

3.5 *Domains*

All the statements about dependence and substitutability apply within some specified domain, the domain being determined either by nature (e.g. silence before and after an utterance) or by the types of environment within which there is regularity (e.g. the narrow restriction of *hood* is only to what precedes it, and only to the first morpheme in that direction). It is often possible to state the co-occurrences of elements within a domain in such a way that that domain then becomes the element whose co-occurrences are regular within a larger domain; e.g. the occurrences of stems and suffixes within word-length, and of words within phrases. Common types of domain are the word, phrase, clause. In many cases the stretches of speech covered by certain long pitch and stress components (or fixed sequences of short pitch and stress components) are identical with the domains of distributional relations: words, sentence.

Although grammar has generally stopped with the sentence, it is possible to find distributional regularities in larger domains. There are certain sentence sequences in which the second can be described as a fixed modification of the first (e.g. with certain restrictions, in the case of questions and answers in English). There are certain types of distributional relation (e.g. between English active and passive, between *buy* and *sell*) which have particular kinds of regularity in (not necessarily immediately) neighbouring sentences. For example, if one sentence contains noun A + active (transitive) verb B + noun C, and a neighbouring sentence contains C + verb + A, there is a certain likelihood that the verb will be the passive of B; or if the neighbouring sentence contains C + passive of B + some noun, there is a certain likelihood that the second noun will be A or some noun which elsewhere in that discourse has similar individual environments (selection) to those of A. And if one sentence contains A *buys* B *from* C, and a neighbouring sentence contains C *sells* B *to*+ some noun, there is a good likelihood that the noun will be A or an environmentally similar noun (and given C + some verb + B *to* A, we may expect the verb to be *sell* or some environmentally similar one).[20]

Finally, if we take a whole connected discourse as environment, we find that there are certain substitution sets of morphemes which occur regularly (relative to the other sets) throughout the discourse of some portion of it;[21] these are not the major substitution sets of the language (e.g. nouns) or its grammatical subclasses, but new groupings which are often relevant only to that one discourse. And there are certain sequences of these sets which constitute the subdomains of the discourse; i.e. such that the sets are regular within these intervals and the intervals are regular within the discourse; these intervals are not necessarily sentences or clauses in the sense of grammatical structure. The regularities in a discourse are far weaker and less interrelated than those within a sentence; but they show that occurrence–dependence (and the environment relevant for distribution) can extend throughout a whole discourse.

3.6 *Data*

The distributional investigations sketched above are carried out by recording utterances (as stretches of changing sound) and comparing them for partial similarities. We do not ask a speaker whether his language contains certain elements or whether they have certain dependences or substitutabilities. Even though his 'speaking habits' (§ 1.2)

---

[20] Such relations as that of active to passive, or *buy* to *sell*, are essentially substitutability relations (§ 3.4), i.e. they show that certain elements have similar environments (e.g. partially inverted ones). The fact that they may appear in neighbouring sentences is a serial relation (§ 3.3) which is a secondary characteristic of certain substitutabilities. Relations like that of active to passive are different from the essentially serial relations of successive intervals of a discourse, discussed at the end of § 3.5.

[21] The fact that a discourse contains several or many occurrences of a given substitution class, often in parallel positions, brings out a rare relation in linguistics; the order of occurrence of various members of the same class. Something like this comes up in compound nouns, or in successions of two or more adjectives (sometimes with preferred order). Usually, if two members of a class occur in one domain, their order is not regular (e.g. in most cases of N *and* N); but in compound nouns, for instance, certain members are frequent in the first N position, and others in the second.

yield regular utterances, they are not sufficiently close to all the distributional details, nor is the speaker sufficiently aware of them. Hence we cannot directly investigate the rules of 'the language' via some system of habits or some neurological machine that generates all the utterances of the language. We have to investigate some actual corpus of utterances, and derive therefrom such regularities as would have generated these utterances—and would presumably generate other utterances of the language than the ones in our corpus. Statements about distribution are always made on the basis of a corpus of occurring utterances; one hopes that these statements will also apply to other utterances which may occur naturally. Thus when we say that the selectional difference in *oculist/lawyer* is greater than in *oculist/eye-doctor* (§ 2.3), or that the selection of nouns around the passive verb is the same as the selection around the active verb, but with inverted order (§ 4.1), we mean that these relations will be approximated in any sufficiently large corpus (especially one built with the aid of eliciting), and that they will presumably apply to any sufficiently large additions to the corpus.

In much linguistic work we require for comparison various utterances which occur so infrequently that searching for them in an arbitrary corpus is prohibitively laborious. To get around this, we can use various techniques of eliciting, i.e. techniques which favour the appearance of utterances relevant to the feature we are investigating (without influencing the speaker in any manner that might bring out utterances which would not have sometimes occurred naturally). In particular, investigations of the selections of particular morphemes (§2.3, 4.1) can hardly be carried out without the aid of eliciting. Eliciting is a method of testing whether a certain utterance (which is relevant to our investigation) would occur naturally: in effect, we try to provide a speaker with an environment in which he could say that utterance—if he ever would naturally say it—without extracting it from him if he wouldn't. For example, if we are testing the active/passive relation we might offer a speaker noun A_1 + transitive verb B_1 and ask him to complete the sentence in many ways, obtaining a particular selection C_1, C_2, . . . after the verb. Then we can offer a speaker the passive verb B_1 + A_1 and ask him to begin the sentence in many ways, checking whether we get about the same selection C_1, C_2, . . . before the verb. We can repeat this for various A_i, and then for various B_i.

4. DISTRIBUTIONAL RELATIONS

The methods of § 3 yield first of all a representation of each utterance as a combination of elements. They also yield a set of statements about the utterances: what elements and regularities of combination suffice to represent the utterances. One can go beyond this and study the kinds of regularities, and the kinds of relations among elements. As was pointed out at the end of § 2.3(*b*), certain correlations may be discovered even in those distributional facts which are too individual to be directly useful.

4.1 As an example of the latter we may consider selectional similarity. For instance, it is impossible to list all the verbs that follow each particular noun, or all the verbs that follow *who*. But it is possible to state the following relation between the verb selection of nouns and the verb selection of *who*: Under an eliciting test as in § 3.6, we will get after *The pianist*—much the same verbs as we will get after *The pianist who* —and so for every noun. This means that the verb selection of *who* is the same as the verb selection of the noun preceding *who*. We have here a distributional characteristic that distinguishes such pronominal elements from ordinary nouns.

Or we may consider the active/passive relation mentioned in § 3.6. If we take a large number of sentences containing a transitive verb in English, e.g. *The kids broke that window last week*, we can elicit sentences consisting of the same verb but with the passive morpheme, the same nouns before and after it but in reverse order, and the same remainder of the sentence, e.g. *That window was broken by the kids last week*. Some of these sentences may be stylistically clumsy, so that they would not occur unless some special circumlocution were involved; but they are obtainable by otherwise valid eliciting techniques.[22] In contrast, if we seek such inversion without the passive, we will fail to elicit many sentences: we can get *The kids saw Mary last week* and *Mary saw the kids last week*; but to *The kids saw the movie* we will never—or hardly ever—get *The movie saw the kids* (even though this sentence is grammatical). Or if we seek such selectional similarity (with or without inversion) for *broke*/*will break* or the like, we will find the same selection as to preceding and following nouns, but not always as to the rest of the sentence: *The kids broke that window* and *The kids will break that window*, but not *The kids will break that window last week* or *The kids broke that window if they don't watch out*. It thus appears that, using only distributional information about an ordinarily elicited corpus, we can find a relation between the active

---

[22] There will be a few exceptions where the passive is not obtainable. And if we try to elicit the active on the basis of the passive, we run into the difficulty of distinguishing between *by* of the passive (*the letter was finished by Carl*) and *by* as preposition (*the letter was finished by noon*).

verb and the passive verb which is different from the relation between -*ed* and *will*.

4.2 The distributional regularities can themselves be a subject of study. One can consider recurrent types of dependence and substitutabilities that are found in a language (or in many languages), and find on one level such relations as 'subject' and 'object' (semantic names for distributional positions), and on a higher level of generality such relations as 'constituent' and 'head of a construction' (if A occurs in environment X, and AB does too, but B does not, then A is the head of AB). One can consider the parts of a grammar which permit alternative distributional analyses, and check their relation to language change and dialect of idiolect interrelations (since probably every linguistic structure has some points which are structurally in flux). One can investigate what are the structural characteristics of those parts of a language which are productive. Furthermore, one can survey what is similar and what is different in a great many language structures, and how linguistic systems in general differ from such partially similar systems as mathematics and logistic 'languages', sign languages, gestures, codes, music.

THE PROBLEM OF MEANING IN
LINGUISTICS

W. V. QUINE

1

LEXICOGRAPHY is concerned, or seems to be concerned, with identification of meanings, and the investigation of semantic change is concerned with change of meaning. Pending a satisfactory explanation of
the notion of meaning, linguists in semantic fields are in the situation of
not knowing what they are talking about. This is not an untenable
situation. Ancient astronomers knew the movements of the planets
remarkably well without knowing what sort of things the planets were.
But it is a theoretically unsatisfactory situation, as the more theoretically
minded among the linguists are painfully aware.

Confusion of meaning with reference[1] has encouraged a tendency to
take the notion of meaning for granted. It is felt that the meaning of the
word 'man' is as tangible as our neighbour and that the meaning of the
phrase 'Evening Star' is as clear as the star in the sky. And it is felt that
to question or repudiate the notion of meaning is to suppose a world
in which there is just language and nothing for language to refer to.
Actually we can acknowledge a worldful of objects, and let our singular
and general terms refer to those objects in their several ways to our
hearts' content, without ever taking up the topic of meaning.

An object referred to, named by a singular term or denoted by a
general term, can be anything under the sun. Meanings, however, purport to be entities of a special sort: the meaning of an expression is the
idea expressed. Now there is considerable agreement among modern
linguists that the idea of an idea, the idea of the mental counterpart

[1] See *From a Logical Point of View*, pp. 9, 21 f.

of a linguistic form, is worse than worthless for linguistic science. I think the behaviourists are right in holding that talk of ideas is bad business even for psychology. The evil of the idea idea is that its use, like the appeal in Molière to a *virtus dormitiva*, engenders an illusion of having explained something. And the illusion is increased by the fact that things wind up in a vague enough state to insure a certain stability, or freedom from further progress.

Let us then look back to the lexicographer, supposed as he is to be concerned with meanings, and see what he is really trafficking in if not in mental entities. The answer is not far to seek: the lexicographer, like any linguist, studies linguistic forms. He differs from the so-called formal linguist only in that he is concerned to correlate linguistic forms with one another in his own special way, namely, synonyms with synonyms. The characteristic feature of semantical parts of linguistics, notably lexicography, comes to be not that there is an appeal to meanings but that there is a concern with synonymy.

What happens in this manœuvre is that we fix on one important context of the baffling word 'meaning', namely the context *'alike in meaning'*, and resolve to treat this whole context in the spirit of a single word 'synonymous', thus not being tempted to seek meanings as intermediary entities. But, even supposing that the notion of synonymy can eventually be provided with a satisfactory criterion, still this manœuvre only takes care of the one context of the word 'meaning'—the context 'alike in meaning'. Does the word also have other contexts that should concern linguists? Yes, there is certainly one more—the context 'having meaning'. Here a parallel manœuvre is in order: treat the context 'having meaning' in the spirit of a single word, 'significant', and continue to turn our backs on the supposititious entities called meanings.

Significance is the trait with respect to which the subject matter of linguistics is studied by the grammarian. The grammarian catalogues short forms and works out the laws of their concatenation, and the end product of this is no more nor less than a specification of the class of all possible linguistic forms, simple and composite, of the language under investigation—the class of all significant sequences, if we accept a liberal standard of significance. The lexicographer, on the other hand, is concerned with not specifying the class of significant sequences for the given language, but rather with specifying the class of pairs of mutually synonymous sequences for the given language or, perhaps, pair of languages. The grammarian and the lexicographer are concerned with meaning to an equal degree, be it zero or otherwise; the grammarian wants to know what forms are significant, or *have* meaning, while the lexicographer wants to know what forms are synonymous, or *alike* in meaning. If it is urged that the grammarian's notion of significant sequences should not be viewed as resting on a prior notion of meaning, I applaud; and I say the lexicographer's notion of synonymy is entitled to the same compliment. What had been the problem of meaning boils down now to a pair of problems in which meaning is best not mentioned; one is the problem of making sense of the notion of significant sequence, and the other is the problem of making sense of the notion of synonymy. What I want to emphasize is that the lexicographer had no monopoly on the problem of meaning. The problem of significant sequence and the problem of synonymy are twin offspring of the problem of meaning.

2

Let us suppose that our grammarian is at work on a hitherto unstudied language, and that his own contact with the language has been limited to his field work. As grammarian he is concerned to discover the bounds of the class K of significant sequences of the language. Synonymy correlations of members of K with English sequences and with one another are not his business; they are the business of the lexicographer.

There is presumably no upper limit to the lengths of members of K. Moreover, parts of significant sequences count as significant, down to the smallest adopted units of analysis; so such units, whatever they are, are the shortest members of K. Besides the length dimension, however, there is a dimension of thickness to consider. For, given two utterances of equal and arbitrary length and fairly similar acoustical make-up, we must know whether to count them as occurrences of two slightly different members of K or as two slightly different occurrences of one and the same member of K. The question of thickness is the question what acoustical differences to count as relevant and what ones to count merely as inconsequential idiosyncrasies of voice and accent.

The question of thickness is settled by cataloguing the *phonemes*— the single sounds, distinguished as coarsely as possible for purposes of the language. Two subtly differing sounds count as the same phoneme unless it is possible, by putting one for the other in some utterance, to change the meaning of the utterance.[2] Now the notion of phoneme, thus formulated, depends obviously and notoriously on the notion of sameness of meaning, or synonymy. Our grammarian, if he is to remain pure grammarian and eschew lexicography, must carry out his

---

[2] Cf. B. Bloch and G. L. Trager, *Outline of Linguistic Analysis*, Linguistic Society of America, Balitmore, 1942, pp. 38–52, or L. Bloomfield, *Language*, Holt, New York, 1933, pp. 74–92.

programme of delimiting K without the help of a notion of phoneme so defined.

There seems indeed, at first glance, to be an easy way out: he can simply enumerate the phonemes needed for the particular language at hand, and dispense with the general notion of phoneme defined in terms of synonymy. This expedient would be quite admissible as a mere technical aid to solving the grammarian's problem of specifying the membership of K, if the problem of specifying the membership of K could itself be *posed* without prior appeal to the general notion of phoneme. But the fact is otherwise. The class K which is the grammarian's empirical business to describe is a class of sequences of phonemes, and each phoneme is a class of brief events. (It will be convenient to swallow this much platonism for present purposes, though some logical manœuvres might serve to reduce it.) The grammarian's problem is in part objectively set for him thus: every speech event which he encounters in his field work counts as a sample of a member of K. But the delimiting of the several members of K, that is, the grouping of mutually resemblant, acoustical histories into bundles of proper thickness to qualify as linguistic forms, needs also to have some objective significance if the task of the field grammarian is to be made sense of as an empirical and objective task at all. This need is fulfilled if the general notion of phoneme is at hand, as a general relative term: 'x is a phoneme for language L', with variable 'x' and 'L', or 'x is a phoneme for speaker s', with variable 'x' and 's'. Thereupon the grammarian's business, with respect to a language L, can be stated as the business of finding what sequences of phonemes of L are significant for L. Statement of the grammarian's purpose thus depends not only on 'significant', as we had been prepared to expect, but also on 'phoneme'.

But we might still seek to free grammar of dependence on the notion of synonymy, by somehow freeing the notion of phoneme itself of such dependence. It has been conjectured, for example, by Bühler, that this might in principle be accomplished. Let the continuum of sounds be arranged in acoustical or physiological order in one or more dimensions, say two, and plotted against frequency of occurrence, so that we come out with a three-dimensional relief map in which altitude represents frequency of occurrence. Then it is suggested that the major humps correspond to the phonemes. There are abundant reasons to suspect that neither this oversimplified account nor anything remotely resembling it can possibly provide an adequate definition of the phoneme; and phonologists have not neglected to adduce such reasons. As a means of isolating other points of comparison between grammar and lexicography, however, let us make the unrealistic assumption that our grammarian has some such nonsemantical definition of phoneme. Then his remaining task is to devise a recursive description of a class K of forms which will comprise all and only those sequences of phonemes which are in fact significant.

The basic point of view is that the class K is objectively determinate before the grammatical research is begun; it is the class of the significant sequences, the sequences capable of occurring in the normal stream of speech (supposing for the moment that this terminology is itself significant). But the grammarian wants to reproduce this same class in other terms, formal terms; he wants to devise, in terms of elaborate conditions of phoneme succession alone, a necessary and sufficient condition for membership of K. He is an empirical scientist, and his result will be right or wrong according as he reproduces that objectively predetermined class K or some other.

Our grammarian's attempted recursive specification of K will follow the orthodox line, we may suppose, of listing 'morphemes' and describing constructions. Morphemes, according to the books,[3] are the significant forms which are not resoluble into shorter significant forms. They comprise affixes, word stems, and whole words in so far as these are not analysable into subsidiary morphemes. But we can spare our grammarian any general problem of defining morpheme by allowing him simply to list his so-called morphemes exhaustively. They become simply a convenient segmentation of heard phoneme sequences, chopped out as convenient building blocks for his purpose. He frames his constructions in the simplest way that will enable him to generate all members of K from his morphemes, and he cuts his morphemes to allow for the simplest constructions. Morphemes, like higher units such as might be called words or free forms, may thus be viewed simply as intermediate stages in a process which, overall, is still describable as reproduction of K in terms of conditions of phoneme succession.

There is no denying that the grammarian's reproduction of K, as I have schematized it, is purely formal, that is, free of semantics. But the setting of the grammarian's problem is quite another matter, for it turns on a prior notion of significant sequence, or possible normal utterance. Without this notion, or something to somewhat the same effect, we cannot say what the grammarian is trying to do—what he is trying to match in his formal reproduction of K—nor wherein the rightness or wrongness of his results might consist. We are thus squarely confronted with one of the twin offspring of the problem of meaning, namely, the problem of defining the general notion of significant sequence.

---

[3] Bloch and Trager, p. 54; Bloomfield, pp. 161-8.

3

It is not satisfactory to say that a significant sequence is simply any sequence of phonemes uttered by any of the *Naturkinder* of our grammarian's chosen valley. What are wanted as significant sequences include not just those uttered but also those which *could* be uttered without reactions suggesting bizarreness of idiom. The joker here is 'could'; we cannot substitute 'will'. The significant sequences, being subject to no length limit, are infinite in variety; whereas, from the dawn of the language under investigation to the time when it will have evolved to the point where our grammarian would disown it, only a finite sample of this infinite manifold will have been uttered.

The desired class K of significant sequences is the culmination of a series of four classes of increasing magnitude, H, I, J, and K, as follows. H is the class of observed sequences, excluding any which are ruled inappropriate in the sense of being non-linguistic or belonging to alien dialects. I is the class of all such observed sequences and all that ever will happen to be professionally observed, excluding again those which are ruled inappropriate. J is the class of all sequences ever occurring, now or in the past or future, within or without professional observation—excluding, again, only those which are ruled inappropriate. K, finally, is the infinite class of all those sequences, with exclusion of the inappropriate ones as usual, which *could* be uttered without bizarreness reactions. K is the class which the grammarian wants to approximate in his formal reconstruction, and K is more inclusive even than J, let alone H and I. Now the class H is a matter of finished record; the class I is, or could be, a matter of growing record; the class J goes beyond any record, but still has a certain common-sense reality; but not even this can very confidently be said of K, because of the 'could'.

I expect we must leave the 'could' unreduced. It has some operational import, indeed, but only in a partial way. It does require our grammarian to bring into his formal reconstruction of K all of the actually observed cases, that is, all of H. Further, it commits him to the prediction that all cases to be observed in the future will conform, that is, all of I belongs to K. Further still, it commits him to the scientific hypothesis that all unobserved cases fall in this K, that is, all of J. Now what more does the 'could' cover? What is the rationale behind that infinite additional membership of K, over and above the finite part J? This vast supplementary force of 'could', in the present instance and elsewhere, is perhaps a vestige of Indo-European myth, fossilized in the subjunctive word.

What our grammarian does is evident enough. He frames his formal reconstruction of K along the grammatically simplest lines he can, compatibly with inclusion of H, plausibility of the predicted inclusion of I, plausibility of the hypothesis of inclusion of J, and plausibility, further, of the exclusion of all sequences which ever actually do bring bizarreness reactions. Our basis for saying what 'could' be generally consists, I suggest, in what *is* plus *simplicity* of the laws whereby we describe and extrapolate what is. I see no more objective way of construing the *conditio irrealis*.

Concerning the notions of significant sequences, one of the two survivals of the notion of meaning, we have now observed the following. It is needed in setting the grammarian's task. But it is describable, without appeal to meanings as such, as denoting any sequence which could be uttered in the society under consideration without reactions suggesting bizarreness of idiom. This notion of a reaction suggesting bizarreness of idiom, would want some refinement eventually. A considerable problem of refinement is involved also in the preliminary putting aside of so-called nonlinguistic noises, as well as utterances in alien dialects. Also there is the general methodological problem, of a pretty philosophical kind, which is raised by the word 'could'. This is a problem common to concept-building in most subjects (apart from logic and mathematics, where it happens to be well cleared up); I have outlined one attitude toward it.

We should also remind ourselves of the oversimplification which I made with regard to morphemes, when I treated them merely as convenient phoneme sequences which our grammarian specifies by enumeration in the course of his formal reconstruction of the class of significant sequences from the phonemes. This is unrealistic because it requires our grammarian to exhaust the vocabulary, instead of allowing him to leave certain open categories, comparable to our nouns and verbs, subject to enrichment *ad libitum*. Now if on the other hand we allow him some open morpheme categories, his reconstruction of the class K of significant sequences ceases to be a formal construction from phonemes; the most we can say for it is that it is a formal reconstruction from phonemes and his open morpheme categories. So the problem remains how he is going to characterize his open morpheme categories—since enumeration no longer serves. This gap must be watched for possible intrusion of an unanalysed semantical element.

I do not want to take leave of the topic of significant sequence without mentioning one curious further problem which the notion raises. I shall speak now of English rather than a hypothetical heathen tongue. Any nonsensical and thoroughly un-English string of sounds can occur within a perfectly intelligible English sentence, even a true one, if in effect we quote the nonsense and say in the rest of our sentence that the quoted matter *is* nonsense, or is not English, or consists of four syllables, or rhymes with 'Kalamazoo', etc. If the whole inclusive sentence is to be called normal English speech, then the rubbish inside it has occurred in normal English speech and we have thus lost the means of excluding any pronounceable sequence from the category of significant sequence. Thus we must either narrow our concept of normality to exclude, for present purposes, sentences which use quotation, or else we must narrow our concept of occurrence to exclude occurrence within quotation. In either event we have the problem of identifying the spoken analogue of quotation marks, and of doing so in general enough terms so that our concept of significant sequence will not be limited in advance to some one preconceived language such as English.

In any case we have seen that the problem of significant sequence admits of considerable fragmentation; and this is one of the two aspects into which the problem of meaning seemed to resolve, namely, the aspect of the having of meaning. The fact that this aspect of the problem of meaning is in such halfway tolerable shape accounts, no doubt, for the tendency to think of grammar as a formal, nonsemantical part of linguistics. Let us turn now to the other and more forbidding aspect of the problem of meaning, that of likeness in meaning, or synonymy.

4

A lexicographer may be concerned with synonymy between forms in one language and forms in another or, as in compiling a domestic dictionary, he may be concerned with synonymy between forms in the same language. It is an open question how satisfactorily the two cases can be subsumed under a single general formulation of the synonymy concept, for it is an open question whether the synonymy concept can be satisfactorily clarified for either case. Let us first limit our attention to synonymy within a language.

So-called substitution criteria, or conditions of interchangability, have in one form or another played central roles in modern grammar. For the synonymy problem of semantics such an approach seems more obvious still. However, the notion of the interchangeability of two linguistic forms makes sense only in so far as answers are provided to these two questions: (*a*) In just what sorts of contextual position, if not in all, are the two forms to be interchangeable? (*b*) The forms are to be interchangeable *salvo quo*? Supplanting one form by another in any context changes something, namely, form at least; and (*b*) asks what feature the interchange is to leave invariant. Alternative answers to (*a*) and (*b*) give alternative notions of interchangeability, some suited to defining grammatical correspondences and others, conceivably, to defining synonymy.

In § 3 of Essay II we tried answering (*b*), for purposes of synonymy, with *veritate*.[4] We found that something had still to be done about (*a*), in view, for example, of the difficulty presented by quotation. So we answered (*a*), lamely appealing to a prior conception of 'word'. Then we found that interchangeability *salva veritate* was too weak a condition for synonymy if the language as a whole was 'extensional', and that in other languages it was an unilluminating condition, involving something like a vicious circle.

It is not clear that the problem of synonymy discussed in those pages is the same as the lexicographer's problem. For in those pages we were concerned with 'cognitive' synonymy, which abstracts from much that the lexicographer would want to preserve in his translations and paraphrases. Even the lexicographer is indeed ready to equate, as synonymous, many forms which differ perceptibly in imaginative associations and poetic value;[5] but the optimum sense of synonymy for his purpose is probably narrower than synonymy in the supposed cognitive sense. However this may be, certainly the negative findings which were summed up in the preceding paragraph carry over; the lexicographer cannot answer (*b*) with *veritate*. The interchangeability which he seeks in synonymy must not merely be such as to assure that true statements remain true, and false ones false, when synonyms are substituted within them; it must assure further that statements go over into statements with which they as wholes are somehow synonymous.

This last observation does not recommend itself as a definition, because of its circularity: forms are synonymous when their interchange leaves their contexts synonymous. But it has the virtue of hinting that substitution is not the main point, and that what we need in the first place is some notion of synonymy for long segments of discourse. The hint is opportune; for, independently of the foregoing considerations, three reasons can be adduced for approaching the problem of synonymy from the point of view of long segments of discourse.

First, any interchangeability criterion for synonymy of short forms would obviously be limited to synonymy within a language; otherwise interchange would produce polyglot jumbles. *Inter*linguistic synonymy must be a relation, primarily, between segments of discourse which are long enough to bear consideration in abstraction from a containing context peculiar to one or the other particular language. I say 'primarily'

---

[4] W. V. Quine, *From a Logical Point of View*.
[5] See *From a Logical Point of View*, p. 28.

because interlinguistic synonymy might indeed be defined for the component forms afterward in some derivative way.

Second, a retreat to longer segments tends to overcome the difficulty of ambiguity or homonymy. Homonymy gets in the way of the law that if a is synonymous with b and b with c, then a is synonymous with c. For, if b has two meanings (to revert to the ordinary parlance of meanings), a may be synonymous with b in one sense of b with c in the other sense of b. This difficulty is sometimes dealt with by treating an ambiguous form as two forms, but this expedient has the drawback of making the concept of form depend on that of synonymy.

Third, there is the circumstance that in glossing a word we have so frequently to content ourselves with a lame partial synonym plus stage directions. Thus in glossing 'addled' we say 'spoiled' and add 'said of an egg'. This widespread circumstance reflects the fact that synonymy in the small is no primary concern of the lexicographer; lame synonyms plus stage directions are quite satisfactory in so far as they expedite his primary business of explaining how to translate or paraphrase long speeches. We may continue to characterize the lexicographer's domain squarely as synonymy, but only by recognizing synonymy as primarily a relation of sufficiently long segments of discourse.

So we may view the lexicographer as interested, ultimately, only in cataloguing synonym pairs which are sequences of sufficient length to admit of synonymy in some primary sense. Naturally he cannot catalogue these true synonym pairs directly, in any exhaustive way, because they are altogether limitless in number and variety. His case is parallel to that of the grammarian, who for the same reason was unable to catalogue the significant sequences directly. The grammarian accomplished his end indirectly, by fixing on a class of atomic units capable of enumeration and then propounding rules for compounding them to get all significant sequences. Similarly the lexicographer accomplishes his end indirectly, the end of specifying the infinitely numerous genuine pairs of long synonyms, and this he does by fixing on a class of short forms capable of enumeration and then explaining as systematically as he can how to construct genuine synonyms for all sufficiently long forms compounded of those short ones. These short forms are in effect the word entries in his glossary, and the explanations of how to construct genuine synonyms of all sufficiently long compounds are what appear as the glosses in his glossary, typically a mixture of quasi synonyms and stage directions.

Thus the lexicographer's actual activity, his glossing of short forms by appeal to quasi synonyms and stage directions, is not antithetical to his being concerned purely and simply with genuine synonymy on the part of forms sufficiently long to admit of genuine synonymy. Something like his actual activity is indeed the only possible way of cataloguing, in effect, the limitless class of pairs of genuinely synonymous longer forms.

I exploited just now a parallelism between the grammarian's indirect reconstruction of the limitless class of significant sequences and the lexicographer's indirect reconstruction of the limitless class of genuine synonym pairs. This parallelism bears further exploiting. It brings out that the lexicographer's reconstruction of the class of synonym pairs is just as formal in spirit as the grammarian's reconstruction of the class of significant sequences. The invidious use of the word 'formal', to favour grammar as against lexicography, is thus misleading. Both the lexicographer and the grammarian would simply list the membership of the respective classes in which they are interested, were it not for the vastness, the infinitude even, of the numbers involved. On the other hand, just as the grammarian needs over and above his formal constructions a prior notion of significant sequence for the setting of his problem, so the lexicographer needs a prior notion of synonym for the setting of his. In the setting of their problems, the grammarian and the lexicographer draw equally on our heritage from the old notion of meaning.

It is clear from the foregoing reflections that the notion of synonymy needed in the statement of the lexicographer's problem is synonymy only as between sequences which are long enough to be pretty clean-cut about their synonymy connections. But in conclusion I want to stress what a baffling problem this remaining problem of synonymy, even relatively clean-cut and well-behaved synonymy, is.

5

Synonymy of two forms is supposed vaguely to consist in an approximate likeness in the situations which evoke the two forms, and an approximate likeness in effect of either form on the hearer. For simplicity let us forget this second requirement and concentrate on the first —the likeness of situations. What I have to say from here on will be so vague, at best, that this further inaccuracy will not much matter.

As everyone is quick to point out, no two situations are quite alike; situations in which even the same form is uttered are unlike in myriad ways. What matters rather is likeness in *relevant respects*. Now the problem of finding the relevant respects is, if we think of the matter in a sufficiently over-simplified way, a problem typical of empirical science. We observe a speaker of Kalaba, say—to adopt Pike's myth

—and we look for correlations or so-called causal connections between the noises he makes and the other things that are observed to be happening. As in any empirical search for correlations or so-called causal connections, we guess at the relevance of one or another feature and then try by further observation, or even experiment, to confirm or refute our hypothesis. Actually, in lexicography this guessing at possible relevances is expedited by our natural familiarity with the basic lines of human interest. Finally, having found fair evidence for correlating a given Kalaba sound sequence with a given combination of circumstances, we conjecture synonymy of that sound sequence with another, in English, say, which is correlated with the same circumstances.

As I unnecessarily remarked, this account is over-simplified. Now I want to stress one serious respect in which it is over-simplified: the relevant features of the situation issuing in a given Kalaba utterance are in large part concealed in the person of the speaker, where they were implanted by his earlier environment. This concealment is partly good, for our purposes, and partly bad. It is good in so far as it isolates the subject's narrowly linguistic training. If we could assume that our Kalaba speaker and our English speaker, when observed in like external situations, differed only in how they say things and not in *what* they say, so to speak, then the methodology of synonymy determinations would be pretty smooth; the narrowly linguistic part of the causal complex, different for the two speakers, would be conveniently out of sight, while all the parts of the causal complex decisive of synonymy or heteronymy were open to observation. But of course the trouble is that not only the narrowly linguistic habits of vocabulary and syntax are imported by each speaker from his unknown past.

The difficulty here is not just that those subjective components of the situation are hard to ferret out. This difficulty, if it were all, would make for practical uncertainty and frequent error in lexicographical pronouncements, but it would be irrelevant to the problem of a theoretical definition of synonymy—irrelevant, that is, to the problem of coherently stating the lexicographer's purpose. Theoretically the more important difficulty is that, as Cassirer and Whorf have stressed, there is in principle no separating language from the rest of the world, at least as conceived by the speaker. Basic differences in language are bound up, as likely as not, with differences in the way in which the speakers articulate the world itself into things and properties, time and space, elements, forces, spirits, and so on. It is not clear even in principle that it makes sense to think of words and syntax as varying from language to language while the content stays fixed; yet precisely this fixation is involved in speaking of synonymy, at least as between expressions of radically different languages.

What provides the lexicographer with an entering wedge is the fact that there are many basic features of men's ways of conceptualizing their environment, of breaking the world down into things, which are common to all cultures. Every man is likely to see an apple or bread-fruit or rabbit first and foremost as a unitary whole rather than as a congeries of smaller units or as a fragment of a larger environment, though from a sophisticated point of view all these attitudes are tenable. Every man will tend to segregate a mass of moving matter as a unit, separate from the static background, and to pay it particular attention. Again there are conspicuous phenomena of weather which one man may be expected to endow with much the same conceptual boundaries as another; and similarly perhaps for some basic internal states such as hunger. As long as we adhere to this presumably common fund of conceptualization, we can successfully proceed on the working assumption that our Kalaba speaker and our English speaker, observed in like external situations, differ only in how they say things and not in what they say.

The nature of this entering wedge into a strange lexicon encourages the misconception of meaning as reference, since words at this stage are construed, typically, by pointing to the object referred to. So it may not be amiss to remind ourselves that meaning is not reference even here. The reference might be the Evening Star, to return to Frege's example, and hence also the Morning Star, which is the same thing; but 'Evening Star' might nevertheless be a good translation and 'Morning Star' a bad one.

I have suggested that our lexicographer's obvious first moves in picking up some initial Kalaba vocabulary are at bottom a matter of exploiting the overlap of our cultures. From this nucleus he words out-ward, even more fallibly and conjecturally, by a series of clues and hunches. Thus he begins with a fund of correlations of Kalaba sentences with English sentences at the level where our cultures meet. Most of these sentences classify conspicuously segregated objects. Then he breaks these Kalaba sentences down into short component elements, and makes tentative English translations of these elements, compatible with his initial sentence translations. On this basis, he frames hypotheses as to the English translations of new combinations of those elements— combinations which as wholes have not been translated in the direct way. He tests his hypotheses as best he can by making further observa-tions and keeping an eye out for conflicts. But, as the sentences under-going translation get further and further from mere reports of common observations, the clarity of any possible conflict decreases; the lexi-cographer comes to depend increasingly on a projection of himself, with his Indo-European *Weltanschauung*, into the sandals of his Kalaba informant. He comes also to turn increasingly to that last refuge of all scientists, the appeal to internal simplicity of his growing system.

The finished lexicon is a case, evidently, of *ex pede Herculem*. But there is a difference. In projecting Hercules from the foot we risk error, but we may derive comfort from the fact that there is something to be wrong about. In the case of the lexicon, pending some definition of synonymy, we have no statement of the problem; we have nothing for the lexicographer to be right or wrong about.

Quite possibly the ultimately fruitful notion of synonymy will be one of degree: not the dyadic relation of *a* as synonymous with *b*, but the tetradic relation of *a* as more synonymous with *b* than *c* with *d*. But to classify the notion as a matter of degree is not to explain it; we shall still want a criterion or at least a definition for our tetradic relation. The big difficulty to be surmounted in devising a definition, whether of a dyadic relation of absolute synonymy or a tetradic rela-tion of comparative synonymy, is the difficulty of making up our minds as to just what we are trying to do when we translate a Kalaba statement which is not a mere report on fairly directly observable features of the surrounding situation.

The other branch of the problem of meaning, namely the problem of defining significant sequence, led us into a contrary-to-fact condi-tional: a significant sequence is one that *could* be uttered without such and such adverse reactions. I urged that the operational content of this 'could' is incomplete, leaving scope for free supplementary determina-tions of a grammatical theory in the light of simplicity considerations. But we are well schooled in acquiescing in contrary-to-fact conditionals. In the case of synonymy the tyranny of the developing system, the paucity of explicit objective controls, is more conspicuous.

B. CONCEPTUALIST FOUNDATIONS

4

THE PSYCHOLOGICAL REALITY OF PHONEMES

E. SAPIR

THE CONCEPT of the 'phoneme' (a functionally significant unit in the rigidly defined pattern or configuration of sounds peculiar to a language), as distinct from that of the 'sound' or 'phonetic element' as such (an objectively definable entity in the articulated and perceived totality of speech), is becoming more and more familiar to linguists. The difficulty that many still seem to feel in distinguishing between the two must eventually disappear as the realization grows that no entity in human experience can be adequately defined as the mechanical sum or product of its physical properties. These physical properties are needed of course to give us the signal, as it were, for the identification of the given entity as a functionally significant point in a complex system of relatednesses; but for any given context it is notorious how many of these physical properties are, or may be, overlooked as irrelevant, how one particular property, possessing for the moment or by social understanding an unusual sign value, may have a determinedness in the definition of the entity that is out of all proportion to its 'physical weight'.

As soon, however, as we admit that all significant entities in experience are thus revised from the physically given by passing through the filter of the functionally or relatedly meaningful, as soon as we see that we can never set up a scale of added or changed meanings that is simply congruent to the scale of physical increments, we implicitly make a distinction whether we know it or not, between the phoneme and the sound in that particular framework of experience which is known as language (actualized as speech). To say that a given phoneme is not sufficiently defined in articulatory or acoustic terms but needs to be fitted into the total system of sound relations peculiar to the language

From 'Language' by Edward Sapir. A portion of this article is reprinted by permission of the publisher from the *Encyclopedia of the Social Sciences*, Edwin R. A. Seligman, Editor in Chief. Volume 9, pp. 155–168. Copyright 1933, renewed 1961 by Macmillan Publishing Company.

is, at bottom, no more mysterious than to say that a club is not defined for us when it is said to be made of wood and to have such and such a shape and such and such dimensions. We must understand why a roughly similar object, not so different to the eye, is no club at all, and why a third object, of very different colour and much longer and heavier than the first, is for all that very much of a club.

Some linguists seem to feel that the phoneme is a useful enough concept in an abstract linguistic discussion—in the theoretical presentation of the form of a language or in the comparison of related languages—but that it has small relevance for the actualities of speech. This point of view seems the reverse of realistic to the present writer. Just as it takes a physicist or philosopher to define an object in terms of such abstract concepts as mass, volume, chemical structure, and location, so it takes very much of a linguistic abstractionist, a phonetician pure and simple, to reduce articulate speech to simple physical processes. To the physicist, the three wooden objects are equally distinct from each other, 'clubs' are romantic intrusions into the austere continuities of nature. But the naïve human being is much surer of his clubs and poles than of unnamed objects to be hereinafter defined in physical terms. So, in speech, precise phonetic stations can be abstracted only by patient observation and frequently at the expense of a direct flouting of one's phonetic (one should say 'phonemic') intuitions. In the physical world the naïve speaker and hearer actualize and are sensitive to sounds, but what they feel themselves to be prounouncing and hearing are 'phonemes'. They order the fundamental elements of linguistic experience into functionally and aesthetically determinate shapes, each of which is carved out by its exclusive laws of relationship within the complex total of all possible sound relationships. To the naïve speaker and hearer, sounds (i.e. phonemes) do not differ as five-inch or six-inch entities differ, but as clubs and poles differ. If the phonetician discovers in the flow of actual speech something that is neither 'club' nor 'pole', he, as phonetician, has the right to set up a 'halfway between club and pole' entity. Functionally, however, such an entity is a fiction, and the naïve speaker or hearer is not only driven by its relational behaviour to classify it as a 'club' or a 'pole', but actually hears and feels it to be such.

If the phonemic attitude is more basic, psychologically speaking, than the more strictly phonetic one, it should be possible to detect it in the unguarded speech judgements of naïve speakers who have a complete control of their language in a practical sense but have no rationalized or consciously systematic knowledge of it. 'Errors' of analysis, or what the sophisticated onlooker is liable to consider such, may be expected to occur which have the characteristic of being phonetically unsound or inconsistent but which at the same time register a feeling for what is phonemically accurate. Such 'errors', generally overlooked by the practical field linguist, may constitute valuable evidence for the dynamic reality of the phonemic structure of the language.

In the course of many years of experience in the recording and analysis of unwritten languages, American Indian and African, I have come to the practical realization that what the naïve speaker hears is not phonetic elements but phonemes. The problem reaches the stage of a practical test when one wishes to teach an intelligent native, say one who can read and write English reasonably well and has some intellectual curiosity besides, how to write his own language. The difficulty of such a task varies, of course, with the intelligence of the native and the intrinsic difficulty of his language, but it varies also with the 'phonemic intuitiveness' of the teacher. Many well-meaning linguists have had disappointing experiences in this regard with quite intelligent natives without ever suspecting that the trouble lay, not with the native, but with themselves. It is exceedingly difficult, if not impossible, to teach a native to take account of purely mechanical phonetic variations which have no phonemic reality for him. The teacher who comes prepared with a gamut of absolute phonetic possibilities and who unconsciously, in spite of all his training, tends to project the phonemic valuations of his own language into what he hears and records of the exotic one may easily befuddle a native. The native realizes when what he is taught 'clicks' with what his phonological intuitions have already taught him; but he is made uncomfortable when purely phonetic distinctions are pointed out to him which seem real enough when he focuses his attention on them but which are always fading out of his consciousness because their objective reality is not confirmed by these intuitions.

I have selected for brief discussion five examples of phonemic versus phonetic hearing and writing out of many which have come to me in the course of my experience with natives and students. In each of these, it will be observed, we have clear evidence of the unconscious reinterpretation of objective facts because of a disturbing phonological preparedness not precisely adjusted to these facts.

1

When working on the Southern Paiute language of south-western Utah and north-western Arizona I spent a little time in trying to teach my native interpreter, a young man of average intelligence, how to write his language phonetically. Southern Paiute is an unusually involved language from the phonological standpoint and, as my point of view at that time stressed phonetic accuracy rather than phonemic adequacy, I doubt if I could have succeeded in teaching him well enough to satisfy my standard even if I had devoted far more time to the effort than I did. As an example of a comparatively simple word I selected *pá·βa'* 'at the water' (voiceless labial stop; stressed long *a*; voiced bilabial spirant; unstressed short *a*; final aspiration). I instructed Tony to divide the word into its syllables and to discover by careful hearing what sounds entered into the composition of each of the syllables, and in what order, then to attempt to write down the proper symbol for each of the discovered phonetic elements. To my astonishment Tony then syllabified: *pa·*, pause, *pa'*. I say 'astonishment' because I at once recognized the paradox that Tony was not 'hearing' in terms of the actual sounds (the voiced bilabial *β* was objectively very different from the initial stop) but in terms of an etymological reconstruction: *pa·-* 'water' plus postposition **-pa'* 'at'. The slight pause which intervened after the stem was enough to divert Tony from the phonetically proper form of the postposition to a theoretically real but actually non-existent form.

To understand Tony's behaviour, which was not in the least due to mere carelessness nor to a tendency of the speakers of this language 'to confuse sounds', to quote the time-worn shibboleth, we must have recourse to the phonology of Southern Paiute. The treatment of the stopped consonants may be summarized in the following table:

	Initial	Postvocalic		
		1. Spirantized	2. Nasalized	3. Geminated
				(*a*) After voiced vowel / (*b*) After unvoiced vowel
Labial	*p*	*β*	*mp*	*p·* *p*
Dental	*t*	*r*	*nt*	*t·* *t*
Guttural	*k*	*γ*	*ŋk*	*k·* *k*
Labialized guttural	*kw*	*γw*	*ŋkw*	*k·w* *kw*

The postvocalic forms of the stops of types 1, 2, and 3*a* are further modified before an unvoiced vowel, the voiced spirants becoming un-

unvoiced spirants (ϕ, R, χ, χ^W),[1] and the nasalized and geminated stops becoming aspirated ($mp\lq$; $p\lq$; $nt\lq$, $t\cdot\lq$; $\eta k\lq$; $k\cdot\lq$; ηkW, $k\cdot W$). It is impossible here to give a systematic idea of the phonological processes which bring about the sound interchanges within a given articulatory series, but it is important to know that the spirantized, nasalized, and geminated stops can occur only in postvocalic position and that they are largely determined by the nature of the element (stem or suffix) which precedes them and which may be said to have an inherently spirantizing, nasalizing, or geminating force. The stem $pa\cdot$- is a spirantizing stem, and the spirantizing of a theoretical *-$pa\lq$ 'at' to -$\beta a\lq$ is parallel to the spirantizing of $p\jmath\cdot$- 'trail' to -$\beta\jmath\cdot$- in such a compound as $pa\cdot$-$\beta\jmath\cdot$-, 'water-trail'. In other words, the language is so patterned that examples of type $p\jmath\cdot$-:-$\beta\jmath\cdot$- lead to the proportion *$pa\lq$: -$\beta a\lq$[2] and, while *$pa\lq$ 'at' does not actually exist as an independent element but must always be actualized in one of the three possible postvocalic forms, its theoretical existence suddenly comes to the light of day when the problem of slowly syllabifying a word is presented to a native speaker for the first time. It then appears that the -$\beta a\lq$ of speech behaviour, as a self-contained syllabic entity without immediately preceding syllable, is actually felt as a phonologic $pa\lq$, from which it differs in two important phonetic respects (voiced, not voiceless, consonant; spirant, not stop).

All this has an important bearing on the construction of a maximally correct orthography of Southern Paiute, if by 'maximally correct' we mean, not most adequate phonetically, but most true to the sound patterning of the language. As it happens, there is reason to believe from both internal and comparative evidence that the spirantized form of a consonant is its normal or primary form after a vowel and that the nasalized and geminated forms are due to the emergence of old nasal and other consonants that had disappeared in the obsolete form of the preceding element.[3] It follows that the postvocalic -β- is more closely related functionally to a simple initial p- than is the postvocalic -p- (after unvoiced vowel), which must always be interpreted as a secondary form of -$p\cdot$-. These relations are summarized in the following table of theoretical non-final forms.

The phonetic orthography is more complex and, in a sense, more

---

[1] W represents voiceless w.

[2] This theoretical *$pa\lq$, occurring only as -$\beta a\lq$, -$mpa\lq$, -$p\cdot a\lq$ in postvocalic position, is not to be confused with secondary (-$pa\lq$ type 3b) < -$p\cdot a\lq$ type 3a).

[3] The analogy to French liaison and, still more, to the three types of consonantal treatment in Old Irish (spirantized or 'aspirated', nasalized or 'eclipsed', and geminated) is obvious.

Phonetic Orthography	Phonologic Orthography
1. pa-	pa-
2. paβa-	papa-
3. paφA-[4]	papa-
4. pap·a-	pap·a-
5. pApa-	pap·a-
6. pap·A-	pap·a-

adequate, but it goes against the grain of the language in one important respect, for it identifies the second p in type 5 with the initial p, which is phonologically unsound. The phonological orthography, on the other hand, is useless for one who has not mastered the phonology of the language, as it leads, or seems to lead, to incorrect pronunciations which would have the cumulative effect of making the language, so read, entirely unintelligible to a native. To a slightly schooled native, however, there can be no serious ambiguity, for the phonetic forms result from the phonologic only by the application of absolutely mechanical phonetic laws of spirantizing, alternating stresses, and unvoicing.[5]

Southern Paiute, then, is a language in which an unusually simple phonemic structure is actualized by a more than ordinarily complex phonetic one. Tony's 'error' unconsciously registered this contrast.

2

When working on Sarcee, an Athabaskan language of Alberta, Canada, I was concerned with the problem of deciding whether certain words that seemed homonymous were actually so or differed in some subtle phonetic respect that was not immediately obvious. One such homonymous, or apparently homonymous, pair of words was dìnì[6] 'this one' and dìní 'it makes a sound'. In the early stage of our work I asked my interpreter, John Whitney, whether the two words sounded alike to him and he answered without hesitation that they were quite different. This statement, however, did not prove that he was objectively correct, as it is possible for perfectly homonymous words to give the speaker the illusion of phonetic difference because of the different contexts in which they appear or because of the different positions they occupy

---

[4] A represents voiceless a.

[5] They are described in detail in E. Sapir, 'The Southern Paiute Language', *Proceedings of the American Academy of Arts and Sciences*, 65 (1930).

[6] The grave accent represents a low tone, the acute accent a high one. Sarcee is a tone language.

in their respective form systems.[7] When I asked him what the difference was, he found it difficult to say, and the more often he pronounced the words over to himself the more confused he became as to their phonetic difference. Yet all the time he seemed perfectly sure that there was a difference. At various moments I thought I could catch a slight phonetic difference, for instance, (1) that the -*ní* of 'this one' was on a slightly lower tone than the -*ní* of 'it makes a sound'; (2) that there was a slight stress on the *dí*- of 'this one' (analysis: stem *dí*- 'this' plus suffix -*ní* 'person') and a similarly slight stress on the -*ní* of 'it makes a sound' (analysis: prefix *dí*- plus verb stem -*ní*); (3) that the -*ní* of 'this one' ended in a pure vowel with little or no breath release, while the -*ní* of 'it makes a sound' had a more audible breath release, was properly -*ní'*. These suggestions were considered and halfheartedly accepted at various times by John, but it was easy to see that he was not intuitively convinced. The one tangible suggestion that he himself made was obviously incorrect, namely, that the -*ní* of 'it makes a sound' ended in a '*t*'. John claimed that he 'felt a *t*' in the syllable, yet when he tested it over and over to himself, he had to admit that he could neither hear a '*t*' nor feel his tongue articulating one. We had to give up the problem, and I silently concluded that there simply was no phonetic difference between the words and that John was trying to convince himself there was one merely because they were so different in grammatical form and function that he felt there ought to be a difference.

I did not then know enough about Sarcee phonology to understand the mysterious '*t*' theory. Later on it developed that there are phonologically distinct types of final vowels in Sarcee: smooth or simple vowels; and vowels with a consonantal latency, i.e. vowels originally followed by a consonant which disappears in the absolute form of the word but which reappears when the word has a suffix beginning with a vowel or which makes its former presence felt in other sandhi

---

[7] Thus, in English, the word *led* (e.g. 'I *led* him away') is felt as having a vowel which has been deflected from the vowel of *lead* (e.g. 'I *lead* him away') and is therefore not psychologically homonymous with the word for a metal, *lead*, in which the vowel is felt to be primary, not deflected (cf. further, 'the *leading* of the windowpane', 'the *leaded* glass', 'the different *leads* now recognized by chemists'). The homonymy of *led* and *lead* (metal) is therefore of a different psychological order from the homonymy of *yard* ('He plays in my *yard*') and *yard* ('I want a *yard* of silk'), for the last two words enter into roughly parallel form systems (e.g. 'Their *yards* were too small to play in': 'I want two *yards* of silk'; '*yard* upon *yard* of railroad tracks': '*yard* upon *yard* of lovely fabrics'). It is probably easier for the naïve speaker, who does not know how to spell either *led* or *lead* (metal), to convince himself that there is a phonetic difference between these two words than between the two words *yard*.

phenomena. One of these disappearing consonants is *-t'*, of which *-'* may be considered a weakened form. Now it happens that all final vowels are pronounced with a breath release in the absolute form of the word and that there is no objective difference between this secondary *-'*, which may be symbolized as *-(')*, phonologically zero, and the etymologically organic *-'*, which may affect certain following consonants of suffixed elements or, in some cases, pass over to one of certain other consonants, such as *t'*. The *-ní* of 'this one', phonetically *-ni'* in absolute form, is phonologically simple *-ní*; the *-ní* of 'it makes a sound', phonetically *-ní'* in absolute form, can be phonologically represented as *-ní'* (*-nít'-*). We can best understand the facts if we test the nature of these two syllables by seeing how they behave if immediately followed by suffixed relative *-í* 'the one who . . .' and inferential *-la*[8] 'it turns out that'.

	plus *-í*	plus *-la*
dini 'this one'	*diná·ᵃ*[9]	*diníla*
dini 'it makes a sound'	*dinít'í*	*diníła*[10]

We see at once that *diní* 'this one' behaves like a word ending in a smooth vowel (witness contraction of *í* + *í* to an over-long vowel and unaffected *l* of *-la*), while *diní* 'it makes a sound' acts as though the final vowel had a voiceless consonantal latency, which registers partly as *-'* (*-'-la* passing, as always, to *-ła*), partly as *-t'-*.

It is clear that, while John was phonetically amateurish, he was phonologically subtle and accurate. His response amounted to an index of the feeling that *diní* 'this one' = *diní*, that *diní* 'it makes a sound' = *diní'*, and that this *-ní'* = *-nít'*. John's certainty of difference in the face of objective identity is quite parallel to the feeling that the average Englishman would have that such words as *sawed* and *soared* are not phonetically identical. It is true that both *sawed* and *soared* can be phonetically represented as *sɔ·d*,[11] but the *-ing* forms of the two verbs (*sawing, soaring*), phonetically *sɔ·-iŋ* and *sɔ·r-iŋ*, and such sentence

---

[8] The lack of a tone mark indicates that this syllable is pronounced on the middle tone.

[9] *a.ᵃ* is an over-long *a*, consisting of a long *a·* followed by a weak rearticulated *a*. Syllables of this type result in Sarcee from contraction of old final vowels with following suffixed vowels. The change in quality from *-í* to *-á·ᵃ* is due to historical factors. *-ní* 'person' is an old *-né* (with pepet vowel), relative *-í* is old *-é*; two pepet vowels contract to long open *-ε·ᵉ*; as Athabaskan ε becomes Sarcee *a*, this older *-é·ᵉ* passes into Sarcee *-á·ᵃ*.

[10] *ł* is voiceless spirantal *l*, as in Welsh *ll*.

[11] These remarks apply to British, not to normal American, usage.

sandhi forms as 'Saw on, my boy!' and 'Soar into the sky!' combine to produce the feeling that the *sɔ·d* of *sawed* = *sɔ·d* but that the *sɔ·d* of *soared* = *sɔ·r-d*. In the one case zero = zero, in the other case zero = *r*. Among educated but linguistically untrained people who discuss such matters differences of orthography are always held responsible for these differences of feeling. This is undoubtedly a fallacy, at least for the great mass of people, and puts the cart before the horse. Were English not a written language, the configuratively determined phonologic difference between such doublets as *sawed* and *soared* would still be 'heard', as a collective illusion, as a true phonetic difference.

3

The most successful American Indian pupil that I have had in practical phonetics is Alex Thomas, who writes his native language, Nootka,[12] with the utmost fluency and with admirable accuracy. Alex's orthography, as is natural, is phonologic in spirit throughout and it is largely from a study of his texts that I have learned to estimate at its ₁true value the psychological difference between a sound and a phoneme. Anyone who knows the phonetic mechanics of Nootka can easily actualize his orthography. Thus, *hi*,[13] phonologically parallel to *si* or *ni*, is actually pronounced *ḥe*, with a vowel which is much nearer to the *e* of English *met* than to that of *sit*. This is due to the peculiar nature of the laryngeal consonants, which favor an *a*-timbre and cause the following vowels *i* and *u* to drop to *ɛ* and *ɔ* respectively. The orthographies *ḥi* and *ḥu* are entirely unambiguous because there can be no phonologically distinct syllables of type *ḥe* and *ḥɔ*.

Another mechanical peculiarity of Nootka is the lengthening of consonants after a short vowel when followed by a vowel. This purely mechanical length has no morphological or phonological significance and is ignored in Alex's orthography. His *hisi·k* and *hisa·* are, then, to be normally pronounced *his·i·k'* and *ḥes·a·*. It sometimes happens, however, that a long consonant, particularly *s·* and *š·*, arises from the meeting of two morphologically distinct consonants (e.g. *s + s > s·* or *š + š > š·* or, less frequently, *š + s* or *s + š > s·*). In such cases the long consonant is not felt to be a mechanical lengthening of the simple consonant but as a cluster of two identical consonants, and so we find Alex writing, for example, *ṭsi·· qšit'łassatłni*[14] 'we went there only to

---

[12] This is spoken on the west coast of Vancouver Island, BC.

[13] *ḥ* is a voiceless laryngeal spirant, almost identical with the Arabic *ḥā*.

[14] I have slightly modified Alex's orthography to correspond to my present orthography, but these changes are merely mechanical substitutions, such as *tł* for L, and in no way affect the argument. *q* is velar *k* (Arabic *ḳ*), *tł* is a lateral affricative, *t'ł* its glottalized form.

speak', to be analyzed into *tsi·qšitł-' as -sa-('a)tł-ni*. The *s* of *-'as* 'to go in order to' and the *s* of *-sa* 'just, only' keep their phonologic independence and the normal intervocalic *-s·-* of *-'as·atł* is interpreted as *-ss-*. Similarly, *kwissiła* 'to do differently', to be analyzed into *kwis-siła*. It does not seem, however, that there is an actual phonetic difference between the *-s-* (phonologically *-s-*) of such words as *tłasatł* 'the stick takes an upright position on the beach' (= *tła-satł*), pronounced *tłas·atł*, and the *-s·-* of *-'assatł* above. Here again we have objectively identical phonetic phenomena which receive different phonologic interpretations.

4

In the earlier system of orthography, which Alex was taught, the glottalized stops and affricatives were treated differently from the glottalized nasals and semivowels. The former were symbolized as *p!, t!, k!, k!w, q!, q!w, ts!, tc!* (= *t͗s*), and *L!* (= *t͗ł*); the latter as *'m, 'n, 'y,* and *'w*. The reason for this was traditional. The glottalized stops and affricatives, as a distinctive type of consonants, had been early recognized by Dr. F. Boas in many American Indian languages, and described as 'fortes', that is, as stops and affricatives 'pronounced with increased stress of articulation'. The type *'m, 'n, 'l, 'y,* and *'w* was not recognized by Dr Boas until much later, first in Kwakiutl, and described as consisting of nasal, voiced lateral, or semivowel immediately preceded by a glottal closure. The orthography for these consonants (later discovered in Tsimshian, Nootka, Haida, and a number of other languages, but not as widely distributed as the so-called 'fortes') suggested their manner of formation, but the orthography for the glottalized stops and affricatives was purely conventional and did not in any way analyze their formation except to suggest that more energy was needed for their pronunciation.[15] As a pure matter

---

[15] This, incidentally, is not necessarily true. In some languages the glottalized stops and affricatives seem to be somewhat more energetic in articulation than the corresponding unglottalized consonants, in others there is no noticeable difference so far as 'stress of articulation' is concerned. In the Athabaskan languages that I have heard (Sarcee, Kutchin, Hupa, Navaho) the aspirated voiceless stops and affricatives (of type *t', k', ts'*) are far more 'fortis' in character than the corresponding glottalized consonants (e.g. *t, k, ts*). There is no necessary correlation between laryngeal type of articulation (voiced, voiceless, glottalized; or any of these with aspiration) and force of articulation (fortis, lenis). So far as Nootka is concerned, it did not seem to me that the glottalized stops and affricatives (Boas' 'fortes') were significantly different in emphasis from the ordinary stops and affricatives. In such languages as recognize a phonological difference of emphatic and nonemphatic and, at the same time, possess glottalized consonants may not appear in both emphatic and nonemphatic form. As Prince Trubetzkoy has

of phonetics, while the Nootka glottalized stops and affricatives are roughly parallel in formation with the glottalized sonantic consonants, they are not and cannot be entirely so. In a glottalized *p*, for instance, our present *p̣* and former *p!*, there is a synchronous closure of lips and glottal cords, a closed air chamber is thus produced between the two, there is a sudden release of the lip closure, a moment of pause, and then the release of the glottal closure. It is the release of the lip (or other oral) closure in advance of the glottal closure that gives consonants of this type their superficial 'click-like' character.[16] On the other hand, in a glottalized *m*, our *'m*, while the lip closure and glottal closure are synchronous as before,[17] the glottal closure must be released at the point of initial sonancy of the *m*. Roughly speaking, therefore, *p̣* may be analysed into *p* + ', while *'m* may be analyzed into ' + *m*. Such an orthographic difference as *p!* versus *'m*, therefore, which I had inherited from the Americanist tradition, was not unjustified on purely phonetic grounds.

We now come to the intuitive phonologic test whether *'p* and *'m* are consonants of the same type or not. Alex learned to write consonants of type *p̣* and *ṭs* very readily (our earlier *p!* and *ts!*), e.g. *p̣api·* 'ear' (earlier *p!ap!ī*), *tsa'ak* 'stream' (earlier *ts!a'ak*). To my surprise Alex volunteered *m!* in such words as *'ma·'mi·qsu* 'the older [brother or sister]', which he wrote *m!ām!īqsu*. In other words, we had valuable evidence here for the phonologic reality of a glottalized class of consonants which included both type *p̣* (with prior release of oral closure) and type *'m* (with prior release of glottal closure). A phonologically consistent orthography would require *p̣* and *ṃ* (or *p!* and *m!*). Once more, a naïve native's phonetic 'ignorance' proved phonologically more accurate than the scientist's 'knowledge'. The phonologic justification for Alex's 'error' is not difficult. Consonants of type *p̣* are entirely analogous to consonants of type *'m* for the following reasons.

1. Each occurs at the beginning of a syllable and, since no word can begin with a cluster of consonants, both *p̣* and *'m* are felt by Nootka speakers to be unanalysable phonologic units. In other words, the glottal stop can no more easily be abstracted from *'m* than from *p̣*. Similarly,

---

shown some of the North Caucasic languages, as a matter of fact, possess both emphatic and nonemphatic glottalized stops and affricatives.

[16] These consonants are apparently identical with the 'ejectives' of Daniel Jones. There is another, apparently less common, type of glottalized stop or affricative in which the oral and glottal releases are synchronous.

[17] The pronunciation of *'m, 'n, 'w*, and *'y* as a simple sequence of glottal stop (') plus *m, n, w*, and *y* is rejected by the Nootka ear as incorrect.

the affricatives and glottalized affricatives are phonologically un-analysable units.

2. All consonants can occur at the end of a syllable except glottalized stops and affricatives, glottalized sonantic consonants (*'m, 'n, 'y, 'w*), semivowels (*y, w*), nasals (*m, n*),[18] the glottal stop ('), and *h*. This rule throws consonants of type *'m* more definitely together with consonants of type *p̓*.

3. Many suffixes which begin with a vowel have the effect of 'hardening'[19] the preceding consonant, in other words, of glottally affecting it. Under the influence of this 'hardening' process *p, t, k* become *p̓, t̓, k̓*, while *m* and *n* become *'m* and *'n*. For example, just as the suffixes *'-a'a*[20] (*'-a·'a*) 'on the rocks' and *'-aḥs* 'in a receptacle' change the stem *wi·nap-* 'to stay, dwell' to *wi·nap̓-* (e.g. *wi·napa'a* 'so stay on the rocks') and *wik-* 'to be not' to *wik̓-* (e.g. *wikaḥs* 'to be not in a receptacle, a canoe is empty'), so *t'łum-* (alternating with *t'łup-*) 'to be hot' becomes *t'łu'm̓-* (alternating with *t'łup̓-*) (e.g. *łłu'ma·'a* 'to be hot on the rocks' and *łłu'maḥs* 'to be hot in a receptacle, there is hot water'; compare *łłupi·tš̌h* 'summer, hot season' = parallel *łłup-* + *'-i·ch* 'season') and *kan-* 'to kneel' (e.g. *kanił* 'to kneel in the house') becomes *ka'n-* (e.g. *ka'naḥs* 'to kneel in a canoe'). As there seem to be no stems ending in *h* or ', the group *'m, 'n, 'w, 'y*[21] is left over as functionally related to the group *m, n, w, y* in the same sense as the group exemplified by *p̓* is related to the group exemplified by *p*. Morphology, in other words, convincingly supports the phonologic proportion *p : p̓ = m : 'm*. It is maintained that it was this underlying phonologic configuration that made Alex hear *'m* as sufficiently similar to *p̓* to justify its being written in an analogous fashion. In other languages, with different phonologic and morphologic understandings, such a parallelism of orthography might not be justified at all and the phonetic differences that actually obtain between *'m* and *p̓* would have a significantly different psychologic weighting.

5

In a course in practical phonetics which I have been giving for a number of years I have so often remarked the following illusion of hearing on

---

[18] *m* and *n* may be followed by a murmured vowel of *i*-timbre which is a reduced form of *a, u*, or *i*. Syllables or half-syllables of type *mi* or *ni* are preceded by *i*, an assimilated product of *a, u* or *i*; *ini* and *imi* result therefore, in part, from sequences of type *ama, umi, anu*. Simple *-am* or *-an* become *-ap, at*.

[19] A term borrowed from Boas' equivalent Kwakiutl phenomenon.

[20] The symbol ' indicates the 'hardening' effect of a suffix.

[21] The phonologic details involving *'w* and *'y* and their relation to *w* and *y* and other consonants are too intricate for a summary statement in this place.

the part of students that there seems no way of avoiding a general phonologic theory to explain it. I find that, after the students have been taught to recognize the glottal stop as a phonetic unit, many of them tend to hear it after a word ending in an accented short vowel of clear timbre (e.g. *a, ε, e, i*). This illusion does not seem to apply so often to words ending in a long vowel or an obscure vowel of relatively undefined quality (ə) or an unaccented vowel. Thus, a dictated non-sense word like *smε* or *pilá* would occasionally be misheard and written as *smε'* and *pilá'* but there seems far less tendency to hear a final glottal stop in words like *pilá* or *pilá·*. What is the reason for this singular type of 'overhearing?' Is it enough to say that students who have learned a new sound like to play with it and that their prepared-ness for it tends to make them project its usage into the stream of acoustic stimuli to which they are asked to attend? No doubt such a general explanation is a correct dynamic formula so far as it goes but it is not precise enough for a phonologist because it does not take sufficient account of the limitations of the illusion.

It must be remembered that the language of my students is English. We may therefore suspect that the illusion of a final glottal stop is due to some feature in the phonologic structure of English. But English has no glottal stops. How, then, can English phonology explain the over-hearing of a consonant which is alien to its genius to begin with? Never-theless, I believe that the students who projected a final glottal stop into the dictated words were handling an exotic phonetic element, the glottal stop, according to a firmly established but quite unconscious phonologic pattern. It requires both the learning process, with its con-sequent alert preparedness to recognize what has been learned, and English phonology to explain the illusion. If we study the kinds of syllables in English which may normally constitute an accented mono-syllabic word or an accented (or secondarily accented) final syllable of a word, we find that they may be classified into three types:

A. Words ending in a long vowel or diphthong, e.g. *sea, flow, shoe, review, apply*.
B. Words ending in a long vowel or diphthong plus one or more con-sonants, e.g. *ball, cease, dream, alcove, amount*.
C. Words ending in a short vowel plus one or more consonants, e.g. *back, fill, come, remit, object*.

The theoretically possible fourth class:

D. Words ending in a short vowel, e.g. French *fait, ami*; Russian *xărăšɔ'* does not exist in English. English-speaking people tend to pronounce words of type D in a 'drawling' fashion which transfers them to type A (e.g. *amĭˑ* for *ami*). Observe that the apparently inconsistent possibility of a non-final accented syllable ending in a short vowel (e.g. *fiddle, butter, double, pheasant*) is justified by the English theory of syllabification, which feels the point of the syllabic division to lie in the following consonant (*d, t, b, z*, in the examples cited), so that the accented syllables of these words really belong phonologically to type C, not to type D. Intervocalic consonants like the *d* of *fiddle* or *z* of *pheasant*, in spite of the fact that they are not phonetically long, are phonologically 'flanking' or two-faced in that they at one and the same time complete one syllable and begin another. Should the point of syllabic division shift back of the consonant, the preceding vowel at once lengthens in spite of its 'short' quality (type A), and we thus get dialectic American pronunciation of words like *fiddle* and *pheasant* in which the accented vowel keeps its original quality but has been lengthened to the unit length of 'long vowels' of type *feeble, reason,* and *ladle*.

We are now prepared to understand the illusion we started with. Such words as *smɛ* and *pilá* are unconsciously tested as possible members of class A or class C. Two illusions are possible, if the hearer is to be a victim of his phonologic system. Inasmuch as a final accented short vowel is an unfamiliar entity, it can be 'legitimized' either by projecting length into it (misheard *smɛˑ* and *piláˑ* fall into class A) or by projecting a final consonant after it (class C). We shall call this imaginary consonant '*x*' and write *smɛx* and *piláx*. Now the fact that one has added the glottal stop to his kit of consonantal tools leads often to the temptation to solve the phonologic problem symbolized as *smɛx* and *piláx* in terms of the glottal stop and to hear *smɛ'* and *pilá'*. The glottal stop is the most unreal or zerolike of consonants to an English or American ear and is admirably fitted, once its existence has been discovered, to serve as the projected actualization of a phonologically required final consonant of minimum sonority. The illusion of the final glottal stop is essentially the illusion of a generalized final consonant ('*x*') needed to classify the dictated words into a known category (type C). Or, to speak more analytically, English phonology creates the groundword (*-x*) of the synthetic illusion, while the learning process colours it to the shape of -'. The error of hearing a glottal stop where there is none, in words of type D, is fundamentally a more sophisticated form of the same error as hearing a dictated final glottal stop as *p* or *t* or *k*, which occurs frequently in an earlier stage of the acquiring of a phonetic technique.

The danger of hearing a glottal stop when the dictated word ends in a long vowel or diphthong is of course rendered very unlikely by the fact that such words conform to a common English pattern (type A). The reason why the error does not so easily occur in hearing dictated words ending in an unaccented short vowel (e.g. *ó·nɛ, sú·li*) is that such words, too, conform to an English pattern, though the range of the qualities allowed a vowel in this position is not as great as when the vowel is covered by a following consonant (e.g. *idea, very, follow*).

METHODOLOGICAL PRELIMINARIES

N. CHOMSKY

1. GENERATIVE GRAMMARS AS THEORIES OF LINGUISTIC COMPETENCE

THIS study will touch on a variety of topics in syntactic theory and English syntax, a few in some detail, several quite superficially, and none exhaustively. It will be concerned with the syntactic component of a generative grammar, that is, with the rules that specify the well-formed strings of minimal syntactically functioning units (*formatives*) and assign structural information of various kinds both to these strings and to strings that deviate from well-formedness in certain respects.

The general framework within which this investigation will proceed has been presented in many places, and some familiarity with the theoretical and descriptive studies listed in the bibliography is presupposed. In this chapter, I shall survey briefly some of the main background assumptions, making no serious attempt here to justify them but only to sketch them clearly.

Linguistic theory is concerned primarily with an ideal speaker-listener, in a completely homogeneous speech-community, who knows its language perfectly and is unaffected by such grammatically irrelevant conditions as memory limitations, distractions, shifts of attention and interest, and errors (random or characteristic) in applying his knowledge of the language in actual performance. This seems to me to have been the position of the founders of modern general linguistics, and no cogent reason for modifying it has been offered. To study actual linguistic performance, we must consider the interaction of a variety of factors, of which the underlying competence of the speaker-hearer is only one. In this respect, study of language is no different from empirical investigation of other complex phenomena.

We thus make a fundamental distinction between *competence* (the speaker-hearer's knowledge of his language) and *performance* (the actual use of language in concrete situations). Only under the idealization set forth in the preceding paragraph is performance a direct reflection of competence. In actual fact, it obviously could not directly reflect competence. A record of natural speech will show numerous false starts, deviations from rules, changes of plan in mid-course, and so on. The problem for the linguist, as well as for the child learning the language, is to determine from the data of performance the underlying system of rules that has been mastered by the speaker-hearer and that he puts to use in actual performance. Hence, in the technical sense, linguistic theory is mentalistic, since it is concerned with discovering a mental reality underlying actual behaviour.[1] Observed use

[1] To accept traditional mentalism, in this way, is not to accept Bloomfield's dichotomy of 'mentalism' versus 'mechanism'. Mentalistic linguistics is simply theoretical linguistics that uses performance as data (along with other data, for example, the data provided by introspection) for the determination of competence, the latter being taken as the primary object of its investigation. The mentalist, in this traditional sense, need make no assumptions about the possible physiological basis for the mental reality that he studies. In particular, he need not deny that there is such a basis. One would guess, rather, that it is the mentalistic studies that will ultimately be of greatest value for the investigation of neurophysiological mechanisms, since they alone are concerned with determining abstractly the properties that such mechanisms must exhibit and the functions they must perform.

In fact, the issue of mentalism versus antimentalism in linguistics apparently has to do only with goals and interests, and not with questions of truth or falsity, sense or nonsense. At least three issues are involved in this rather idle controversy: (*a*) dualism—are the rules that underlie performance represented in a non-material medium?; (*b*) behaviourism—do the data of performance exhaust the domain of interest to the linguist, or is he also concerned with other facts, in particular those pertaining to the deeper systems that underlie behaviour?; (*c*) introspectionism—should one make use of introspective data in the attempt to ascertain the properties of these underlying systems? It is the dualistic position against which Bloomfield irrelevantly inveighed. The behaviourist position is not an arguable matter. It is simply an expression of lack of interest in theory and explanation. This is clear, for example, in Twaddell's critique (1935) of Sapir's mentalistic phonology, which used informant responses and comments as evidence bearing on the psychological reality of some abstract system of phonological elements. For Twaddell, the enterprise has no point because all that interests him is the behaviour itself, 'which is already available for the student of language, though in less concentrated form'. Characteristically, this lack of interest in linguistic theory expresses itself in the proposal to limit the term 'theory' to 'summary of data' (as in Twaddell's paper, or, to take a more recent example, in Dixon, 1963, although the discussion of 'theories' in the latter is sufficiently vague to allow other interpretations of what he may have in mind). Perhaps this loss of interest in theory, in the usual sense, was fostered by certain ideas (e.g. strict operationalism or strong verificationism) that were considered briefly in positivist philosophy

of language or hypothesized dispositions to respond, habits, and so on, may provide evidence as to the nature of this mental reality, but surely cannot constitute the actual subject matter of linguistics, if this is to be a serious discipline. The distinction I am noting here is related to the *langue-parole* distinction of Saussure; but it is necessary to reject his concept of *langue* as merely a systematic inventory of items and to return rather to the Humboldtian conception of underlying competence as a system of generative processes. For discussion, see Chomsky (1964).

A grammar of a language purports to be a description of the ideal speaker-hearer's intrinsic competence. If the grammar is, furthermore, perfectly explicit—in other words, if it does not rely on the intelligence of the understanding reader but rather provides an explicit analysis of his contribution—we may (somewhat redundantly) call it a *generative grammar*.

A fully adequate grammar must assign to each of an infinite range of sentences a structural description indicating how this sentence is understood by the ideal speaker-hearer. This is the traditional problem of descriptive linguistics, and traditional grammars give a wealth of information concerning structural descriptions of sentences. However, valuable as they obviously are, traditional grammars are deficient in that they leave unexpressed many of the basic regularities of the language with which they are concerned. This fact is particularly clear on the level of syntax, where no traditional or structuralist grammar goes beyond classification of particular examples to the stage of formulation of generative rules on any significant scale. An analysis of the best existing grammars will quickly reveal that this is a defect of principle, not just a matter of empirical detail or logical preciseness. Nevertheless, it seems obvious that the attempt to explore this largely uncharted territory can most profitably begin with a study of the kind of structural information presented by traditional grammars and the kind of linguistic processes that have been exhibited, however informally, in these grammars.[2]

of science, but rejected forthwith, in the early 1930s. In any event, question (*b*) poses no substantive issue. Question (*c*) arises only if one rejects the behaviourist limitations of (*b*). To maintain, on grounds of methodological purity, that introspective judgements of the informant (often, the linguist himself) should be disregarded is, for the present, to condemn the study of language to utter sterility. It is difficult to imagine what possible reason might be given for this. For further discussion, see Katz (1964*a*).

[2] This has been denied recently by several European linguists (e.g. Dixon, 1963; Uhlenbeck, 1963, 1964). They offer no reasons for their scepticism concerning traditional grammar, however. Whatever evidence is available today seems to me to show that by and large the traditional views are basically correct, so far

The limitations of traditional and structuralist grammars should be clearly appreciated. Although such grammars may contain full and explicit lists of exceptions and irregularities, they provide only examples and hints concerning the regular and productive syntactic processes. Traditional linguistic theory was not aware of this fact. For example, James Beattie (1788) remarks that

> Languages, therefore, resemble men in this respect, that, though each has peculiarities, whereby it is distinguished from every other, yet all have certain qualities in common. The peculiarities of individual tongues are explained in their respective grammars and dictionaries. Those things, that all languages have in common, or that are necessary to every language, are treated of in a science, which some have called *Universal* or *Philosophical* grammar.

Somewhat earlier, Du Marsais defines universal and particular grammar in the following way (1769; quoted in Sahlin, 1928, pp. 29-30):

> Il y a dans la grammaire des observations qui conviènnent à toutes les langues; ces observations forment ce qu'on appelle la grammaire générale: telles sont les remarques que l'on a faites sur les sons articulés, sur les lettres qui sont les signes de ces sons; sur la nature des mots, et sur les différentes manières dont ils doivent être ou arrangés ou terminés pour faire un sens. Outre ces observations générales, il y en a qui ne sont propres qu'à une langue particulière; et c'est ce qui forme les grammaires particulières de chaque langue.

Within traditional linguistic theory, furthermore, it was clearly understood that one of the qualities that all languages have in common is their 'creative' aspect. Thus an essential property of language is that it provides the means for expressing indefinitely many thoughts and for reacting appropriately in an indefinite range of new situations (for references, cf. Chomsky, 1964). The grammar of a particular language, then, is to be supplemented by a universal grammar that accommodates

as they go, and that the suggested innovations are totally unjustifiable. For example, consider Uhlenbeck's proposal that the constituent analysis of 'the man saw the boy' is [*the man saw*] [*the boy*], a proposal which presumably also implies that in the sentences [*the man put*] [*it into the box*], [*the man aimed*] [*it at John*], [*the man persuaded*] [*Bill that it was unlikely*], etc., the constituents are as indicated. There are many considerations relevant to the determination of constituent structure (cf. n. 7); to my knowledge, they support the traditional analysis without exception against this proposal, for which the only argument offered is that it is the result of a 'pure linguistic analysis'. Cf. Uhlenbeck (1964), and the discussion there. As to Dixon's objections to traditional grammars, since he offers neither any alternative nor any argument (beyond the correct but irrelevant observation they they have been 'long condemned by professional linguists'), there is nothing further to discuss, in this case.

the creative aspect of language use and expresses the deep-seated regularities which, being universal, are omitted from the grammar itself. Therefore it is quite proper for a grammar to discuss only exceptions and irregularities in any detail. It is only when supplemented by a universal grammar that the grammar of a language provides a full account of the speaker-hearer's competence.

Modern linguistics, however, has not explicitly recognized the necessity for supplementing a 'particular grammar' of a language by a universal grammar if it is to achieve descriptive adequacy. It has, in fact, characteristically rejected the study of universal grammar as misguided; and, as noted before, it has not attempted to deal with the creative aspect of language use. It thus suggests no way to overcome the fundamental descriptive inadequacy of structuralist grammars.

Another reason for the failure of traditional grammars, particular or universal, to attempt a precise statement of regular processes of sentence formation and sentence interpretation lay in the widely held belief that there is a 'natural order of thoughts' that is mirrored by the order of words. Hence, the rules of sentence formation do not really belong to grammar but to some other subject in which the 'order of thoughts' is studied. Thus in the *Grammaire générale et raisonnée* (Lancelot *et al.*, 1660) it is asserted that, aside from figurative speech, the sequence of words follows an 'ordre naturel,' which conforms 'à l'expression naturelle de nos pensées.' Consequently, few grammatical rules need be formulated beyond the rules of ellipsis, inversion, and so on, which determine the figurative use of language. The same view appears in many forms and variants. To mention just one additional example, in an interesting essay devoted largely to the question of how the simultaneous and sequential array of ideas is reflected in the order of words, Diderot concludes that French is unique among languages in the degree to which the order of words corresponds to the natural order of thoughts and ideas (Diderot, 1751). Thus 'quel que soit l'ordre des termes dans une langue ancienne ou moderne, l'esprit de l'écrivain a suivi l'ordre didactique de la syntaxe française' (p. 390); 'Nous disons les choses en français, comme l'esprit est forcé de les considérer en quelque langue qu'on écrive' (p. 371). With admirable consistency he goes on to conclude that 'notre langue pédestre a sur les autres l'avantage de l'utile sur l'agréable' (p. 372); thus French is appropriate for the sciences, whereas Greek, Latin, Italian, and English 'sont plus avantageuses pour les lettres.' Moreover,

le bon sens choisirait la langue française; mais . . . l'imagination et les passions donneront la préférence aux langues anciennes et à celles de nos voisins . . . il faut parler français dans la société et dans les écoles de philosophie; et grec, latin, anglais, dans les chaires et sur les théâtres; . . . notre langue sera celle de la vérité, si jamais elle revient sur la terre; et . . . la grecque, la latine et les autres seront les langues de la fable et du mensonge. Le français est fait pour instruire, éclairer et convaincre; le grec, le latin, l'italien, l'anglais, pour persuader, émouvoir et tromper: parlez grec, latin, italien au peuple; mais parlez français au sage. (pp. 371–372)

In any event, in so far as the order of words is determined by factors independent of language, it is not necessary to describe it in a particular or universal grammar, and we therefore have principled grounds for excluding an explicit formulation of syntactic processes from grammar. It is worth noting that this naïve view of language structure persists to modern times in various forms, for example, in Saussure's image of a sequence of expressions corresponding to an amorphous sequence of concepts or in the common characterization of language use as merely a matter of use of words and phrases (for example, Ryle, 1953).

But the fundamental reason for this inadequacy of traditional grammars is a more technical one. Although it was well understood that linguistic processes are in some senses 'creative', the technical devices for expressing a system of recursive processes were simply not available until much more recently. In fact, a real understanding of how a language can (in Humboldt's words) 'make infinite use of finite means' has developed only within the last thirty years, in the course of studies in the foundations of mathematics. Now that these insights are readily available it is possible to return to the problems that were raised, but not solved, in traditional linguistic theory, and to attempt an explicit formulation of the 'creative' processes of language. There is, in short, no longer a technical barrier to the full-scale study of generative grammars.

Returning to the main theme, by a generative grammar I mean simply a system of rules that in some explicit and well-defined way assigns structural descriptions to sentences. Obviously, every speaker of a language has mastered and internalized a generative grammar that expresses his knowledge of his language. This is not to say that he is aware of the rules of the grammar or even that he can become aware of them, or that his statements about his intuitive knowledge of the language are necessarily accurate. Any interesting generative grammar will be dealing, for the most part, with mental processes that are far beyond the level of actual or even potential consciousness; furthermore, it is quite apparent that a speaker's reports and viewpoints about his behaviour and his competence may be in error. Thus a generative grammar attempts to specify what the speaker actually knows, not what he may report about his knowledge. Similarly, a theory of visual perception would attempt to account for what a person actually sees and the mechanisms that determine this rather than his statements about what he sees and why, though these statements may provide useful, in fact, compelling evidence for such a theory.

To avoid what has been a continuing misunderstanding, it is perhaps worth while to reiterate that a generative grammar is not a model for a speaker or a hearer. It attempts to characterize in the most neutral possible terms the knowledge of the language that provides the basis for actual use of language by a speaker-hearer. When we speak of grammar as generating a sentence with a certain structural description, we mean simply that the grammar assigns this structural description to the sentence. When we say that a sentence has a certain derivation with respect to a particular generative grammar, we say nothing about how the speaker or hearer might proceed, in some practical or efficient way, to construct such a derivation. These questions belong to the theory of language use—the theory of performance. No doubt, a reasonable model of language use will incorporate, as a basic component, the generative grammar that expresses the speaker-hearer's knowledge of the language; but this generative grammar does not, in itself, prescribe the character or functioning of a perceptual model or a model of speech production. For various attempts to clarify this point, see Chomsky (1957), Gleason (1961), Miller and Chomsky (1963), and many other publications.

Confusion over this matter has been sufficiently persistent to suggest that a terminological change might be in order. Nevertheless, I think that the term 'generative grammar' is completely appropriate, and have therefore continued to use it. The term 'generate' is familiar in the sense intended here in logic, particularly in Post's theory of combinational systems. Furthermore, 'generate' seems to be the most appropriate translation for Humboldt's term *erzeugen*, which he frequently uses, it seems, in essentialy the sense here intended. Since this use of the term 'generate' is well established both in logic and in the tradition of linguistic theory, I can see no reason for a revision of terminology.

2. TOWARD A THEORY OF PERFORMANCE

There seems to be little reason to question the traditional view that investigation of performance will proceed only so far as understanding of underlying competence permits. Furthermore, recent work on performance seems to give new support to this assumption. To my knowledge, the only concrete results that have been achieved and the only clear suggestions that have been put forth concerning the theory of performance, outside of phonetics, have come from studies of performance models that incorporate generative grammars of specific kinds—that is, from studies that have been based on assumptions about underlying competence.[3] In particular, there are some suggestive observations concerning limitations on performance imposed by organization of memory and bounds on memory, and concerning the exploitation of grammatical devices to form deviant sentences of various types. To clarify further the distinction between competence and performance, it may be useful to summarize briefly some of the suggestions and results that have appeared in the last few years in the study of performance models with limitations of memory, time, and access.

For the purposes of this discussion, let us use the term 'acceptable' to refer to utterances that are perfectly natural and immediately comprehensible without paper-and-pencil analysis, and in no way bizarre or outlandish. Obviously, acceptability will be a matter of degree, along various dimensions. One could go on to propose various operational tests to specify the notion more precisely (for example, rapidity, correctness, and uniformity of recall and recognition, normalcy of intonation).[4] For present purposes, it is unnecessary to delimit it more carefully. To illustrate, the sentences of (1) are somewhat more acceptable, in the intended sense, than those of (2):

(1) (i) I called up the man who wrote the book that you told me about
     (ii) quite a few of the students who you met who come from New York are friends of mine
     (iii) John, Bill, Tom, and several of their friends visited us last night
(2) (i) I called the man who wrote the book that you told me about up
     (ii) the man who the boy who the students recognized pointed out is a friend of mine.

The more acceptable sentences are those that are more likely to be produced, more easily understood, less clumsy, and in some sense more natural.[5] The unacceptable sentences one would tend to avoid and replace by more acceptable variants, wherever possible, in actual discourse.

The notion of 'acceptable' is not to be confused with 'grammatical'.

[3] Furthermore, it seems to me that speech perception is also best studied in this framework. See, for example, Halle and Stevens (1962).

[4] Tests that seem to determine a useful notion of this sort have been described in various places—for example, Miller and Isard (1963).

[5] These characterizations are equally vague, and the concepts involved are equally obscure. The notion 'likely to be produced' or 'probable' is sometimes thought to be more 'objective' and antecedently better defined than the others,

Acceptability is a concept that belongs to the study of performance, whereas grammaticalness belongs to the study of competence. The sentences of (2) are low on the scale of acceptability but high on the scale of grammaticalness, in the technical sense of this term. That is, the generative rules of the language assign an interpretation to them in exactly the way in which they assign an interpretation to the somewhat more acceptable sentences of (1). Like acceptability, grammaticalness is, no doubt, a matter of degree (cf. Chomsky, 1955, 1957, 1961), but the scales of grammaticalness and acceptability do not coincide. Grammaticalness is only one of many factors that interact to determine acceptability. Correspondingly, although one might propose various operational tests for acceptability, it is unlikely that a necessary and sufficient operational criterion might be invented for the much more abstract and far more important notion of grammaticalness. The unacceptable grammatical sentences often cannot be used, for reasons having to do, not with grammar, but rather with memory limitations, intonational and stylistic factors, 'iconic' elements of discourse (for example, a tendency to place logical subject and object early rather than late, and so on). Note that it would be quite

on the assumption that there is some clear meaning to the notion 'probability of a sentence' or 'probability of a sentence type'. Actually, the latter notions are objective and antecedently clear only if probability is based on an estimate of relative frequency and if sentence type means something like 'sequence of word or morpheme classes'. (Furthermore, if the notion is to be at all significant, these classes must be extremely small and of mutually substitutable elements, or else unacceptable and ungrammatical sentences will be as 'likely' and acceptable as grammatical ones.) But in this case, though 'probability of a sentence (type)' is clear and well defined, it is an utterly useless notion, since almost all highly acceptable sentences (in the intuitive sense) will have probabilities empirically indistinguishable from zero and will belong to sentence types with probabilities empirically indistinguishable from zero. Thus the acceptable or grammatical sentences (or sentence types) are no more likely, in any objective sense of this word, than the others. This remains true if we consider, not 'likelihood', but 'likelihood relative to a given situation', as long as 'situations' are specified in terms of observable physical properties and are not mentalistic constructs. It is noteworthy that linguists who talk of hardheaded objective study of use of sentences in real situations, when they actually come to citing examples, invariably describe the 'situations' in completely mentalistic terms. Cf. e.g. Dixon (1963, p. 101), where, in the only illustrative example in the book, a sentence is described as gaining its meaning from the situation 'British Culture'. To describe British culture as 'a situation' is in the first place, a category mistake; furthermore, to regard it as a pattern abstracted from observed behaviour, and hence objectively describable in purely physical terms, betrays a complete misunderstanding of what might be expected from anthropological research. For further discussion, see Katz and Fodor (1964).

impossible to characterize the unacceptable sentences in grammatical terms. For example, we cannot formulate particular rules of the grammar in such a way as to exclude them. Nor, obviously, can we exclude them by limiting the number of reapplications of grammatical rules in the generation of the sentence, since unacceptability can just as well arise from application of distinct rules, each being applied only once. In fact, it is clear that we can characterize unacceptable sentences only in terms of some 'global' property of derivations and the structures they define—a property that is attributable, not to a particular rule, but rather to the way in which the rules interrelate in a derivation.

This observation suggests that the study of performance could profitably begin with an investigation of the acceptability of the simplest formal structures in grammatical sentences. The most obvious formal property of utterances is their bracketing into constituents of various types, that is, the 'tree structure' associated with them. Among such structures we can distinguish various kinds—for example, those to which we give the following conventional technical names, for the purposes of this discussion:

(3)   (i) nested constructions
      (ii) self-embedded constructions
      (iii) multiple-branching constructions
      (iv) left-branching constructions
      (v) right-branching constructions.

The phrases A and B form a nested construction if A falls totally within B, with some non-null element to its left within B and some non-null element to its right within B. Thus the phrase 'the man who wrote the book that you told me about' is nested in the phrase 'called the man who wrote the book that you told me about up', in (2i). The phrase A is self-embedded in B if A is nested in B and, furthermore, A is a phrase of the same type as B. Thus 'who the students recognized' is self-embedded in 'who the boy who the students recognized pointed out', in (2ii), since both are relative clauses. Thus nesting has to do with bracketing, and self-embedding with labelling of brackets as well. A multiple-branching construction is one with no internal structure. In (1iii), the Subject Noun Phrase is multiple-branching, since 'John', 'Bill', 'Tom', and 'several of their friends' are its immediate constituents, and have no further association among themselves. In terms of bracketing, a multiple-branching construction has the form $[[A][B] \ldots [M]]$. A left-branching structure is of the form $[[[\ldots] \ldots] \ldots]$— for example, in English, such indefinitely iterable structures as

[[[*John*]'s *brother*]'s *father*]'s *uncle*] or [[[*the man who you met*] *from Boston*] *who was on the train*], or (1ii), which combines several kinds of left-branching. Right-branching structures are those with the opposite property—for example, the Direct-Object of (1i) or [*this is* [*the cat that caught* [*the rat that stole the cheese*]]] .

The effect of these superficial aspects of sentence structure on performance has been a topic of study since almost the very inception of recent work on generative grammar, and there are some suggestive observations concerning their role in determining acceptability (that is, their role in limiting performance). Summarizing this work briefly, the following observations seem plausible:

(4) (i) repeated nesting contributes to unacceptability
   (ii) self-embedding contributes still more radically to unacceptability
   (iii) multiple-branching constructions are optimal in acceptability
   (iv) nesting of a long and complex element reduces acceptability
   (v) there are no clear examples of unacceptability involving only left-branching or only right-branching, although these constructions are unnatural in other ways—thus, for example, in reading the right-branching construction 'this is the cat that caught the rat that stole the cheese', the intonation breaks are ordinarily inserted in the wrong places (that is, after 'cat' and 'rat', instead of where the main brackets appear).

In some measure, these phenomena are easily explained. Thus it is known (cf. Chomsky, 1959*a*; and for discussion, Chomsky, 1961, and Miller and Chomsky, 1963) that an optimal perceptual device, even with a bounded memory, can accept unbounded left-branching and right-branching structures, though nested (hence ultimately self-embedded) structures go beyond its memory capacity. Thus case (4i) is simply a consequence of finiteness of memory, and the unacceptability of such examples as (2ii) raises no problem.

If (4ii) is correct,[6] then we have evidence for a conclusion about

[6] That it may be true is suggested by several (for the moment, quite untested) observations. For example, in Chomsky and Miller (1963, p. 286) the following example is cited: 'anyone who feels that if so many more students whom we haven't actually admitted are sitting in on the course than ones we have that the room had to be changed, then probably auditors will have to be excluded, is likely to agree that the curriculum needs revision'. This contains six nested dependencies (along with other dependencies that go beyond nesting) with no self-embedding. Though hardly a model of felicitious style, it seems fairly comprehensible, and not extremely low on the scale of acceptability. In comparison, self-embedding of degree two or three seems to disturb acceptability much more severely. The

organization of memory that goes beyond the triviality that it must be finite in size. An optimal finite perceptual device of the type discussed in Chomsky (1959a) need have no more difficulty with self-embedding than with other kinds of nesting (see Bar-Hillel, Kasher, and Shamir, 1963, or a discussion of this point). To account for the greater unacceptability of self-embedding (assuming this to be a fact), we must add other conditions on the perceptual device beyond mere limitation of memory. We might assume, for example, that the perceptual device has a stock of analytic procedures available to it, one corresponding to each kind of phrase, and that it is organized in such a way that it is unable (or finds it difficult) to utilize a procedure ϕ while it is in the course of executing ϕ. This is not a necessary feature of a perceptual model, but it is a rather plausible one, and it would account for (4ii). See, in this connection, Miller and Isard (1964).

The high acceptability of multiple-branching, as in case (4iii), is easily explained on the rather plausible assumption that the ratio of number of phrases to number of formatives (the node-to-terminal node ratio, in a tree-diagram of a sentence) is a rough measure of the amount of computation that has to be performed in analysis. Thus multiple co-ordination would be the simplest kind of construction for an analytic device—it would impose the least strain on memory.[7] For discussion, see Miller and Chomsky (1963).

matter is worth studying, since a positive result concerning (4ii) would, as noted, support a conclusion about organization of memory which is not entirely obvious.

[7] It has sometimes been claimed that the traditional co-ordinated structures are necessarily right-recursive (Yngve, 1960) or left-recursive (Harman, 1963, p. 613, rule 3i). These conclusions seem to me equally unacceptable. Thus to assume (with Harman) that the phrase 'a tall, young, handsome, intelligent man' has the structure [[[[*tall young*] *handsome*] *intelligent*] *man*] seems to me no more justifiable than to assume that it has the structure [*tall* [*young* [*intelligent man*]]]. In fact, there is no grammatical motivation for any internal structure, and, as I have just noted, the assumption that there is no structure is also supported on grounds of acceptability, with extremely weak and plausible assumptions about organization of memory. Notice that there are cases where further structure might be justified (e.g. [*intelligent* [*young man*]] or, perhaps [YOUNG [*intelligent man*]], with contrastive stress on 'young'), but the issue is rather whether it is always necessary.

The same is true if we consider the very different type of Adjective-Noun construction that we find in such phrases as 'all the young, old, and middle-aged voters' (for an interesting discussion of these various kinds of modification relations, see Ornan, 1964). Here, too, neither the structure [[*young, old*] *and middle-aged*] nor [*young* [*old and middle-aged*]] has any justification.

Similarly, it is surely impossible to assume, with Yngve, that in the phrase 'John, Mary, and their two children' the structure is [*John*] [[*Mary*] [*and their two children*]], so that 'John' is co-ordinated with 'Mary and their two children',

Case (4iv) suggests decay of memory, perhaps, but raises unsolved problems (see Chomsky, 1961, n. 19).

Case (4v) follows from the result about optimal perceptual models mentioned earlier. But it is unclear why left- and right-branching structures should become unnatural after a certain point, if they actually do.[8]

the latter being analysed into the co-ordinated items 'Mary' and 'their two children'. This is entirely counter to the sense. Notice, again, that conjunction *can* have this structure (e.g. 'John, as well as Mary and her child'), but surely it is false to claim that it *must* have this structure.

In these cases all known syntactic, phonetic, and perceptual considerations converge in support of the traditional view that these constructions are typically co-ordinating (multiple-branching). Notice also that this is the weakest assumption. The burden of proof rests on one who claims additional structure beyond this. There are various ways of justifying assignment of constituent structure. For example, in such a phrase as 'all (none) of the blue, green, red, and (or) yellow pennants', if one wanted to argue that 'blue, green, red' is a constituent (i.e. that the structure is left-branching), or that 'green, red, and (or) yellow' is a constituent (that the structure is right-branching), then he would have to show that these analyses are required for some grammatical rule, that the postulated intermediate phrases must receive a semantic interpretation, that they define a phonetic contour, that there are perceptual grounds for the analysis, or something or this sort. All of these claims are patently false in this case, and the other cases mentioned here. Thus no semantic interpretation can be assigned to 'old and middle-aged' in 'young, old, and middle-aged voters' or to 'green, red, or yellow' in 'none of the blue, green, red, or yellow pennants' or to 'Mary and their two children' in 'John, Mary, and their two children'; the phonetic rules explicitly preclude such constituent analysis; there are no grammatical rules that require these analyses; there are no perceptual or other arguments to support them. It seems difficult, then, to see any grounds for objecting to the traditional analysis and insisting on additional intermediate categorization, in such cases as these.

[8] Yngve (1960, and several other papers) has proposed a different theory to account for certain observations such as those of (4). Beyond the obvious condition of finiteness of memory, his theory assumes also that order of generation is identical with order of production—that the speaker and hearer produce sentences 'from top-to-bottom' (they first decide on the major structures, then the substructures of these, etc., leaving to the very end of the process the choice of lexical items). Under this highly restrictive additional assumption, the optimal perceptual device mentioned earlier is no longer constructible, and left-branching and multiple-branching, as well as nesting and self-embedding, contribute to 'depth' in Yngve's sense, hence to unacceptability. To support this hypothesis, it would be necessary to show (*a*) that it has some initial plausibility, and (*b*) that left-branching and multiple-branching in fact contribute to unacceptability exactly as do nesting and self-embedding. As to (*a*), I see no plausibility at all to the assumption that the speaker must uniformly select sentence type, then determine subcategories, etc., finally, at the last stage, deciding what he is going to talk about; or that the hearer should invariably make all higher-level decisions before doing any lower-level analysis. As to (*b*), the hypothesis is supported by no evi-

One might ask whether attention to less superficial aspects of grammatical structure than those of (3) could lead to somewhat deeper conclusions about performance models. This seems entirely possible. For example, in Miller and Chomsky (1963) some syntactic and perceptual considerations are adduced in support of a suggestion (which is, to be sure, highly speculative) as to the somewhat more detailed organization of a perceptual device. In general, it seems that the study of performance models incorporating generative grammars may be a fruitful study; furthermore, it is difficult to imagine any other basis on which a theory of performance might develop.

There has been a fair amount of criticism of work in generative grammar on the grounds that it slights study of performance in favour of study of underlying competence. The facts, however, seem to be that the only studies of performance, outside of phonetics (but see n. 3), are those carried out as a by-product of work in generative grammar. In particular, the study of memory limitations just summarized and the study of deviation from rules, as a stylistic device, have developed in this way. Furthermore, it seems that these lines of investigation can provide some insight into performance. Consequently, this criticism is unwarranted, and, furthermore, completely misdirected. It is the descriptivist limitation-in-principle to classification and organization of data, to 'extracting patterns' from a corpus of observed speech, to describing 'speech habits' or 'habit structures', in so far as these may exist, etc. that precludes the development of a theory of actual performance.

3. THE ORGANIZATION OF A GENERATIVE GRAMMAR

Returning now to the question of competence and the generative grammars that purport to describe it, we stress again that knowledge of a language involves the implicit ability to understand indefinitely many

dence at all. The examples given by Yngve all involve nesting and self-embedding and hence are irrelevant to the hypothesis, since the unacceptability in this case follows from the assumption of finiteness alone without the additional assumption of 'top-to-bottom' production for speaker and hearer. Furthermore, the hypothesis is contradicted by the observation (4iii) that multiply co-ordinated structures (cf. n. 7) are the most acceptable (rather than the least acceptable, as predicted) and that left-branching structures are far more acceptable than nested structures of equal 'depth', in Yngve's sense. It also fails to explain why examples of type (4iv), such as (2i), though very low in 'depth', are still unacceptable.

However, Yngve makes one important point in these papers, namely, that some transformations can be used to decrease nesting, hence to reduce the perceptual load. This suggests an interesting argument as to why grammars should contain transformational rules. Some additional weight to this argument is given by the discussion of performance models involving transformational grammars in Miller and Chomsky (1963, Part 2).

sentences.[9] Hence, a generative grammar must be a system of rules that can iterate to generate an indefinitely large number of structures. This system of rules can be analyzed into three major components of a generative grammar: the syntactic, phonological, and semantic components.[10]

The syntactic component specifies an infinite set of abstract formal objects, each of which incorporates all information relevant to a single interpretation of a particular sentence.[11] Since I shall be concerned here only with the syntactic component, I shall use the term 'sentence' to refer to strings of formatives rather than to strings of phones. It will be recalled that a string of formatives specifies a string of phones uniquely (up to free variation), but not conversely.

The phonological component of a grammar determines the phonetic form of a sentence generated by the syntactic rules. That is, it relates a structure generated by the syntactic component to a phonetically represented signal. The semantic component determines the semantic interpretation of a sentence. That is, it relates a structure generated by the syntactic component to a certain semantic representation. Both the phonological and semantic components are therefore purely interpretive. Each utilizes information provided by the syntactic component concerning formatives, their inherent properties, and their interrelations in a given sentence. Consequently, the syntactic component of a grammar must specify, for each sentence, a *deep structure* that determines its semantic interpretation and a *surface structure* that determines its phonetic interpretation. The first of these is interpreted

---

[9] It is astonishing to find that even this truism has recently been challenged. See Dixon (1963). However, it seems that when Dixon denies that a language has infinitely many sentences, he is using the term 'infinite' in some special and rather obscure sense. Thus on the same page (p. 83) on which he objects to the assertion 'that there are an infinite number of sentences in a language' he states that 'we are clearly unable to say that there is any definite number, N, such that no sentence contains more than N clauses' (that is, he states that the language is infinite). Either this is a blatant self-contradiction, or else he has some new sense of the word 'infinite' in mind. For further discussion of his remarks in this connection, see Chomsky (1966).

[10] Aside from terminology, I follow here the exposition in Katz and Postal (1964). In particular, I shall assume throughout that the semantic component is essentially as they describe it and that the phonological component is essentially as described in Chomsky, Halle, and Lukoff (1956); Halle (1959a, 1959b, 1962); Chomsky (1962b); Chomsky and Miller (1963); Halle and Chomsky (1960).

[11] I assume throughout that the syntactic component contains a lexicon, and that each lexical item is specified in the lexicon in terms of its intrinsic semantic features, whatever these may be.

by the semantic component; the second, by the phonological component.[12]

It might be supposed that surface structure and deep structure will always be identical. In fact, one might briefly characterize the syntactic theories that have arisen in modern structural (taxonomic) linguistics as based on the assumption that deep and surface structures are actually the same (cf. Postal, 1964*a*, Chomsky, 1964). The central idea of transformational grammar is that they are, in general, distinct

[12] In place of the terms 'deep structure' and 'surface structure', one might use the corresponding Humboldtian notions 'inner form' of a sentence and 'outer form' of a sentence. However, though it seems to me that 'deep structure' and 'surface structure', in the sense in which these terms will be used here, do correspond quite closely to Humboldtian 'inner form' and 'outer form', respectively (as used of a sentence), I have adopted the more neutral terminology to avoid the question, here, of textual interpretation. The terms 'depth grammar' and 'surface grammar' are familiar in modern philosophy in something roughly like the sense here intended (cf. Wittgenstein's distinction of *Tiefengrammatik* and *Oberflächengrammatik*, 1953, p. 168); Hockett uses similar terminology in his discussion of the inadequacy of taxonomic linguistics (Hockett, 1958, Chapter 29). Postal has used the terms 'underlying structure' and 'superficial structure' (Postal, 1964*b*) for the same notions.

The distinction between deep and surface structure, in the sense in which these terms are used here, is drawn quite clearly in the Port-Royal *Grammar* (Lancelot *et al.*, 1660). See Chomsky (1964, pp. 15–16) for some discussion and references. In philosophical discussion, it is often introduced in an attempt to show how certain philosophical positions arise from false grammatical analogies, the surface structure of certain expressions being mistakenly considered to be semantically interpretable by means appropriate only to other, superficially similar sentences. Thus Thomas Reid (1785) holds a common source of philosophical error to lie in the fact that

in all languages, there are phrases which have a distinct meaning; while at the same time, there may be something in the structure of them that disagrees with the analogy of grammar or with the principles of philosophy. . . . Thus, we speak of feeling pain as if pain was something distinct from the feeling of it. We speak of pain coming and going, and removing from one place to another. Such phrases are meant by those who use them in a sense that is neither obscure nor false. But the philosopher puts them into his alembic, reduces them to their first principles, draws out of them a sense that was never meant, and so imagines that he has discovered an error of the vulgar [pp. 167–168].

More generally, he criticizes the theory of ideas as based on a deviation from the 'popular meaning', in which 'to have an idea of anything signifies nothing more than to think of it' (p. 105). But philosophers take an idea to be 'the object that the mind contemplates' (p. 105); to have an idea, then, is to possess in the mind such an image, picture, or representation as the immediate object of thought. It follows that there are two objects of thought: the idea, which is in the mind, and the thing represented by it. From this conclusion follow the absurdities, as Reid regards them, of the traditional theory of ideas. One of the sources of these absurdities is the failure of the philosopher to attend 'to the distinction between

and that the surface structure is determined by repeated application of certain formal operations called 'grammatical transformations' to objects of a more elementary sort. If this is true (as I assume, henceforth), then the syntactic component must generate deep and surface structures, for each sentence, and must interrelate them. This idea has been clarified substantially in recent work. For the moment, it is sufficient to observe that although the Immediate Constituent analysis (labelled bracketing) of an actual string of formatives may be adequate as an account of surface structure, it is certainly not adequate as an account of deep structure. My concern here is primarily with deep structure and, in particular, with the elementary objects of which deep structure is constituted.

To clarify exposition, I shall use the following terminology, with occasional revisions as the discussion proceeds.

The *base* of the syntactic component is a system of rules that generate a highly restricted (perhaps finite) set of *basic strings*, each with an associated structural description called a *base Phrase-marker*. These base Phrase-markers are the elementary units of which deep structures are constituted. I shall assume that no ambiguity is introduced by rules of the base. This assumption seems to me correct, but has no important consequences for what follows here, though it simplifies exposition. Underlying each sentence of the language there

the operations of the mind and the objects of these operations . . . although this distinction be familiar to the vulgar, and found in the structure of all languages . . . ' (p. 110). Notice that these two senses of 'having an idea' are distinguished by Descartes in the Preface to the *Meditations* (1641, p. 138). Reid's linguistic observation is made considerably earlier by Du Marsais, in a work published posthumously in 1769, in the following passage (pp. 179–80):

Ainsi, comme nous avons dit *j'ai un livre, j'ai un diamant, j'ai une montre,* nous disons par imitation, *j'ai la fièvre, j'ai envie, j'ai peur, j'ai un doute, j'ai pitié, j'ai une idèe,* etc. Mais *livre, diamant, montre* sont autant de noms d'objects réels qui existent indépendamment de notre manière de penser; au lieu que *santé, fièvre, peur, doute, envie,* ne sont que des termes métaphysiques qui ne désignent que des manières d'êtres considérés par des points de vue particuliers de l'esprit.

Dans cet exemple, *j'ai une montre,* j'ai est une expression qui doit être prise dans le sens propre: mais dans *j'ai une idèe,* j'ai n'est dit que par une imitation. C'est une expression empruntée. *J'ai une idèe,* c'est-à-dire, *je pense, je conçois de telle ou telle manière. J'ai envie,* c'est-à-dire, *je désire; j'ai la volonté,* c'est-à-dire, *je veux,* etc.

Ainsi, *idée, concept, imagination,* ne marquent point d'objects réels, et encore moins des êtres sensibles que l'on puisse unir l'un avec l'autre.

In more recent years, it has been widely held that the aims of philosophy should, in fact, be strictly limited to 'the detection of the sources in linguistic idioms of recurrent misconstructions and absurd theories' (Ryle, 1931).

is a sequence of base Phrase-markers, each generated by the base of the syntactic component. I shall refer to this sequence as the *basis* of the sentence that it underlies.

In addition to its base, the syntactic component of a generative grammar contains a *transformational* subcomponent. This is concerned with generating a sentence, with its surface structure, from its basis. Some familiarity with the operation and effects of transformational basis is henceforth presupposed.

Since the base generates only a restricted set of base Phrase-markers, most sentences will have a sequence of such objects as an underlying basis. Among the sentences with a single base Phrase-marker as basis, we can delimit a proper subset called 'kernel sentences'. These are sentences of a particularly simple sort that involve a minimum of transformational apparatus in their generation. The notion 'kernel sentence' has, I think, an important intuitive significance, but since kernel sentences play no distinctive role in generation or interpretation of sentences, I shall say nothing more about them here. One must be careful not to confuse kernel sentences with the basic strings that underlie them. The basic strings and base Phrase-markers do, it seems, play a distinctive and crucial role in language use.

Since transformations will not be considered here in detail, no careful distinction will be made, in the case of a sentence with a single element in its basis, between the basic string underlying this sentence and the sentence itself. In other words, at many points in the exposition I shall make the tacit simplifying (and contrary-to-fact) assumption that the underlying basic string *is* the sentence, in this case, and that the base Phrase-marker is the surface structure as well as the deep structure. I shall try to select examples in such a way as to minimize possible confusion, but the simplifying assumption should be borne in mind throughout.

4. JUSTIFICATION OF GRAMMARS

Before entering directly into an investigation of the syntactic component of a generative grammar, it is important to give some thought to several methodological questions of justification and adequacy.

There is, first of all, the question of how one is to obtain information about the speaker-hearer's competence, about his knowledge of the language. Like most facts of interest and importance, this is neither presented for direct observation nor extractable from data by inductive procedures of any known sort. Clearly, the actual data of linguistic performance will provide much evidence for determining the correctness of hypotheses about underlying linguistic structure, along with introspective reports (by the native speaker, or the linguist who has learned the language). This is the position that is universally adopted in practice, although there are methodological discussions that seem to imply a reluctance to use observed performance or introspective reports as evidence for some underlying reality.

In brief, it is unfortunately the case that no adequate formalizable techniques are known for obtaining reliable information concerning the facts of linguistic structure (nor is this particularly surprising). There are, in other words, very few reliable experimental or data-processing procedures for obtaining significant information concerning the linguistic intuition of the native speaker.

It is important to bear in mind that when an operational procedure is proposed, it must be tested for adequacy (exactly as a theory of linguistic intuition—a grammar—must be tested for adequacy) by measuring it against the standard provided by the tacit knowledge that it attempts to specify and describe. Thus a proposed operational test for, say, segmentation into words, must meet the empirical condition of conforming, in a mass of crucial and clear cases, to the linguistic intuition of the native speaker concerning such elements. Otherwise, it is without value. The same, obviously, is true in the case of any proposed operational procedure or any proposed grammatical description. If operational procedures were available that met this test, we might be justified in relying on their results in unclear and difficult cases. This remains a hope for the future rather than a present reality, however. This is the objective situation of present-day linguistic work; allusions to presumably well-known 'procedures of elicitation' or 'objective methods' simply obscure the actual situation in which linguistic work must, for the present, proceed. Furthermore, there is no reason to expect that reliable operational criteria for the deeper and more important theoretical notions of linguistics (such as 'grammaticalness' and 'paraphrase') will ever be forthcoming.

Even though few reliable operational procedures have been developed, the theoretical (that is, grammatical) investigation of the knowledge of the native speaker can proceed perfectly well. The critical problem for grammatical theory today is not a paucity of evidence but rather the inadequacy of present theories of language to account for masses of evidence that are hardly open to serious question. The problem for the grammarian is to construct a description and, where possible, an explanation for the enormous mass of unquestionable data concerning the linguistic intuition of the native speaker (often, himself); the problem for one concerned with operational procedures is to develop tests that give the correct results and make relevant distinctions. Neither the study of grammar nor the attempt to develop useful tests is hampered by lack of evidence with which to check results, for the present. We may hope that these efforts will converge, but they must obviously converge on the tacit knowledge of the native speaker if they are to be of any significance.

One may ask whether the necessity for present-day linguistics to give such priority to introspective evidence and to the linguistic intuition of the native speaker excludes it from the domain of science. The answer to this essentially terminological question seems to have no bearing at all on any serious issue. At most, it determines how we shall denote the kind of research that can be effectively carried out in the present state of our technique and understanding. However, this terminological question actually does relate to a different issue of some interest, namely the question whether the important feature of the successful sciences has been their search for insight or their concern for objectivity. The social and behavioural sciences provide ample evidence that objectivity can be pursued with little consequent gain in insight and understanding. On the other hand, a good case can be made for the view that the natural sciences have, by and large, sought objectivity primarily in so far as it is a tool for gaining insight (for providing phenomena that can suggest or test deeper explanatory hypotheses).

In any event, at a given stage of investigation, one whose concern is for insight and understanding (rather than for objectivity as a goal in itself) must ask whether or to what extent a wider range and more exact description of phenomena is relevant to solving the problems of the data by more objective tests is a matter of small importance for the problems at hand. One who disagrees with this estimate of the present situation in linguistics can justify his belief in the current importance of more objective operational tests by showing how they can lead to new and deeper understanding of linguistic structure. Perhaps the day will come when the kinds of data that we now can obtain in abundance will be insufficient to resolve deeper questions concerning the structure of language. However, many questions that can realistically and significantly be formulated today do not demand evidence of a kind that is unavailable or unattainable without significant improvements in objectivity of experimental technique.

Although there is no way to avoid the traditional assumption that the speaker-hearer's linguistic intuition is the ultimate standard that determines the accuracy of any proposed grammar, linguistic theory, or operational test, it must be emphasized, once again, that this tacit knowledge may very well not be immediately available to the user of the language. To eliminate what has seemed to some an air of paradox in this remark, let me illustrate with a few examples.

If a sentence such as 'flying planes can be dangerous' is presented in an appropriate constructed context, the listener will interpret it immediately in a unique way, and will fail to detect the ambiguity. In fact, he may reject the second interpretation, when this is pointed out to him, as forced or unnatural (independently of which interpretation he originally selected under contextual pressure). Nevertheless, his intuitive knowledge of the language is clearly such that both of the interpretations (corresponding to 'flying planes are dangerous' and 'flying planes is dangerous') are assigned to the sentence by the grammar he has internalized in some form.

In the case just mentioned, the ambiguity may be fairly transparent. But consider such a sentence as

(5) I had a book stolen.

Few hearers may be aware of the fact that their internalized grammar in fact provides at least three structural descriptions for this sentence. Nevertheless, this fact can be brought to consciousness by consideration of slight elaborations of sentence (5), for example: (i) 'I had a book stolen from my car when I stupidly left the window open', that is, 'someone stole a book from my car'; (ii) 'I had a book stolen from his library by a professional thief who I hired to do the job', that is, 'I had someone steal a book'; (iii) 'I almost had a book stolen, but they caught me leaving the library with it', that is, 'I had almost succeeded in stealing a book'. In bringing to consciousness the triple ambiguity of (5) in this way, we present no new information to the hearer and teach him nothing new about his language but simply arrange matters in such a way that his linguistic intuition, previously obscured, becomes evident to him.

As a final illustration, consider the sentences

(6) I persuaded John to leave
(7) I expected John to leave.

The first impression of the hearer may be that these sentences receive the same structural analysis. Even fairly careful thought may fail to show him that his internalized grammars assigns very different syntactic descriptions to these sentences. In fact, so far as I have been able to discover, no English grammar has pointed out the fundamental distinction between these two constructions (in particular, my own sketches of English grammar in Chomsky, 1955, 1962a, failed to note this). However, it is clear that the sentences (6) and (7) are not parallel in structure. The difference can be brought out by consideration of the sentences

(8)   (i) I persuaded a specialist to examine John
      (ii) I persuaded John to be examined by a specialist
(9)   (i) I expected a specialist to examine John
      (ii) I expected John to be examined by a specialist.

The sentences (9i) and (9ii) are 'cognitively synonymous': one is true if and only if the other is true. But no variety of even weak paraphrase holds between (8i) and (8ii). Thus (8i) can be true or false quite independently of the truth or falsity of (8ii). Whatever difference of connotation or 'topic' or emphasis one may find between (9i) and (9ii) is just the difference that exists between the active sentence 'a specialist will examine John' and its passive counterpart 'John will be examined by a specialist'. This is not at all the case with respect to (8), however. In fact, the underlying deep structure for (6) and (8ii) must show that 'John' is the Direct-Object of the Verb Phrase as well as the grammatical Subject of the embedded sentence. Furthermore, in (8ii) 'John' is the logical Direct-Object of the embedded sentence, whereas in (8i) the phrase 'a specialist' is the Direct-Object of the Verb Phrase and the logical Subject of the embedded sentence. In (7), (9i), and (9ii), however, the Noun Phrases 'John', 'a specialist', and 'John', respectively, have no grammatical functions other than those that are internal to the embedded sentence; in particular, 'John' is the logical Direct-Object and 'a specialist' the logical Subject in the embedded sentences of (9). Thus the underlying deep structures for (8i), (8ii), (9i), and (9ii) are, respectively, the following:[13]

(10) (i) Noun Phrase—Verb—Noun Phrase—Sentence
          (*I—persuaded—a specialist—a specialist will examine John*)
      (ii) Noun Phrase—Verb—Noun Phrase—Sentence
          (*I—persuaded—John—a specialist will examine John*)
(11) (i) Noun Phrase—Verb—Sentence
          (*I—expected—a specialist will examine John*)
      (ii) Noun Phrase—Verb—Sentence
          (*I—expected—a specialist will examine John*).

---

[13] These descriptions are not fully accurate. In fact, the sentential complement in (10) should, more properly, be regarded as embedded in a Prepositional-Phrase, and, as Peter Rosenbaum has pointed out, the sentential complement of (ii) should be regarded as embedded in the Noun-Phrase Object of 'expect'. Furthermore, the treatment of the Verbal Auxiliaries in (10) and (11) is incorrect, and there are other modifications relating to the marking of the passive transformation.

In the case of (10ii) and (11ii), the passive transformation will apply to the embedded sentence, and in all four cases other operations will give the final surface forms of (8) and (9). The important point in the present connection is that (8i) differs from (8ii) in underlying structure, although (9i) and (9ii) are essentially the same in underlying structure. This accounts for the difference in meaning. Notice, in support of this difference in analysis, that we can have 'I persuaded John that (of the fact that) Sentence', but not 'I expected John that (of the fact that) Sentence'.

The examples (6)–(7) serve to illustrate two important points. First, they show how unrevealing surface structure may be as to underlying deep structure. Thus (6) and (7) are the same in surface structure, but very different in the deep structure that underlies them and determines their semantic interpretations. Second, they illustrate the elusiveness of the speaker's tacit knowledge. Until such examples as (8) and (9) are adduced, it may not be in the least clear to a speaker of English that the grammar that he has internalized in fact assigns very different syntactic analyses to the superficially analogous sentences (6) and (7).

In short, we must be careful not to overlook the fact that surface similarities may hide underlying distinctions of a fundamental nature, and that it may be necessary to guide and draw out the speaker's intuition in perhaps fairly subtle ways before we can determine what is the actual character of his knowledge of his language or of anything else. Neither point is new (the former is a commonplace of traditional linguistic theory and analytic philosophy; the latter is as old as Plato's *Meno*); both are too often overlooked.

A grammar can be regarded as a theory of a language; it is *descriptively adequate* to the extent that it correctly describes the intrinsic competence of the idealized native speaker. The structural descriptions assigned to sentences by the grammar, the distinctions that it makes between well-formed and deviant, and so on, must, for descriptive adequacy, correspond to the linguistic intuition of the native speaker (whether or not he may be immediately aware of this) in a substantial and significant class of crucial cases.

A linguistic theory must contain a definition of 'grammar', that is, a specification of the class of potential grammars. We may, correspondingly, say that *a linguistic theory is descriptively adequate* if it makes a descriptively adequate grammar available for each natural language.

Although even descriptive adequacy on a large scale is by no means easy to approach, it is crucial for the productive development of linguistic theory that much higher goals than this be pursued. To facilitate the clear formulation of deeper questions, it is useful to consider the abstract problem of constructing an 'acquisition model' for language, that is, a theory of language learning or grammar construction. Clearly, a child who has learned a language has developed an internal representation of a system of rules that determines how sentences are to be formed, used, and understood. Using the term 'grammar' with a systematic ambiguity (to refer, first, to the native speaker's internally represented "theory of his language" and, second, to the linguist's account of this), we can say that the child has developed and internally represented a generative grammar, in the sense described. He has done this on the basis of observation of what we may call *primary linguistic data*. This must include examples of linguistic performance that are taken to be well-formed sentences, and may include also examples designated as non-sentences, and no doubt much other information of the sort that is required for language learning, whatever this may be (see pp. 108–10). On the basis of such data, the child constructs a grammar—that is, a theory of the language of which the well-formed sentences of the primary linguistic data constitute a small sample.[14] To learn a language, then, the child must have a method for devising an appropriate grammar, given primary linguistic data. As a precondition for language learning, he must possess, first, a linguistic theory that specifies the form of the grammar of a possible human language, and, second, a strategy for selecting a grammar of the appropriate form that is compatible with the primary linguistic data. As a long-range task for general linguistics, we might set the problem of developing an account of this innate linguistic theory that provides the basis for language learning. (Note that we are again using the term 'theory'—in this case 'theory of language' rather than 'theory of a particular language'—with a systematic ambiguity, to refer both to the child's innate predisposition to learn a language of a certain type and to the linguist's account of this.)

[14] It seems clear that many children acquire first or second languages quite successfully even though no special care is taken to teach them and no special attention is given to their progress. It also seems apparent that much of the actual speech observed consists of fragments and deviant expressions of a variety of sorts. Thus it seems that a child must have the ability to 'invent' a generative grammar that defines well-formedness and assigns interpretations to sentences even though the primary linguistic data that he uses as a basis for this act of theory construction may, from the point of view of the theory he constructs, be deficient in various respects. In general, there is an important element of truth in the traditional view that 'the pains which everyone finds in conversation . . . is not to comprehend what another thinketh, but to extricate his thought from the signs or words which often agree not with it' (Cordemoy, 1667), and the problem this poses for speech perception is magnified many times for the language learner.

To the extent that a linguistic theory succeeds in selecting a descriptively adequate grammar on the basis of primary linguistic data, we can say that it meets the condition of *explanatory adequacy*. That is, to this extent, it offers an explanation for the intuition of the native speaker on the basis of an empirical hypothesis concerning the innate predisposition of the child to develop a certain kind of theory to deal with the evidence presented to him. Any such hypothesis can be falsified (all too easily, in actual fact) by showing that it fails to provide a descriptively adequate grammar for primary linguistic data from some other language—evidently the child is not predisposed to learn one language rather than another. It is supported when it does provide an adequate explanation for some aspect of linguistic structure, an account of the way in which such knowledge might have been obtained.

Clearly, it would be utopian to expect to achieve explanatory adequacy on a large scale in the present state of linguistics. Nevertheless, considerations of explanatory adequacy are often critical for advancing linguistic theory. Gross coverage of a large mass of data can often be attained by conflicting theories; for precisely this reason it is not, in itself, an achievement of any particular theoretical interest or importance. As in any other field, the important problem in linguistics is to discover a complex of data that differentiates between conflicting conceptions of linguistic structure in that one of these conflicting theories can describe these data only by *ad hoc* means whereas the other can explain it on the basis of some empirical assumption about the form of language. Such small-scale studies of explanatory adequacy have, in fact, provided most of the evidence that has any serious bearing on the nature of linguistic structure. Thus whether we are comparing radically different theories of grammar or trying to determine the correctness of some particular aspect of one such theory, it is questions of explanatory adequacy that must, quite often, bear the burden of justification. This remark is in no way inconsistent with the fact that explanatory adequacy on a large scale is out of reach, for the present. It simply brings out the highly tentative character of any attempt to justify an empirical claim about linguistic structure.

To summarize briefly, there are two respects in which one can speak of 'justifying a generative grammar'. On one level (that of descriptive adequacy), the grammar is justified to the extent that it correctly describes its object, namely the linguistic intuition—the tacit competence—of the native speaker. In this sense, the grammar is justified on *external* grounds, on grounds of correspondence to linguistic fact. On a much deeper and hence much more rarely attainable level (that of explanatory adequacy), a grammar is justified to the extent that it is a *principled* descriptively adequate system, in that the linguistic theory with which it is associated selects this grammar over others, given primary linguistic data with which all are compatible. In this sense, the grammar is justified on *internal* grounds, on grounds of its relation to a linguistic theory that constitutes an explanatory hypothesis about the form of language as such. The problem of internal justification—of explanatory adequacy—is essentially the problem of constructing a theory of language acquisition, an account of the specific innate abilities that make this achievement possible.

5. FORMAL AND SUBSTANTIVE UNIVERSALS

A theory of linguistic structure that aims for explanatory adequacy incorporates an account of linguistic universals, and it attributes tacit knowledge of these universals to the child. It proposes, then, that the child approaches the data with the presumption that they are drawn from a language of a certain antecedently well-defined type, his problem being to determine which of the (humanly) possible languages is that of the community in which he is placed. Language learning would be impossible unless this were the case. The important question is: What are the initial assumptions concerning the nature of language that the child brings to language learning, and how detailed and specific is the innate schema (the general definition of 'grammar') that gradually becomes more explicit and differentiated as the child learns the language? For the present we cannot come at all close to making a hypothesis about innate schemata that is rich, detailed, and specific enough to account for the fact of language acquisition. Consequently, the main task of linguistic theory must be to develop an account of linguistic universals that, on the one hand, will not be falsified by the actual diversity of languages and, on the other, will be sufficiently rich and explicit to account for the rapidity and uniformity of language learning, and the remarkable complexity and range of the generative grammars that are the product of language learning.

The study of linguistic universals is the study of the properties of any generative grammar for a natural language. Particular assumptions about linguistic universals may pertain to either the syntactic, semantic, or phonological component, or to interrelations among the three components.

It is useful to classify linguistic universals as *formal* or *substantive*. A theory of substantive universals claims that items of a particular kind in any language must be drawn from a fixed class of items. For example, Jakobson's theory of distinctive features can be interpreted as making an assertion about substantive universals with respect to the phonological component of a generative grammar. It asserts that each output of this component consists of elements that are characterized in terms of some small number of fixed, universal, phonetic features (perhaps on the order of fifteen or twenty), each of which has a substantive acoustic-articulatory characterization independent of any particular language. Traditional universal grammar was also a theory of substantive universals, in this sense. It not only put forth interesting views as to the nature of universal phonetics, but also advanced the position that certain fixed syntactic categories (Noun, Verb, etc.) can be found in the syntactic representations of the sentences of any language, and that these provide the general underlying syntactic structure of each language. A theory of substantive semantic universals might hold, for example, that certain designative functions must be carried out in a specified way in each language. Thus it might assert that each language will contain terms that designate persons or lexical items referring to certain specific kinds of objects, feelings, behaviour, and so on.

It is also possible, however, to search for universal properties of a more abstract sort. Consider a claim that the grammar of every language meets certain specified formal conditions. The truth of this hypothesis would not in itself imply that any particular rule must appear in all or even in any two grammars. The property of having a grammar meeting a certain abstract condition might be called a *formal* linguistic universal, if shown to be a general property of natural languages. Recent attempts to specify the abstract conditions that a generative grammar must meet have produced a variety of proposals concerning formal universals, in this sense. For example, consider the proposal that the syntactic component of a grammar must contain transformational rules (these being operations of a highly special kind) mapping semantically inter-preted deep structures into phonetically interpreted surface structures, or the proposal that the phonological component of a grammar consists of a sequence of rules, a subset of which may apply cyclically to successively more dominant constituents of the surface structure (a transformational cycle, in the sense of much recent work on phono-logy). Such proposals make claims of a quite different sort from the claim that certain substantive phonetic elements are available for phonetic representation in all languages, or that certain specific cate-gories must be central to the syntax of all languages, or that certain semantic features or categories provide a universal framework for semantic description. Substantive universals such as these concern the vocabulary for the description of language; formal universals involve rather the character of the rules that appear in grammars and the ways in which they can be interconnected.

On the semantic level, too, it is possible to search for what might be called formal universals, in essentially the sense just described. Consider, for example, the assumption that proper names, in any language, must designate objects meeting a condition of spatiotemporal contiguity,[15] and that the same is true of other terms designating objects; or the condition that the colour words of any language must subdivide the colour spectrum into continuous segments; or the condition that artefacts are defined in terms of certain human goals, needs, and functions instead of solely in terms of physical qualities.[16] Formal constraints of this sort on a system of concepts may severely limit the choice (by the child, or the linguist) of a descriptive grammar, given primary linguistic data.

The existence of deep-seated formal universals, in the sense suggested by such examples as these, implies that all languages are cut to the same pattern, but does not imply that there is any point by point correspondence between particular languages. It does not, for example, imply that there must be some reasonable procedure for translating between languages.[17]

[15] For example, Russell (1940, p. 33: 'from a logical point of view, a proper name may be assigned to any continuous portion of space-time') if we interpret his notion of 'logically proper name' as embodying an empirical hypothesis. Interpreted in this way, Russell is stating what is, no doubt, a psychological truth. Interpreted otherwise, he is giving an unmotivated definition of 'proper name'. There is no logical necessity for names or other 'object words' to meet any condition of spatiotemporal contiguity or to have other Gestalt qualities, and it is a non-trivial fact that they apparently do, in so far as the designated objects are of the type that can actually be perceived (for example, it is not true of 'United States'—similarly, it need not be true of somewhat more abstract and functionally defined notions such as 'barrier'). Thus there are no logical grounds for the apparent non-existence in natural languages of words such as 'LIMB', similar to 'limb' except that it designates the single object consisting of a dog's four legs, so that 'its LIMB is brown' (like 'its head is brown') would mean that the object consisting of the four legs is brown. Similarly, there is no a priori reason why a natural language could not contain a word 'HERD', like the collective 'herd' except that it denotes a single scattered object with cows as parts, so that 'a cow lost a leg' implies 'the HERD lost a leg', etc.

[16] Thus for Aristotle (*De Anima*, 403*b*), the 'essence of a house is assigned in such a formula as "a shelter against destruction by wind, rain, and heat",' though 'the physicist would describe it as "stones, bricks, and timbers" '. For interesting comments on such definitions, see Foot (1961), Katz (1964*b*).

[17] By a 'reasonable procedure' I mean one that does not involve extralinguistic information—that is, one that does not incorporate an 'encyclopedia'. See Bar-Hillel (1960) for discussion. The possibility of a reasonable procedure for translation between arbitrary languages depends on the sufficiency of substantive universals. In fact, although there is much reason to believe that languages are to a significant extent cast in the same mold, there is little reason to suppose that reasonable procedures of translation are in general possible.

In general, there is no doubt that a theory of language, regarded as a hypothesis about the innate 'language-forming capacity' of humans, should concern itself with both substantive and formal universals. But whereas substantive universals have been the traditional concern of general linguistic theory, investigations of the abstract conditions that must be satisfied by any generative grammar have been undertaken only quite recently. They seem to offer extremely rich and varied possibilities for study in all aspects of grammar.

6. FURTHER REMARKS ON DESCRIPTIVE AND EXPLANATORY THEORIES

Let us consider with somewhat greater care just what is involved in the construction of an 'acquisition model' for language. A child who is capable of language learning must have

(12) (i) a technique for representing input signals
 (ii) a way of representing structural information about these signals
 (iii) some initial delimitation of a class of possible hypotheses about language structure
 (iv) a method for determining what each such hypothesis implies with respect to each sentence
 (v) a method for selecting one of the (presumably, infinitely many) hypotheses that are allowed by (iii) and are compatible with the given primary linguistic data.

Correspondingly, a theory of linguistic structure that aims for explanatory adequacy must contain

(13) (i) a universal phonetic theory that defines the notion 'possible sentence'
 (ii) a definition of 'structural description'
 (iii) a definition of 'generative grammar'
 (iv) a method for determining the structural description of a sentence, given a grammar
 (v) a way of evaluating alternative proposed grammars.

Putting the same requirements in somewhat different terms, we must require of such a linguistic theory that it provide for

(14) (i) an enumeration of the class $s_1, s_2, \ldots$ of possible sentences
 (ii) an enumeration of the class $SD_1, SD_2, \ldots$ of possible structural descriptions
 (iii) an enumeration of the class $G_1, G_2, \ldots$ of possible generative grammars

(iv) specification of a function f such that $SD_{f(i,j)}$ is the structural description assigned to sentences s_i by grammar G_j, for arbitrary i,j[18]

(v)   specification of a function m such that $m(i)$ is an integer associated with the grammar G_i as its value (with, let us say, lower value indicated by higher number).

Conditions of at least this strength are entailed by the decision to aim for explanatory adequacy.

A theory meeting these conditions would attempt to account for language learning in the following way. Consider first the nature of primary linguistic data. This consists of a finite amount of information about sentences, which, furthermore, must be rather restricted in scope, considering the time limitations that are in effect, and fairly degenerate in quality (cf. n. 14). For example, certain signals might be accepted, as properly formed sentences, while others are classed as nonsentences, as a result of correction of the learner's attempts on the part of the linguistic community. Furthermore, the conditions of use might be such as to require the structural description be assigned to these objects in certain ways. That the latter is a prerequisite for language acquisition seems to follow from the widely accepted (but, for the moment, quite unsupported) view that there must be a partially semantic basis for the acquisition of syntax or for the justification of hypotheses about the syntactic component of a grammar. Incidentally, it is often not realized how strong a claim this is about the innate concept-forming abilities of the child and the system of linguistic universals that these abilities imply. Thus what is maintained, presumably, is that the child has an innate theory of potential structural descriptions that is sufficiently rich and fully developed so that he is able to determine, from a real situation in which a signal occurs, which structural descriptions may be appropriate to this signal, and also that he is able to do this in part in advance of any assumption as to the linguistic structure of this signal. To say that the assumption about innate capacity is extremely strong is, of course, not to say that it is incorrect. Let us, in any event, assume tentatively that the primary linguistic data consist of signals classified

---

[18] Actually, a set of structural descriptions should be assigned by f to each s_i (and each structural description must be assigned to exactly one s_i), given G_j, one for each way of interpreting the sentence s_i with respect to G_j. Thus an unambiguous sentence should receive one structural description, a doubly ambiguous sentence two structural descriptions, etc. We assume that mappings are effective—that there is an algorithm for enumerating sentences, structural descriptions, and grammars and (throughout this is less obvious) for determining the values of f and m in all cases.

as sentences and nonsentences, and a partial and tentative pairing of signals with structural descriptions.

A language-acquisition device that meets conditions (i)-(iv) is capable of utilizing such primary linguistic data as the empirical basis for language learning. This device must search through the set of possible hypotheses $G_1, G_2, \ldots$, which are available to it by virtue of condition (iii), and must select grammars that are compatible with the primary linguistic data, represented in terms of (i) and (ii). It is possible to test compatibility by virtue of the fact that the device meets conditon (iv). The device would then select one of these potential grammars by the evaluation measure guaranteed by (v).[19] The selected grammar now provides the device with a method for interpreting an arbitrary sentence, by virtue of (ii) and (iv). That is to say, the device has now constructed a theory of the language of which the primary linguistic data are a sample. The theory that the device has now selected and internally represented specifies its tacit competence, is knowledge of the language. The child who acquires a language in this way of course knows a great deal more than he has 'learned'. His knowledge of the language, as this is determined by his internalized grammar, goes far beyond the presented primary linguistic data and is in no sense an 'inductive generalization' from these data.

This account of language learning can, obviously, be paraphrased directly as a description of how the linguist whose work is guided by a linguistic theory meeting conditions (i)-(v) would justify a grammar that he constructs for a language on the basis of given primary linguistic data.[20]

[19] Obviously, to construct an actual theory of language learning, it would be necessary to face several other very serious questions involving, for example, the gradual development of an appropriate hypothesis, simplification of the technique for finding a compatible hypothesis, and the continual accretion of linguistic skill and knowledge and the deepening of the analysis of language structure that may continue long after the basic form of the language has been mastered. What I am describing is an idealization in which only the moment of acquisition of the correct grammar is considered. Introduction of these additional considerations might affect the general discussion in many ways. For example, in some limited but nevertheless real way, the preconditions (i)-(v) themselves might possibly be developed on the basis of deeper innate structure, in ways that depend in part on primary linguistic data and the order and manner in which they are presented. Furthermore, it might very well be true that a series of successively more detailed and highly structured schemata (corresponding to maturational stages, but perhaps in part themselves determined in form by earlier steps of language acquisition) are applied to the data at successive stages of language acquisition. There are, a priori, many possibilities that can be considered here.

[20] It is instructive to see how modern structural linguistics has attempted to

Notice, incidentally, that care must be taken to distinguish several different ways in which primary linguistic data may be necessary for language learning. In part, such data determine to which of the possible languages (that is, the languages provided with grammars in accordance with the a priori constraint (iii)) the language learner is being exposed, and it is this function of the primary linguistic data that we are considering here. But such data may play an entirely different role as well; namely, certain kinds of data and experience may be required in order to set the language-acquisition device into operation, although they may not affect the manner of its functioning in the least. Thus it has been found that semantic reference may greatly facilitate performance in a syntax-learning experiment, even though it does not, apparently, affect the *manner* in which acquisition of syntax proceeds; that is, it plays no role in determining which hypotheses are selected by the learner (Miller and Norman, 1964). Similarly, it would not be at all surprising to find that normal language learning requires use of language in real-life situations, in some way. But this, if true, would not be sufficient to show that information regarding situational context (in particular, a pairing of signals with structural descriptions that is at least in part prior to assumptions about syntactic structure) plays any role in determining how language is acquired, once the mechanism is put to work and the task of language learning is undertaken by the child. This distinction is quite familiar outside of the domain of language acquisition. For example, Richard Held has shown in numerous experiments that under certain circumstances reafferent stimulation (that is, stimulation resulting from voluntary activity) is a prerequisite to the development of a concept of visual space, although it may not determine the character of this concept (cf. Held and Hein, 1963; Held and Freedman, 1963, and references cited there). Or, to take one of innumerable examples from studies of animal learning, it has been observed (Lemmon and Patterson, 1964) that depth perception in lambs is considerably

meet these conditions. It assumes that the technique for discovering the correct hypothesis (grammar) must be based on procedures of successive segmentation and classification of the items in the corpus (which constitute the primary linguistic data, when supplemented, perhaps, by certain kinds of semantic information the exact relevance of which to the problem at hand has never been clarified). To compensate for this extremely strong demand on the procedure of grammar discovery, it was necessary to sacrifice descriptive adequacy, over a wide range of cases. In fact, the methodological discussions of modern linguistics pay very little attention to considerations (ii)–(iv) (though they do imply certain conclusions about them) and concentrate almost solely on development of constructive, step-by-step procedures of classification and segmentation. For discussion, see Lees (1957), Chomsky (1964).

facilitated by mother-neonate contact, although again there is no reason to suppose that the nature of the lamb's 'theory of visual space' depends on this contact.

In studying the actual character of learning, linguistic or otherwise, it is of course necessary to distinguish carefully between these two functions of external data—the function of initiating or facilitating the operation of innate mechanisms and the function of determining in part the direction that learning will take.[21]

Returning now to the main theme, we shall call a theory of linguistic structure that meets conditions (i)-(v) an *explanatory theory*, and a theory that meets conditions (i)-(iv) a *descriptive theory*. In fact, a linguistic theory that is concerned only with descriptive adequacy will limit its attention to topics (i)-(iv). Such a theory must, in other words, make available a class of generative grammars containing, for each language, a descriptively adequate grammar of this language—a grammar that (by means of (iv)) assigns structural descriptions to sentences in accordance with the linguistic competence of the native speaker. A theory of language is empirically significant only to the extent that it meets conditions (i)-(iv). The further question of explanatory adequacy arises only in connection with a theory that also meets condition (v) (but see pp. 113-14). In other words, it arises only to the extent that the theory provides a principled basis for selecting a descriptively adequate grammar on the basis of primary linguistic data by the use of a well-defined evaluation measure.

This account is misleading in one important respect. It suggests that to raise a descriptively adequate theory to the level of explanatory adequacy one needs only to define an appropriate evaluation measure. This is incorrect, however. A theory may be descriptively adequate, in the sense just defined, and yet provide such a wide range of potential grammars that there is no possibility of discovering a formal property distinguishing the descriptively adequate grammars, in general, from among the mass of grammars compatible with whatever data are available. In fact, the real problem is almost always to restrict the range of possible hypotheses by adding additional structure to the notion 'generative grammar'. For the construction of a reasonable acquisition model, it is necessary to reduce the class of attainable[22] grammars

---

[21] This point has some historical interest. In fact, as has generally been noted by commentators, Locke's attempt to refute the doctrine of innate ideas is largely vitiated by his failure to observe the distinction we have just been discussing, although this was clear to Descartes (and was later re-emphasized by Leibniz, in his critique of Locke's *Essay*).

[22] See n. 19. An actual acquisition model must have a strategy for finding hypotheses. Suppose, for example, that the strategy is to consider only grammars

compatible with given primary linguistic data to the point where selection among them can be made by a formal evaluation measure. This requires a precise and narrow delimitation of the notion 'generative grammar'—a restrictive and rich hypothesis concerning the universal properties that determine the form of language, in the traditional sense of this term.

The same point can be put in a somewhat different way. Given a variety of descriptively adequate grammars for natural languages, we are interested in determining to what extent they are unique and to what extent there are deep underlying similarities among them that are attributable to the form of language as such. Real progress in linguistics consists in the discovery that certain features of given languages can be reduced to universal properties of language, and explained in terms of these deeper aspects of linguistic form. Thus the major endeavor of the linguist must be to enrich the theory of linguistic form by formulating more specific constraints and conditions on the notion 'generative grammar'. Where this can be done, particular grammars can be simplified by eliminating from them descriptive statements that are attributable to the general theory of grammar (cf. 5). For example, if we conclude that the transformational cycle[23] is a universal feature of the phonological component, it is unnecessary, in the grammar of English, to describe the manner of functioning of those phonological rules that involve syntactic structure. This description will now have been abstracted from the grammar of English and stated as a formal linguistic universal, as part of the theory of generative grammar. Obviously, this conclusion, if justified, would represent an important advance in the theory of language, since it would then have been shown that what appears to be a peculiarity of English is actually explicable in terms of a general and deep empirical assumption about the nature of language, an assumption that can be refuted, if false, by study of descriptively adequate grammars of other languages.

In short, the most serious problem that arises in the attempt to achieve explanatory adequacy is that of characterizing the notion 'generative grammar' in a sufficiently rich, detailed, and highly

---

that have better than a certain value (in terms of the evaluation measure (v)), at each stage in the process of language learning. What is required of a significant linguistic theory, then, is that given primary linguistic data D, the class of grammars compatible with D be sufficiently scattered, in terms of value, so that the intersection of the class of grammars compatible with D and the class of grammars which are highly valued be reasonably small. Only then can language learning actually take place.

[23] See references of n. 10.

structured way. A theory of grammar may be descriptively adequate and yet leave unexpressed major features that are defining properties of natural language and that distinguish natural languages from arbitrary symbolic systems. It is for just this reason that the attempt to achieve explanatory adequacy—the attempt to discover linguistic universals—is so crucial at every stage of understanding of linguistic structure, despite the fact that even descriptive adequacy on a broad scale may be an unrealized goal. It is not necessary to achieve descriptive adequacy before raising questions of explanatory adequacy. On the contrary, the crucial questions, the questions that have the greatest bearing on our concept of language and on descriptive practice as well, are almost always those involving explanatory adequacy with respect to particular aspects of language structure.

To acquire language, a child must devise a hypothesis compatible with presented data—he must select from the store of potential grammars a specific one that is appropriate to the data available to him. It is logically possible that the data might be sufficiently rich and the class of potential grammars sufficiently limited so that no more than a single permitted grammar will be compatible with the available data at the moment of successful language acquisition, in our idealized 'instantaneous' model (cf. nn. 19 and 22). In this case, no evaluation procedure will be necessary as a part of linguistic theory—that is, an innate property of an organism or a device capable of language acquisition. It is rather difficult to imagine how in detail this logical possibility might be realized, and all concrete attempts to formulate an empirically adequate linguistic theory certainly leave ample room for mutually inconsistent grammars, all compatible with primary data of any conceivable sort. All such theories therefore require supplementation by an evaluation measure if language acquisition is to be accounted for and selection of specific grammars is to be justified; and I shall continue to assume tentatively, as heretofore, that this is an empirical fact about the innate human *faculté de langage* and consequently about general linguistic theory as well.

7. ON EVALUATION PROCEDURES

The status of an evaluation procedure for grammars (see conditions (v) of (12)–(14)) has often been misconstrued. It must first of all be kept clearly in mind that such a measure is not given a priori, in some manner. Rather, any proposal concerning such a measure is an empirical hypothesis about the nature of language. This is evident from the preceding discussion. Suppose that we have a descriptive theory, meeting conditions (i)–(iv) of (12)–(14) in some fixed way. Given primarily linguistic data D, different choices of an evaluation measure will assign quite different ranks to alternative hypotheses (alternative grammars) as to the language of which D is a sample, and will therefore lead to entirely different predictions as to how a person who learns a language on the basis of D will interpret new sentences not in D. Consequently, choice of an evaluation measure is an empirical matter, and particular proposals are correct or incorrect.

Perhaps confusion about this matter can be traced to the use of the term 'simplicity measure' for particular proposed evaluation measures, it being assumed that 'simplicity' is a general notion somehow understood in advance outside of linguistic theory. This is a misconception, however. In the context of this discussion, 'simplicity' (that is, the evaluation measure m of (v)) is a notion to be defined within linguistic theory along with 'grammar', 'phoneme', etc. Choice of a simplicity measure is rather like determination of the value of a physical constant. We are given, in part, an empirical pairing of certain kinds of primary linguistic data with certain grammars that are in fact constructed by people presented with such data. A proposed simplicity measure constitutes part of the attempt to determine precisely the nature of this association. If a particular formulation of (i)-(iv) is assumed, and if pairs (D_1,G_1), (D_2,G_2), . . . of primary linguistic data and descriptively adequate grammars are given, the problem of defining 'simplicity' is just the problem of discovering how G_i is determined by D_i, for each i. Suppose, in other words, that we regard an acquisition model for language as an input-output device that determines a particular generative grammar as 'output', given certain primary linguistic data as input. A proposed simplicity measure, taken together with a specification of (i)-(iv), constitutes a hypothesis concerning the nature of such a device. Choice of a simplicity measure is therefore an empirical matter with empirical consequences.

All of this has been said before. I repeat it at such length because it has been so grossly misunderstood.

It is also apparent that evaluation measure of the kinds that have been discussed in the literature on generative grammar cannot be used to compare different theories of grammar; comparison of a grammar from one class of proposed grammars with a grammar from another class, *by such a measure*, is utterly without sense. Rather, an evaluation measure of this kind is an essential part of a particular theory of grammar that aims at explanatory adequacy. It is true that there is a sense in which alternative theories of language (or alternative theories in other domains) can be compared as to simplicity and elegance. What we have been discussing here, however, is not this general question but rather the problem of comparing two theories of a language—two grammars of this language—in terms of a particular general linguistic theory. This is, then, a matter of formulating an explanatory theory of language; it is not to be confused with the problem of choosing among competing theories of language. Choice among competing theories of language is of course a fundamental question and should also be settled, in so far as possible, on empirical grounds of descriptive and explanatory adequacy. But it is not the question involved in the use of an evaluation measure in the attempt to achieve explanatory adequacy.

As a concrete illustration, consider the question of whether the rules of a grammar should be unordered (let us call this the linguistic theory T_U) or ordered in some specific way (the theory T_O). A priori, there is no way to decide which of the two is correct. There is no known absolute sense of 'simplicity' or 'elegance', developed within linguistic theory of general epistemology, in accordance with which T_U and T_O can be compared. It is quite meaningless, therefore, to maintain that in absolute sense T_U is 'simpler' than T_O or conversely. One can easily invent a general concept of 'simplicity' that will prefer T_U to T_O, or T_O to T_U; in neither case will this concept have any known justification. Certain measures of evaluation have been proposed and in part empirically justified within linguistics—for example, minimization of feature specification (as discussed in Halle, 1959a, 1961, 1962a, 1964) or the measure based on abbreviatory notations (discussed on pp. 119–22). These measures do not apply, because they are internal to a specific linguistic theory and their empirical justification relies essentially on this fact. To choose between T_U and T_O, we must proceed in an entirely different way. We must ask whether T_U or T_O provides descriptively adequate grammars for natural languages, or leads to explanatory adequacy. This is a perfectly meaningful empirical question if the theories in question are stated with sufficient care. For example, if T_U^S is the familiar theory of phrase structure grammar and T_O^S is the same theory, with the further condition that the rules are linearly ordered and apply cyclically, with at least one rule $A \rightarrow X$ being obligatory for each category A, so as to guarantee that each cycle is non-vacuous, then it can be shown that T_U^S and T_O^S are incomparable in descriptive power (in 'strong generative capacity'; see Chomsky, 1955, chs. 6 and 7, and Chomsky, 1956, for some discussion of such systems). Consequently, we might ask whether natural languages in fact fall under T_U^S or T_O^S, these being non-equivalent and empirically distinguishable theories. Or, supposing T_U^P and T_O^P to be theories of the phonological component (where T_U^P holds phonological rules to be unordered and T_O^P holds them to be partially ordered), it is easy to invent hypothetical 'languages' for which significant generalizations are expressible in terms of T_O^P but not T_U^P, or conversely. We can therefore try to determine whether there are significant generalizations that are expressible in terms of one but not the other theory in the case of empirically given languages. In principle, either result is possible; it is an entirely factual question, having to do with the properties of natural languages. We shall see later that T_O^S is rather well motivated as a theory of the base, and strong arguments have been offered to show that T_O^P is correct and T_U^P is wrong, as a theory of phonological processes (cf. Chomsky, 1951, 1964; Halle, 1959*a*, 1959*b*, 1962*a*, 1964). In both cases, the argument turns on the factual question of expressibility of linguistically significant generalizations in terms of one or the other theory, not on any presumed absolute sense of 'simplicity' that might rank T_U and T_O relative to one another. Failure to appreciate this fact has led to a great deal of vacuous and pointless discussion.

Confusion about these questions may also have been engendered by the fact that there are several different senses in which one can talk of 'justifying' a grammar, as noted on pp. 104–5. To repeat the major point: on the one hand, the grammar can be justified on external grounds of descriptive adequacy—we may ask whether it states the facts about the language correctly, whether it predicts correctly how the idealized native speaker would understand arbitrary sentences and gives a correct account of the basis for this achievement; on the other hand, a grammar can be justified on internal grounds if, given an explanatory linguistic theory, it can be shown that this grammar is the highest-valued grammar permitted by the theory and compatible with given primary linguistic data. In the latter case, a principled basis is presented for the construction of this grammar, and it is therefore justified on much deeper empirical grounds. Both kinds of justification are of course necessary; it is important, however, not to confuse them. In the case of a linguistic theory that is merely descriptive, only one kind of justification can be given—namely, we can show that it permits grammars that meet the external conditions of descriptive adequacy.[24]

[24] Failure of attempts to justify an explanatory theory may be interpreted in various ways, of course. It may indicate that the theory is wrong, or that its consequences were incorrectly determined—in particular, that the grammar tested for descriptive adequacy was not the most highly valued one. Since any reasonable evaluation measure must be a systematic measure, and since language is a tightly interconnected system, the latter possibility is not to be discounted. In short, justification of linguistic theory does not avoid the problems faced by justification of any substantive and non-trivial empirical hypothesis.

It is only when all of the conditions (i)–(v) of (12)–(14) are met that the deeper question of internal justification can be raised.

It is also apparent that the discussion as to whether an evaluation measure is a 'necessary' part of linguistic theory is quite without substance (see, however, pp. 113-15). If the linguist is content to formulate descriptions one way or another with little concern for justification, and if he does not intend to proceed from the study of facts about particular languages to an investigation of the characteristic properties of natural language as such, then construction of an evaluation procedure and the associated concerns that relate to explanatory adequacy need not concern him. In this case, since interest in justification has been abandoned, neither evidence nor argument (beyond minimal requirements of consistency) has any bearing on what the linguist presents as a linguistic description. On the other hand, if he wishes to achieve descriptive adequacy in his account of language structure, he must concern himself with the problem of developing an explanatory theory of the form of grammar, since this provides one of the main tools for arriving at a descriptively adequate grammar in any particular case. In other words, choice of a grammar for a particular language L will always be much underdetermined by the data drawn from L alone. Moreover, other relevant data (namely, successful grammars for other languages or successful fragments for other subparts of L) will be available to the linguist only if he possesses an explanatory theory. Such a theory limits the choice of grammar by the dual method of imposing formal conditions on grammar and providing an evaluation procedure to be applied for the language L with which he is now concerned. Both the formal conditions and the evaluation procedure can be empirically justified by their success in other cases. Hence, any far-reaching concern for descriptive adequacy must lead to an attempt to develop an explanatory theory that fulfills these dual functions, and concern with explanatory adequacy surely requires an investigation of evaluation procedures.

The major problem in constructing an evaluation measure for grammars is that of determining which generalizations about a language are significant ones; an evaluation measure must be selected in such a way as to favour these. We have a generalization when a set of rules about distinct items can be replaced by a single rule (or, more generally, partially identical rules) about the whole set, or when it can be shown that a 'natural class' of items undergoes a certain process or set of similar processes. Thus, choice of an evaluation measure constitutes a decision as to what are 'similar processes' and 'natural classes'—in short, what are significant generalizations. The problem is to devise a procedure that will assign a numerical measure of valuation to a grammar in terms of the degree of linguistically significant generalization that this grammar achieves. The obvious numerical measure to be applied to a grammar is length, in terms of number of symbols. But if this is to be a meaningful measure, it is necessary to devise notations and to restrict the form of rules in such a way that significant considerations of complexity and generality are converted into considerations of length, so that real generalizations shorten the grammar and spurious ones do not. Thus it is the notational conventions used in presenting a grammar that define 'significant generalization', if the evaluation measure is taken as length.

This is, in fact, the rationale behind the conventions for use of parentheses, brackets, etc. that have been adopted in explicit (that is, generative) grammars. For a detailed discussion of these, see Chomsky (1951, 1955), Postal (1962), and Matthews (1964). To take just one example, consider the analysis of the English Verbal Auxiliary. The facts are that such a phrase must contain Tense (which is, furthermore, *Past* or *Present*), and then may or may not contain a Modal and either the *Perfect* or *Progressive* Aspect (or both), where the elements must appear in the order just given. Using familiar notational conventions, we can state this rule in the following form:

(15) Aux → Tense (Modal) (*Perfect*) (*Progressive*)

(omitting details that are not relevant here). Rule (15) is an abbreviation for eight rules that analyse the element Aux into its eight possible forms. Stated in full, these eight rules would involve twenty symbols, whereas rule (15) involves four (not counting Aux, in both cases). The parenthesis notation, in this case, has the following meaning. It asserts that the difference between four and twenty symbols is a measure of the degree of linguistically significant generalization achieved in a language that has the forms given in list (16), for the Auxiliary Phrase, as compared with a language that has, for example, the forms given in list (17) as the representatives of this category:

(16) Tense, Tense͡ Modal, Tense͡ *Perfect*, Tense͡ *Progressive*, Tense͡ Modal͡ *Perfect*, Tense͡ Modal͡ *Progressive*, Tense͡ *Perfect*͡ *Progressive*, Tense͡ Modal͡ *Perfect*͡ *Progressive*

(17) Tense͡ Modal͡ *Perfect*͡ *Progressive*, Modal͡ *Perfect*͡ *Progressive*͡ Tense, *Perfect*͡ *Progressive*͡ Tense͡ Modal, *Progressive*͡ Tense͡ Modal͡ *Perfect*, Tense͡ *Perfect*, Modal͡ *Progressive*

In the case of both list (16) and list (17), twenty symbols are involved. List (16) abbreviates to rule (15) by the notational convention;

list (17) cannot be abbreviated by this convention. Hence, adoption of the familiar notational conventions involving the use of parentheses amounts to a claim that there is a linguistically significant generalization underlying the set of forms in list (16) but not the set of forms in list (17). It amounts to the empirical hypothesis that regularities of the type exemplified in (16) are those found in natural languages, and are of the type that children learning a language will expect; whereas cyclic regularities of the type exemplified in (17), though perfectly genuine, abstractly, are not characteristic of natural language, are not of the type for which children will intuitively search in language materials, and are much more difficult for the language-learner to construct on the basis of scattered data or to use. What is claimed, then, is that when given scattered examples from (16), the language learner will construct the rule (15) generating the full set with their semantic interpretations, whereas when given scattered examples that could be subsumed under a cyclic rule, he will not incorporate this 'generalization' in his grammar—he will not, for example, conclude from the existence of 'yesterday John arrived' and 'John arrived yesterday' that there is a third form 'arrived yesterday John', or from the existence of 'is John here' and 'here is John' that there is a third form 'John here is', etc. One might easily propose a different notational convention that would abbreviate list (17) to a shorter rule than list (16), thus making a different empirical assumption about what constitutes a linguistically significant generalization. There is no a priori reason for preferring the usual convention; it simply embodies a factual claim about the structure of natural language and the predisposition of the child to search for certain types of regularity in natural language.

The illustrative examples of the preceding paragraph must be regarded with some caution. It is the full set of notational conventions that constitute an evaluation procedure, in the manner outlined earlier. The factual content of an explanatory theory lies in its claim that the most highly valued grammar of the permitted form will be selected, on the basis of given data. Hence, descriptions of particular subsystems of the grammar must be evaluated in terms of their effect on the entire system of rules. The extent to which particular parts of the grammar can be selected independently of others is an empirical matter about which very little is known, at present. Although alternatives can be clearly formulated, deeper studies of particular languages than are presently available are needed to settle the questions that immediately arise when these extremely important issues are raised. To my knowledge, the only attempt to evaluate a fairly full and complex subsystem of a grammar is in Chomsky (1951), but even here all that is shown is that the value of the system is a 'local maximum' in the sense that inter-change of adjacent rules decreases value. The effect of modifications on a larger scale is not investigated. Certain aspects of the general question, relating to lexical and phonological structure, are discussed in Halle and Chomsky (1968).

One special case of this general approach to evaluation that has been worked out in a particularly convincing way is the condition of mini-mization of distinctive feature specifications in the phonological com-ponent of the grammar. A very plausible argument can be given to the effect that this convention defines the notions of 'natural class' and 'significant generalization' that have been relied on implicitly in des-criptive and comparative-historical phonological investigations, and that determine the intuitively given distinction between 'phonologically possible' and 'phonologically impossible' nonsense forms. For discus-sion, see Halle, (1959*a*, 1959*b*, 1961, 1962, 1964), Halle and Chomsky (1968). It is important to observe that the effectiveness of this particular evaluation measure is completely dependent on a strong assumption about the form of grammar, namely, the assumption that only feature notation is permitted. If phonemic notation is allowed in addition to feature notation, the measure gives absurd consequences, as Halle shows.

It is clear, then, that choice of notations and other conventions is not an arbitrary or 'merely technical' matter, if length is to be taken as the measure of valuation for a grammar. It is, rather, a matter that has immediate and perhaps quite drastic empirical consequences. When particular notational devices are incorporated into a linguistic theory of the sort we are discussing, a certain empirical chain is made, implicitly, concerning natural language. It is implied that a person learning a language will attempt to formulate generalizations that can easily be expressed (that is, with few symbols) in terms of the notations available in this theory, and that he will select grammars containing these generalizations over other grammars that are also compatible with the given data but that contain different sorts of generalization, different concepts of 'natural class', and so on. These may be very strong claims, and need by no means be true on any a priori grounds.

To avoid any possible lingering confusion on this matter, let me repeat once more that this discussion of language learning in terms of formulation of rules, hypotheses, etc., does not refer to conscious formulation and expression of these but rather to the process of arriv-ing at an internal representation of a generative system, which can be appropriately described in these terms.

In brief, it is clear that no present-day theory of language can hope to attain explanatory adequacy beyond very restricted domains. In other words, we are very far from being able to present a system of formal and substantive linguistic universals that will be sufficiently rich and detailed to account for the facts of language learning. To advance linguistic theory in the direction of explanatory adequacy, we can attempt to refine the evaluation measure for grammars or to tighten the formal constraints on grammars so that it becomes more difficult to find a highly valued hypothesis compatible with primary linguistic data. There can be no doubt that present theories of grammar require modification in both of these ways, the latter, in general, being the more promising. Thus the most crucial problem for linguistic theory seems to be to abstract statements and generalizations from particular descriptively adequate grammars and, wherever possible, to attribute them to the general theory of linguistic structure, thus enriching this theory and imposing more structures on the schema for grammatical description. Whenever this is done, an assertion about a particular language is replaced by a corresponding assertion, from which the first follows, about language in general. If this formulation of a deeper hypothesis is incorrect, this fact should become evident when its effect on the description of other aspects of the language or the description of other languages is ascertained. In short, I am making the obvious comment that, wherever possible, general assumptions about the nature of language should be formulated from which particular features of the grammars of individual languages can be deduced. In this way, linguistic theory may move toward explanatory adequacy and contribute to the study of human mental processes and intellectual capacity—more specifically, to the determination of the abilities that make language learning possible under the empirically given limitations of time and data.

REFERENCES

Aristotle. *De Anima*. Translated by J. A. Smith. In R. McKeon (ed.), *The Basic Works of Aristotle*. New York: Random House, 1941.

Bar-Hillel, Y. (1960). 'The present status of automatic translation of languages.' In F. L. Alt (ed.), *Advances in Computers*, vol. i, pp. 91–163. New York: Academic Press.

——, A. Kasher, and E. Shamir (1963). *Measures of Syntactic Complexity*. Report for U. S. Office of Naval Research, Information Systems Branch. Jerusalem.

Beattie, J. (1788). *Theory of Language*. London.

Chomsky, N. (1952). 'Morphophonemics of Modern Hebrew', Unpublished Master's thesis, University of Pennsylvania.

—— (1955) 'The Logical Structure of Linguistic Theory'. Mimeographed, M. L. T. Library, Cambridge, Mass.

—— (1956). 'Three models for the description of language'. *I. R. E. Transactions on Information Theory*, vol. IT-2, pp. 113-24. Reprinted, with corrections, in

R. D. Luce, R. Bush, and E. Galanter (eds.) *Readings in Mathematical Psychology*, vol. ii. New York: Wiley 1965.

— (1957). *Syntactic Structures*. The Hague: Mouton & Co.

— (1959*a*). 'On certain formal properties of grammars.' *Information and Control*, 2, pp. 137–67. Reprinted in R. D. Luce, R. Bush, and E. Galanter (eds.), *Readings in Mathematical Psychology*, vol. ii. New York. Wiley 1965.

— (1959*b*). Review of Skinner (1957). *Language*, 35, pp. 26–58. Reprinted in Fodor and Katz (1964).

— (1961). 'Some methodological remarks on generative grammar.' *Word*, 17, pp. 219, 239. Reprinted in part in Fodor and Katz (1964).

— (1962*a*). 'A transformational approach to syntax.' In A. A. Hill (ed.), *Proceedings of the 1958 Conference on Problems of Linguistic Analysis in English*, pp. 124–48. Austin, Texas. Reprinted in Fodor and Katz (1964).

— (1962*b*). 'Explanatory models in linguistics.' In E. Nagel, P. Suppes, and A. Tarski, *Logic, Methodology and Philosophy of Science*. Stanford, California: Stanford University Press.

— (1963). 'Formal properties of grammars.' In R. D. Luce, R. Bush, and E. Galanter (eds.), *Handbook of Mathematical Psychology*, vol. ii, pp. 232–418. New York: Wiley.

— (1964). *Current Issues in Linguistic Theory*. The Hague: Mouton & Co. A slightly earlier version appears in Fodor and Katz (1964). This is a revised and expanded version of a paper presented to the session 'The logical basis of linguistic theory', at the Ninth International Congress of Linguistics, Cambridge, Mass., 1962. It appears under the title of the session in H. Lunt (ed.), *Proceedings* of the Congress. The Hague: Mouton & Co., 1964.

— (1966). 'Topics in the theory of generative grammar.' In T. A. Sebcok (ed.), *Current Trends in Linguistics*, vol. iii. *Linguistic Theory*. The Hague: Mouton & Co.

— (forthcoming). 'Cartesian Linguistics.'

—, M. Halle, and F. Lukoff (1956). 'On accent and juncture in English.' In M. Halle, H. Lunt, and H. MacLean (eds.), *For Roman Jakobson*, pp. 65–80. The Hague: Mouton & Co.

—, and G. A. Miller (1963). 'Introduction to the formal analysis of natural languages.' In R. D. Luce, R. Bush, and E. Galanter (eds.), *Handbook of Mathematical Psychology*, vol. ii, pp. 269–322. New York: Wiley.

—, and M. P. Schützenberger (1963). 'The algebraic theory of context-free languages.' In P. Braffort and D. Hirschberg (eds.), *Computer Programming and Formal Systems*, pp. 119–61, Studies in Logic Series. Amsterdam: North-Holland.

Cordemoy, G. de (1667). *A Philosophical Discourse Concerning Speech*. The English translation is dated 1668.

Descartes, R. (1641). *Meditations*.

Diderot, D. (1751). *Lettre sur les Sourds et Muets*. Page references are to J. Assezat (ed.), *Oeuvres Complètes de Diderot*, vol. i (1875). Paris: Carnier Frères.

Dixon, R. W. (1963). *Linguistic Science and Logic*. The Hague: Mouton & Co.

Du Marsais, C. Ch. (1769). *Les Véritables Principes de la grammaire*.

Fodor, J. A. and Katz, J. J., eds. (1964). *The Structure of Language: Readings in the Philosophy of Language*, Prentice-Hall Inc., Englewood Cliffs, N.J.

Foot, P. (1961). 'Goodness and Choice'. *Proceedings of the Aristotelian Society*, Supplementary Volume 35, pp. 45–80.

Frishkopf, L. S., and M. H. Goldstein (1963). 'Responses to acoustic stimuli from single units in the eighth nerve of the bullfrog.' *Journal of the Acoustical Society of America*, 35, pp. 1219-28.

Gleason, H. A. (1961). *Introduction to Descriptive Linguistics*, 2nd ed. New York: Holt, Rinehart & Winston.

Halle, M. (1959a). 'Questions of linguistics.' *Nuovo Cimento*, 13, pp. 494-517.

— (1959b). *The Sound Pattern of Russian*. The Hague: Mouton & Co.

— (1961). 'On the role of the simplicity in linguistic description.' In R. Jakobson (ed.), *Structure of Language and its Mathematical Aspects, Proceedings of the Twelfth Symposium in Applied Mathematics*, pp. 89-94. Providence, R. I.: American Mathematical Society.

— (1962). 'Phonology in generative grammar.' *Word*, 18, pp. 54-72. Reprinted in Fodor and Katz (1964).

— (1964). 'On the bases of phonology.' In Fodor and Katz (1964).

—, and N. Chomsky (1960). 'The morphophonemics of English.' *Quarterly Progress Report*, No. 58, Research Laboratory of Electronics, M. I. T., pp. 275-81.

— (1968). *The Sound Pattern of English*, New York: Harper & Row.

—, and K. Stevens (1962). 'Speech regulation: A model and a program for research.' *I. R. E. Transactions in Information Theory*, vol. IT-8, pp. 155-9. Reprinted in Fodor and Katz (1964).

Harman, G. H. (1963). 'Generative grammars without transformational rules: a defense of phrase structure.' *Language*, 39, pp. 597-616.

Held, and A. Hein (1963). 'Movement-produced stimulation in the development of visually guided behaviour.' *Journal of Comparative and Physiological Psychology*, 56, pp. 872-6.

Hockett, C. F. (1958). *A Course in Modern Linguistics*. New York: Macmillan.

Hubel, D. H. and T. N. Wisesel (1962). 'Receptive fields, binocular interaction and functional architecture in the cat's visual cortex.' *Journal of Physiology*, 160, pp. 106-54.

Katz, J. J. (1964a). 'Mentalism in linguistics.' *Language*, 40, pp. 124-37.

— (1964b). 'Semantic theory and the meaning of "good".' *Journal of Philosophy*.

—, and J. A. Fodor. 'The structure of a semantic theory.' *Language*, 39, pp. 170-210. Reprinted in Fodor and Katz (1964).

—, and J. A. Fodor (1964). 'A reply to Dixon's "A trend in semantics".' *Linguistics*, 3, pp. 19-29.

Lancelot, C. A., Arnauld, *et al.* (1660). *Grammaire générale et raisonée*.

Lees, R. B. (1957). Review of Chomsky (1957). *Language*, 33, pp. 375-407.

Leibniz, G. W. *New Essays Concerning Human Understanding*. Translated by A. G. Langley, La Salle Ill.: Open Court, 1949.

Lemmon, W. B., and G. H. Patterson (1964). 'Depth perception in sheep.' *Science*, 145, p. 835.

Lenneberg, E. (1960). 'Language, evolution, and purposive behavior.' In S. Diamond (ed.), *Culture in History: Essays in Honor of Paul Radin*. New York: Columbia University Press. Reprinted in a revised and extended version under the title 'The capacity for language acquisition' in Fodor and Katz (1964).

— (1967). *The Biological Bases of Language*. New York: John Wiley & Sons, Inc.

Lettvin, J. Y., H. R. Maturana, W. S. McCulloch, and W. H. Pitts (1959). 'What the frog's eye tells the frog's brain.' *Proceedings of the I. R. E.*, 47, pp. 1940-51.

Matthews, G. H. (1964). *Hidatsa Syntax*. The Hague: Mouton & Co.

Miller, G. A., and N. Chomsky (1963). 'Finitary models of language users.' In R. D. Luce, R. Bush, and E. Galanter (eds.), *Handbook of Mathematical Psychology*, vol. ii, Ch. 13, pp. 419–92. New York: Wiley.

——, and S. Isard (1964). 'Some perceptual consequences of linguistic rules.' *Journal of Verbal Learning and Verbal Behavior*, 2, No. 3, pp. 217–28.

——, and D. A. Norman (1964). *Research on the Use of Formal Language in the Behavioural Sciences*. Semi-annual Technical Report, Department of Defense, Advanced Research Projects Agency, January–June, 1964, pp. 10–11. Cambridge: Harvard University Center for Cognitive Studies.

Ornan, U. (1964). *'National compounds in modern literary Hebrew.'* Unpublished doctoral dissertation, Jerusalem, Hebrew University.

Postal, P. M. (1962). 'On the limitations of context-free phrase structure description.' *Quarterly Progress Report* No. 64, Research Laboratory of Electronics, M. I. T., pp. 231–8.

—— (1964*a*). *Constituent Structure: A Study of Contemporary Models of Syntactic Description*. The Hague: Mouton & Co.

—— (1964*b*). 'Underlying and superficial linguistic structure.' *Harvard Educational Review*, 34, pp. 246–66.

—— (1964*c*). 'Limitations of phrase structure grammars.' In Fodor and Katz (1964).

Quine, W. V. (1960). *Word and Object*. Cambridge, Mass.: M. I. T. Press, and New York: Wiley.

Reid, T. (1785). *Essays on the Intellectual Powers of Man*. Page references are to the abridged edition by A. D. Woozley, 1941. London: Macmillan and Co.

Russell, B. (1940). *An Inquiry into Meaning and Truth*. London: Allen & Unwin.

Ryle, G. (1931). 'Systematically misleading expressions.' *Proceedings of the Aristotelian Society*. Reprinted in A. G. N. Flew (ed.), *Logic and Language*, first series. Oxford: Blackwell, 1951.

—— (1953). 'Ordinary Language.' *Philosophical Review*, 62, pp. 167–86.

Sahlin, G. (1928). *César Chesneau de Marsais et son rôle dans l'évolution de la grammaire générale*, Paris: Presses Universitaires.

Skinner, B. F. (1957). *Verbal Behavior*. New York: Appleton-Century-Crofts.

Sutherland, N. S. (1959). 'Stimulus analyzing mechanisms.' *Mechanization of Thought Processes*, vol. ii. National Physical Laboratory Symposium, No. 10, London.

—— (1964). 'Visual discrimination in animals.' *British Medical Bulletin*, 20, pp. 54–9.

Twaddell, W. F. (1935). *On Defining the Phoneme*. Language Monograph No. 16. Reprinted in part in M. Joos (ed.), *Readings in Linguistics*. Washington: 1957.

Uhlenbeck, E. M. (1963). 'An appraisal of transformation theory.' *Lingua*, 12, pp. 1–18.

—— (1964). Discussion in the session 'Logical basis of linguistic theory.' In H. Lunt (ed.), *Proceedings of the Ninth Congress of Linguistics*, pp. 981–3. The Hague: Mouton & Co.

Wittgenstein, L. (1953). *Philosophical Investigations*. Oxford: Blackwell.

Ynvge, V. (1960). 'A model and a hypothesis for language structure.' *Proceedings of the American Philosophical Society*, 104, pp. 444–66.

6

GRAMMAR, PSYCHOLOGY AND INDETERMINACY

S. STICH

> Significance is the trait with respect to which the subject matter of linguistics is studied by the grammarian.
> Pending a satisfactory explanation of the notion of meaning, linguists in semantic fields are in the position of not knowing what they are talking about. W. V. Quine

ACCORDING to Quine, the linguist qua grammarian does not know what he is talking about. The goal of this essay is to tell him. My aim is to provide an account of what the grammarian is saying of an expression when he says it is grammatical, or a noun phrase, or ambiguous, or the subject of a certain sentence. More generally, I want to give an account of the nature of a generative grammatical theory of a language —of the data for such a theory, the relation between the theory and the data, and the relation between the theory and a speaker of the language.

1

Prominent among a linguist's pronouncements are attributions of grammaticality. What are we saying about a sentence when we say it is grammatical? One strategy for answering this question is to attend to the work of the grammarian. To be grammatical, a sentence must have those characteristics which the grammarian seeks in deciding whether a sentence is grammatical. So a reconstruction of the grammarian's work is a likely path to an explication of 'grammatical'. This is the strategy adopted by Quine,[1] and it will be of value to study his remarks in some detail. On Quine's account, *significance* rather than *grammati-*

From *Journal of Philosophy*, vol. 79, No. 22 (7 Dec. 1972), pp. 799–818. Reprinted by permission of the author and The Journal of Philosophy.

[1] *From a Logical Point of View*, 2nd edn., revised (Harper & Row, New York, 1963), essay III. [Reprinted as Essay 3 in the present volume; references are to the present volume.]

cality 'is the trait with respect to which the subject matter of linguistics is studied by the grammarian' (49). If the two are different, there is some inclination to take the grammarian at his name. So let us see what can be learned by taking Quine's proposal as an explication of *grammaticality*.

The problem for the grammarian may be posed as the segregating of a class K of sequences that we will call *grammatical*. On Quine's view, he attends to four nested classes of sequences, H, I, J, and K.

H is the class of observed sequences, excluding any which are ruled inappropriate in the sense of being non-linguistic or belonging to alien dialects. I is the class of all such observed sequences and all that ever will happen to be professionally observed, excluding again those which are ruled inappropriate. J is the class of all sequences ever occurring, now or in the past or future, within or without professional observation —excluding, again, only those which are ruled inappropriate. K, finally, is the infinite class of all those sequences, with the exclusion of the inappropriate ones as usual, which *could* be uttered without bizarreness reactions. K is the class which the grammarian wants to approximate in his formal reconstruction (53).

The linguist's data are H, and he checks his predictions against I minus H hoping that this will be a representative sample of J. It is when we come to K that philosophical eyebrows are raised; for what is the force of the 'could' which extends the class beyond J, commonly infinitely beyond? Quine's answer is that, besides H and future checks against I, the 'could' is the reflection of the scientist's appeal to simplicity. 'Our basis for saying what "could" be generally consists . . . in what *is* plus simplicity of the laws whereby we describe and extrapolate what is' (54).

Quine's proposal shares with other operational definitions the virtue of objectivity. Yet his solution is beset with problems. For Quine's procedure just does not pick out anything like the class we would pre-systematically hold to be grammatical—and this because his account fails to portray what the grammarian *actually does*. To see this, consider the case of a Quinean linguist ignorant of English setting out to segregate grammatical English sequences. He starts with H, the class of sequences he observes. But H, in addition to samples of what we would pre-systematically hold to be grammatical sequences, contains all manner of false starts, 'lost thoughts', peculiar pauses ('aahhhh!') and, unless he is uncommonly fortunate, a liberal sprinkling of blatantly incoherent speech. Yet Quine, if we take him literally, would have H included as a subset of K. What the resulting projection might be is hard to imagine. But K, so constructed, would not be the class of grammatical sequences in English.

It might be thought that, appealing to simplicity, the linguist could toss out an occasional member of *H*, much as he excludes from *H* what he takes to be nonlinguistic noise or intrusion from another tongue. But an hour spent attending carefully to unreflective speech will dispel this notion. There is simply too much to exclude.[2]

Quine succeeds in muddying the waters a bit by sprinkling the restriction that the sentences to be studied are those which could be uttered 'without bizarreness reactions'. It is not clear whether he takes such sentences to be excluded from *H* and *I* by virtue of their being observed *in situ* or whether he would have *H* and *I* further filtered. But it seems clear that, in either case, either this move is inadequate or it begs the question. If by 'bizarreness' Quine means *bizarreness*, then the exclusion will hardly accomplish his purpose. For many sorts of sequences that we would want to exclude from *K* (those with 'aahhhh's' interspersed, for example, or those which change subject mid-sentence) are uttered all the time without bizarreness reactions. And many sentences we would want to include in *K* would surely evoke the strongest of bizarreness reactions. Indeed, though *K* will be infinite, only members of a finite subset could be uttered without evoking a bizarreness reaction. Sentences that take more than six months to utter are bizarre. If, however, the reaction Quine has in mind is the reaction (whatever it may be) characteristically displayed when an ungrammatical sequence is uttered, then, until he has provided some account of how this reaction is to be recognized, he has begged the question.[3]

2

Taking Quine's proposal as an explication of grammaticality has led to an impasse. In seeking our way around it we might do well to return to Quine's original insight and attend more closely to what the grammarian actually does. From the first, the generative grammarian has relied heavily on the fact that, with a modicum of instruction, speakers can be brought to make all manner of judgements about their language. In particular, they can be brought to make firm judgements on the oddness or acceptability of indefinitely many sequences. Provided with a few examples, speakers can go on to judge new sequences in point of

---

[2] Much the same point is made by Jerrold Katz and Jerry Fodor in 'What's Wrong with the Philosophy of Language?,' *Inquiry*, 5 (1962) 197–237.

[3] Significance is likely a more inclusive notion than grammaticality, more liberal in the constructions it will allow and tolerating a richer sprinkling of 'aahhh's', 'I mean's', and 'you knows's'. Thus perhaps Quine's proposal does rather better when taken as advertised. But whatever its interest, significance as characterized by Quine is not the property studied by grammarians of a generative bent.

grammaticality, and do so with considerable consistency for large numbers of cases. This suggests that we might try to remedy the difficulties with Quine's proposal by substituting *intuitive judgements* for observed utterances. On the revised account, H would be the class of those sequences which to date have been considered and judged to be grammatical. I would be the class of sequences ever reflected upon and judged clearly grammatical. And K is the infinite class projected along simplest lines from H and checked against I.

This modified account nicely circumvents the major shortcoming we found in Quine's proposal. Read literally, Quine's method did not pick out the class of sequences we would pre-systematically call grammatical. The class H on which his projection was based was already tainted with ungrammatical sequences. Our modified version avoids this difficulty by basing its projection on sequences intuitively taken to be grammatical. The projected class K can still miss the mark, failing to be compatible with I minus H. But this potential failure is the normal inductive one.[4]

We can now make a plausible first pass at depicting the grammarian's work. He proceeds by eliciting intuitive judgements about which sequences are in the informant's language and which are not. He then projects these clear cases along simplest lines, checking his projected class against speakers' intuitions. Thus the task of the generative grammarian may be viewed as that of constructing a system of rules and a definition of 'generate' that define a terminal language containing phonetic representations for all the sequences judged by speakers to be clearly acceptable and containing no sequence judged to be clearly unacceptable. The sequences about which speakers have no firm or consistent intuitions can be relegated to the class of 'don't cares' and decided by the simplest grammar that handles the clear cases.

Yet as it stands the account still will not do. One fault is its myopic concentration on intuitions. Speakers' judgements about acceptability are the most important data for the grammarian. But they are not his only data, nor are they immune from being corrected or ignored. The attentive grammarian will attend to many aspects of his subjects' behaviour in addition to their response to questions about sentences' acceptability. And a proper explication of the grammarian's job must provide some account of the role these additional data play.

Perhaps the most important sort of evidence for the grammarian besides intuitions of acceptability is the actual unreflective speech of

---

[4] Note that Quine's 'bizarreness reactions' could be taken as negative judgements when the subject is queried about a sequence's acceptability. If this is Quine's intention, his proposal and the present account converge.

his subjects. An informant's protest that a given sequence is unacceptable may be ignored if he is caught in the act, regularly uttering unpremeditatedly what, on meditation, he alleges he doesn't say. In addition to actual speech, there is a host of further clues for the grammarian. Stress patterns, facts about how sentences are heard and data on short-term verbal recall are among them.[5] Others might be mentioned. To what use does the grammarian put this further evidence? Principally, I suggest, to shore up the evidence provided by the speakers' intuitive judgements or to justify his neglect of them. A sentence whose acceptability to speakers is in some doubt will, with good conscience, be generated by a grammar if it ranks high in the other tests. And, on the other side, a sentence that has the blessings of speakers may be rejected—not generated by the grammar—if it fails to display the other characteristics of grammatical sequences.

We now have one justification the grammarian may use for rejecting speakers' intuitions. There is another. And consideration of it will lead to a fundamental revision of our account of grammaticality. Intuitive oddness may be explained by many factors. Some sentences seem odd because they are pragmatically odd, describing a situation that is bizarre. Others, perhaps, may be rejected as obscene or taboo. Most importantly, sentences may seem odd because they are simply too long and complicated. If the grammarian suspects that any of these factors explain speakers' rejection of a sentence, he may classify it as grammatical *even though it lacks all the characteristics in the cluster associated with grammaticality*.

Note that at this juncture two notions we have been conflating part company. Thus far I have been interchanging 'acceptability' and 'grammaticality' with studied equivocation. Intuitions of acceptability and the cluster of further characteristics usually accompanying sentences judged acceptable have been taken as (more or less) necessary and sufficient conditions for grammaticality. But the picture changes when a sentence may be classed as grammatical in spite of failing each relevant test. The motivation for separating acceptability and grammaticality is *broad theoretic simplicity*. It is simpler to generate an infinite class including the acceptable sentences than it is to draw a boundary around just those sentences which rank high in the several tests for acceptability. But in thus choosing the simpler task we must assume that some further theory or theories will account for those grammatical sentences which are unacceptable. And we must also assume that the new theory

<hr>

[5] Cf. George A. Miller and Stephen Isard, 'Some Perceptual Consequences of Linguistic Rules', *Journal of Verbal Learning and Verbal Behavior*, 2 (1963), 217-28.

combined with a grammatical theory will together be simpler than any theory attempting directly to generate all and only the acceptable sequences. In short, we are venturing that the best theory to account for *all* the data will include a grammar of infinite generative capacity. This is hardly a step to be taken lightly. For in allowing his grammar to generate an infinite number of sentences, the grammarian is countenancing as grammatical an infinite number of sentences that fail each test of acceptability. It might be thought that such prodigality could be avoided by simply cutting off the class of sentences generated by a grammar at an appropriately high point. But this is not the case. For there is no natural point to draw the line—no point at which the addition of another conjunct or another clause regularly changes a clearly acceptable sentence into a clearly unacceptable one. Nor would it do to pick an *arbitrary* high cut-off point. This would leave the grammarian as before with generated sentences that are unacceptable. And any account of *why* these sentences were unacceptable would likely also account for the sequences beyond the arbitrary cut-off point.

By now it is evident that grammaticality is best viewed as a *theoretical* notion. Like other theoretical notions, it is related to relevant data in several and complex ways. Simple grammatical sentences generally have several or all of the cluster of characteristics typical of acceptable sequences. More complex grammatical sentences may share none of these characteristics. They are grammatical in virtue of being generated by the grammar that most simply generates all the clearly acceptable sentences and holds the best promise of fitting into a simple total theory of acceptability.

There is, thus, a conjecture built into a proposed grammar—the conjecture that this generative system will fit comfortably into a total theory that accounts for all the data. In this respect a grammar is similar to the theory of ideal gases. The ideal-gas laws do a good job at predicting the behaviour of light gases at high temperatures and low pressures. In less favourable cases, the laws predict poorly. They were acceptable in the hope, later fulfilled, that further laws could be found to explain the difference between the behaviour of real gases and the predicted behaviour of ideal ones. The adoption of a given grammar or form of grammar might be viewed as setting up a 'paradigm'[6] or framework for future investigation. The grammar serves to divide those phenomena still needing explanation (viz. unacceptable grammatical sequences) from those already adequately handled.

---

[6] In a sense that may be intended by T. S. Kuhn, *The Structure of Scientific Revolutions* (University Press, Chicago, 1962).

In our portrait of the grammarian's job, the emphasis has shifted from the concept of grammaticality to the notion of a correct grammar. A sequence is grammatical if and only if it is generated by a correct grammar for the language in question. And a grammar is correct only if it excels in the virtues lately adumbrated. But there are higher virtues to which a grammar may aspire, and more data to be reckoned with. So far we have taken into account data about speakers' intuitions of acceptability and data about a cluster of further characteristics common among acceptable sequences. But we have hardly exhausted the speaker's intuitions about matters linguistic. There is a host of other properties of sentences and their parts about which speakers have firm intuitions. With a bit of training speakers can judge pairs of sentences to be related as active and passive, or as affirmative and negative. They can pick out parts of speech, detect subjects and objects, and spot syntactic ambiguities. The list of these grammatical intuitions could easily be extended. A grammatical theory will not only try to specify which sequences are acceptable; it will also try to specify the grammatical properties and relations of sentences as intuited by speakers. As in the case of intuitions of acceptability, the grammatical theory will be expected to agree with grammatical intuitions only for relatively short and simple sentences. The theory is an idealization, and, as before, we permit it to deviate from the intuited data in the expectation that further theory will account for the differences.

3

It might seem our job is finished. We set ourselves to giving an account of the grammarian's doings in building a grammar, and this we have done. But the reader conversant with competing accounts[7] will expect more. For, commonly, such accounts go on to talk of *linguistic theory, acquisition models, evaluation measures* and other notions related to the question of how a speaker acquires his grammar. Moreover the discussion of these notions is not a simple addition to the account of the grammarian's work in constructing a grammar. Rather it is an intrinsic part of that account. Yet why this is so is far from obvious. Constructing a theory of grammar acquisition is surely a fascinating project and one which would naturally catch a grammarian's eye. But, at first blush at least, it would seem to be a new project, largely distinct

---

[7] For example, those in Noam Chomsky, 'Current Issues in Linguistic Theory', in Fodor and Katz, eds., *The Structure of Language* (Prentice-Hall, Englewood Cliffs, N.J. 1964); in Chomsky, *Aspects of the Theory of Syntax* (MIT Press, Cambridge, Mass., 1965), ch. I; and Katz, *The Philosophy of Language* (Harper & Row, New York, 1966).

from the job of constructing grammars for individual languages. Why, then, do Chomsky and others view the study of acquisition as intrinsic to the construction of grammars for individual languages? This is the riddle that will occupy us in the present section. In the course of untangling it we will come upon some unexpected facts about grammar and its place among the sciences.

Let me begin with a puzzle. A grammar of English will generate structural descriptions for English sentences in the form of phrase markers or labelled bracketings. The labels on these brackets will be the familiar NP, VP, etc. But now imagine a perverse variant of our grammar created by systematically interchanging the symbols NP and VP throughout the theory. If the change is thoroughgoing (made in all appropriate generative rules and definitions), then presumably the original theory and the variant will make exactly the same predictions about intuitions, etc. So the two would appear to be empirically indistinguishable. On what basis, then, are we to select one over the other?

To underscore the puzzle, consider a grammarian attending to the hitherto neglected tongue of some appropriately exploited and unlettered people. His grammar will likely end up generating labelled bracketings among whose labels are the familiar NP and VP. But what justification can there be for this grammar as contrasted with a variant interchanging NP and VP throughout, or yet another variant in which NP and VP are systematically replaced with a pair of symbols that occur nowhere in any grammar of English?[8]

There is a related puzzle that focuses not on the vocabulary of a grammar but on its rules. Consider any grammar or fragment of a grammar for English. With the grammar at hand it requires only modest ingenuity to produce a variant set of rules and definitions whose consequences (the entailed chains about grammaticality, grammatical relations and the rest) are identical with those of the original. Among the variants that might be produced some will differ only trivially, adding a superfluous rule perhaps, or capturing a generalization in two rules rather than one. But other variants exist which differ quite radically from the original.[9] A grammar is but an axiomatized theory, and it is a truism that a theory that can be axiomatized at all can be axiomatized in radically different ways. Yet each of these variants makes identical

---

[8] Much the same puzzle is hinted at by Quine in 'Methodological Reflections on Current Linguistic Theory', *Synthèse*, 21, 3/4 (Oct. 1970), 386–398, pp. 390 ff.

[9] Such variants often require considerable effort to construct. Nor is it always a trivial matter to prove their equivalence of a pair of grammars.

claims about the grammarian's data—not only the data on hand, but *all* the data he might acquire. They may, of course, predict incorrectly on a given point; but if one variant predicts incorrectly they all will. How then is the grammarian to decide among them?

The point of these puzzles is that grammar is afflicted with an embarrassment of riches. It is a task demanding wit and perseverance to construct a grammar that correctly captures a broad range of speakers' intuitions. Yet when the job has been done there are indefinitely many variants each of which captures the known intuitions equally well and predicts unprobed intuitions equally well (or poorly). Somehow the grammarian does come up with a single theory. What principle can he use to guide his choice?

It is in attempting to answer this question that the study of acquisition looms large in Chomsky's writings. But exactly how a theory of grammar acquisition is supposed to motivate a choice among alternative grammars is far from clear. Part of the obscurity, I suspect, stems from the fact that Chomsky, perhaps without realizing it, pursues two rather different strategies in relating the study of acquisition to the problem of choosing among alternative grammars. One of these strategies, I will contend, is thoroughly misguided and rests on a mistaken picture of what grammar is. The other is quite compatible with the account of grammar developed above and suggests an illuminating solution to the puzzles of alternative grammars. Our first project will be to dissect out these alternatives for closer inspection.

Before we begin, some terminology will be helpful. Let us call a grammar *descriptively adequate* for a given language if it correctly captures the intuitions of the speakers of the language (and the rest of the grammarian's data) within the limits of accuracy allowed by idealization. The grammarian's embarrassment of riches arises from the fact that for each descriptively adequate grammar of a language there are indefinitely many alternatives all of which are also descriptively adequate.

Now the strategy I would disparage unfolds like this:[10] When a child learns a language, he learns a descriptively adequate grammar (*dag*). He somehow 'internally represents' the rules of the grammar. So if we could discover which set of rules the child has 'internalized' we would be able to choose a right one from among the *dags* of the child's language. The right one is simply that grammar which the child has in

<hr/>

[10] I think this strategy is often suggested by what Chomsky says (e.g. in *Aspects of the Theory of Syntax*, pp. 24–7 and elsewhere). But my concern here is to scotch the view, not to fix the blame. So I will not bother to document details of its parentage.

fact internally represented. The study of acquisition will be designed to give us a lead on which descriptively adequate grammar the child has learned.

Let us reflect on what the child must do to acquire his grammar. The learner is exposed to what Chomsky calls *primary linguistic data (pld)* which 'include examples of linguistic performance that are taken to be well formed sentences, and may include also examples designated as non-sentences, and no doubt much other information of the sort that is required for language learning, whatever this may be' (ibid., p. 25). When he has succeeded in learning his language the child will have internalized a *dag*. In two rather different ways this grammar will specify more information about the language than is to be gleaned from the *pld*. First, the *pld* contain a modest sample of the grammatical sentences of the language; the grammar acquired generates all the grammatical sentences. Second, the *pld* contain little or no information about the structural descriptions of sentences and the grammatical relations among them; the grammar assigns structural descriptions to each grammatical sentence and entails all the appropriate facts about grammatical relations. Thus a theory of grammar acquisition must explain how the child can acquire and internalize a grammar that is significantly more informative about the sentences of the language than the *pld* he has been exposed to.

How might we build a theory that accounts for the child's accomplishment? What we seek is a model (or function) which, when given a complete account of the *pld* available to the child as input (or argument), will produce, as output (or value), the *dag* that the child acquires. Our problem is to design the model with sufficient structure so that it can correctly project from the limited *pld* to the full grammar of the language from which the data are drawn. What sort of information should the model contain?

Suppose it were discovered that certain features were shared by all *dags*. If the grammars that shared the features were sufficiently numerous and diverse we might reasonably hypothesize that these features were universal among *dags* of natural language. We would, in effect, be hypothesizing that there is a restricted set of grammars that humans can in fact learn (in the normal way). Were such universal features to be found, our strategy suggests that we take account of them in our acquisition model. Since the output of the model must be a *dag*, we would want to build our model in such a way that the possible outputs (the range of the acquisition function) each had the features that were universal to all *dags*. We would thus take the specification of universal features to define the class of *humanly possible grammars (hpgs)*. The task of the acquisition model is to discover the correct grammar, the grammar of the language the child is actually exposed to, from among the humanly possible grammars.

There is great gain for the builder of an acquisition theory in discovering as rich a set of universal features as possible. For the stronger the restrictions on the *hpgs*, the smaller the class of such grammars will be. Thus the easier the task relegated to the other parts of the model. What remains for the rest of the model is to compare the *pld* with the class of *hpgs* and exclude those possible grammars which are incompatible with the data.

Now it might happen that the universal features we discover so narrow down the class of *hpgs* that only one *hpg* is compatible with the *pld*.[11] If this is commonly the case, our acquisition theory need contain only a specification of *hpgs* and a device for excluding those *hpgs* which are incompatible with the *pld*. If, however, there are several *hpgs* compatible with all the data the child as accumulated by the time acquisition is essentially complete, we will have to seek some further principle of selection. The principle, the strategy suggests, is to be found in an evaluation measure or weighting of *hpgs*. Some of the *hpgs* that are compatible with all the *pld* will still fail to be descriptively adequate for the child's language. Some of these may simply project incorrectly beyond the sample of the language available to the child. They will then classify as grammatical sequences that are not grammatical. Others, while projecting correctly, may miss the mark on structural descriptions or grammatical relations, specifying that sentences are related in ways other than the ways speakers in fact intuit them to be related. So what we seek in our evaluation measure is some ranking of *hpgs* that has the following property: when we exclude from the *hpgs* those grammars which are incompatible with the *pld*, the highest ranked of the *remaining* grammars is a descriptively adequate grammar of the language the child acquires. The acquisition model would then proceed by first eliminating those *hpgs* which are not compatible with the *pld*, then selecting from among those which remain the one that is highest ranked. The grammar selected is unique among *dags*, for it is chosen by a model that explains how a child might go about acquiring the grammar he does acquire. It is this 'explanatorily adequate' grammar which the child actually internalizes and which the linguist seeks to uncover.

A more detailed account of the strategy we are sketching might now go on to worry about how the appropriate evaluation measure could

---

[11] Chomsky suggests this possibility, ibid., pp. 36–7.

be discovered or what we can say about linguistic universals in the light of present knowledge. But this will not be our course. For I think we have said enough to see that the strategy is wholly wrongheaded. To begin, let us consider the possibility, mentioned briefly a paragraph back, that the universals so constrict the class of *hpgs* that only one *hpg* will be compatible with the *pld*. A moment's reflection will reveal that this is not a real possibility at all. For recall the pair of puzzles that initially prodded our interest in acquisition models. Each puzzle pointed to the superabundance of descriptively adequate grammars for any natural language. For every *dag* there are alternatives which are also descriptively adequate. But the linguistic universals were taken to be properties of all *dags*.[12] Thus each *dag* for every natural language will be among the *hpgs*. So if any *dag* is compatible with the *pld*, all its alternatives will be as well. And we have made no progress at selecting a single *dag* as the right one.

What is more, the hunt for an evaluation measure is of no real value in narrowing down the class of *dags*. The job that was set for the evaluation measure was not a trivial one. Given any body of *pld*, the evaluation measure had to rank as highest among the *hpgs* which are compatible with the *pld* a *dag* of the language from which the data are drawn. Finding such a measure would likely be a task of considerable difficulty. But, and this is the crucial point, once a measure *has* been found there will be indefinitely many alternative measures which select different *dags* for the same body of *pld*. If the sub-class of *hpgs* compatible with a given body of *pld* contains *one dag* of the language of which the data are a sample, it will contain many. Thus if we can design a measure which ranks any one of these *dags* highest in the sub-class, there will be another measure which ranks a different *dag* highest.[13] But whatever justification there is for holding the *dag* selection by one measure to be the grammar actually internalized is equally justification for holding that the other is. And we are back

---

[12] It is essential that the linguistic universals be taken as the properties common to each descriptively adequate grammar of every natural language. An alternative notion that took the linguistic universals as the features common to each of the actually internalized grammars of every natural language would be useless in the present context, since our project is to discover which among the *dags* of a given language is internalized. And until we *know* which grammars are internalized we cannot discover which features are universal to such grammars.

[13] As is the case with alternative *dags*, some alternative measure functions will be trivially cooked up variants of the original (e.g. simply select an arbitrary *dag* of the language from which the *pld* is drawn and place it highest under the evaluation measure, leaving the rest of the measure unchanged). Others will exist which differ from the original in more substantial ways.

where we started, with too many *dags* each with equal claim to be the 'right one'.

The second strategy for solving the problem, the strategy I would endorse, sets out in quite a different direction from the first. It does not propose to select among *dags* by finding the one actually internalized. Indeed it is compatible with (but does not entail) the view that *no* grammar is, in any illuminating sense, internally represented in the speaker's mind or brain, and that there is no good sense to be made of the notion of 'internal representation'. The second strategy approaches the multiplicity of *dag* as a practical problem for the working linguist. At numerous junctures a linguist may find himself with data to account for and a variety of ways of doing so. Among the alternatives, more than one will handle all the data available and will coincide with their predictions about facts as yet unrecorded. How is the linguist to choose? What the linguist seeks, according to this strategy, is not the grammar actually in the head (whatever that may mean) but some motivated way to select among *dags*.

The motivation is to be found through the study of acquisition models, though the goals of an acquisition model must be reinterpreted. If we suspend interest in which grammar is 'internally represented' we need no longer demand of an acquisition model that, for a given body of *pld*, it produce as output a grammar that a learner exposed to the data would internalize. Instead, we ask only that the acquisition model have as output *some* grammar that is true of the accomplished speaker (i.e. some grammar that correctly describes the sentences acceptable to him, his intuitions about grammatical relations, etc). But let it not be thought that this is a trivial task. Such a model would be able to specify a grammar true of the speaker given only the (relatively scant) primary linguistic data to which the speaker was exposed. To do this would be a monumentally impressive feat realizable, for the foreseeable future, only in linguistic science fiction.

How can such a model be built? In attending to the more demanding model of the first strategy, our first move was to linguistic universals, the properties shared by all *dags*. The analogous role in the present strategy can be played by properties less difficult to discover. For suppose we have a single descriptively adequate grammar of a particular natural language. Might it not be reasonable to take as many properties of that grammar as possible as 'quasi-universals'? 'Quasi-universal' properties play just the role that universals did in the first strategy— they constrain the output of the acquisition model. The quasi-universals, then, define a class of 'quasi-humanly possible grammars' which are the only possible outputs of the acquisition model. The terminology is adopted to stress the parallel with the first strategy. But there are important differences. For quasi-universals are in no sense universals —there is no claim that all *dags* must share them. Nor does the class of quasi-humanly possible grammars pretend to exhaust the class of grammars that humans can learn;[14] it simply coincides with the possible outputs of the acquisition model.

As was the case at the analogous point in the first strategy, there is profit in taking the quasi-universals to be as strong as we can. For the stronger the quasi-universals, the smaller the class of quasi-*hpgs* and thus the easier the task that remains for the rest of the model. Indeed, it would not be unreasonable as a first guess to take *all* the properties of the single *dag* as quasi-universals.[15] But this clearly will not do. For then the output class of the acquisition model would have but a single member. Rather, our principle in deciding whether to take features of our single *dag* as quasi-universal is this: take as quasi-universal as many features of the *dag* as possible, provided only that the resultant class of quasi-*hpgs* contains at least one quasi-*hpg* for each natural language. The remainder of the model will contain (at least) a component testing the compatibility of quasi-*hpgs* with the accumulated *pld*. Note that, on this second strategy, it is indeed possible that the quasi-universals so narrow down the class of quasi-*hpgs* that only one *hpg* will be compatible with any given body of *pld*. If this is the case, then a specification of the quasi-universals and a compatibility-testing device of the sort lately considered would complete an acquisition model. But if we cannot discover quasi-universals of this strength, we will again resort to an evaluation measure. As with the first strategy, what we seek is a ranking of quasi-*hpgs* which, when we exclude from the quasi-*hpgs* those grammars incompatible with a given body of *pld*, ranks highest among the remaining quasi-*hpgs* a grammar that is descriptively adequate for the language from which the *pld* was drawn. Since we are making no claim that the selected grammar is 'actually internalized' we need not be concerned that there may be several such

---

[14] Indeed, if we abandon the notion of internal representation, it is no longer clear that it makes sense to speak of a child 'learning' a grammar. When the child succeeds in mastering his mother tongue, each *dag* of that tongue is true of him. But he surely has not learned *all* these *dags*. What, then, is the 'cash value' of the claim that he has learned any one of them?

[15] During the John Locke Lectures at Oxford in 1969, Chomsky suggested that were a Martian linguist to come to earth in the midst of an English-speaking community, his most reasonable first hypothesis would be that the ability to speak English is entirely innate. I suspect that Chomsky's remark and the present observation are directed at basically the same point.

evaluation measures. Our project is the highly nontrivial project of producing a model that takes *pld* as input and yields an appropriate *dag* as
output. *Any* evaluation measure that does the trick will be suitable.

The outline we have given of the construction of an acquisition
model is, in a crucial respect, misleading. For it suggests that the model
builder is bound irrevocably by the first *dag* he constructs. He takes as
quasi-universal as many properties of this grammar as he can get away
with, weakening the quasi-universals only when he comes upon some
language no *dag* of which could be included among the quasi-*hpgs* if
the stronger quasi-universals are retained. Actually, of course, matters
are much more flexible. There is room for substantial feedback in both
directions as work proceeds on the model and on individual grammars.
The overriding concern is to make both the individual grammars and
the acquisition model as simple and as powerful as possible. If at a given
juncture it is found that adhering to the working hypothesis about the
acquisition model will substantially complicate construction of grammars for one or more languages, he will try to alter the model, even
if this may require altering or abandoning the original grammar from
which the earliest hypothesis about quasi-universals was drawn. And,
on the other side, if in constructing a particular *dag* a certain choice of
how to proceed would accord well with the working hypothesis about
the acquisition model, then he will be inclined to make that choice even
if the resulting grammar is somewhat less elegant than another which
would result from an alternative choice. There is no circularity here, or
at least, to crib a phrase, the circularity is virtuous. Through this
process of mutual adjustment progress on the acquisition model and on
particular grammars can take place simultaneously.

Notice, now, that the strategy we have been detailing will solve the
puzzles with which we began. An acquisition model provides motivation for selecting one *dag* over another, though both do equally well
at predicting intuitions and such. The grammar to be chosen is that
which accords with the quasi-universals. And, if several do, the grammar
chosen is the one the evaluation measure ranks highest. Thus the grammar chosen will be preferred to its descriptively adequate competitors
because it is more closely parallel to successful grammars for other
languages and integrates more successfully into a model of grammar
acquisition.

The account we have given of the second strategy has the further
virtue of according well with actual linguistic practice. It is simply not
the case that, when speculating about 'linguistic universals', Chomsky
and his followers set out to survey a broad range of languages and
collect those features common to all the grammars. Rather, speculation

is based on the study of a single language, or at best a few closely related languages. A feature of a grammar will be tentatively taken as 'universal' if it is sufficiently abstract (or nonidiosyncratic) to make it plausible that the feature could be readily incorporated into a grammar of every natural language. If 'universals' are taken to be features common to all *dags*, this speculation about universals would be quite mad. But in the light of the second strategy the speculation appears as a thoroughly reasonable way to proceed.

An element of indeterminacy still lurks in our second strategy. And if I am right in identifying this strategy with the generative grammarian's practice, then the indeterminacy infuses his theory as well. In constructing an acquisition model, the first few plausible (approximations of) descriptively adequate grammars have a profound influence. For it is the abstract features of these grammars which are taken as quasi-universals. Yet the selection of these first *dags* over indefinitely many alternatives is completely unmotivated by any linguistic evidence. Which *dag* is first constructed is largely a matter of historical accident. But the accident casts its shadow over all future work. The acquisition model serves to direct future research into the channel forged by these first grammars, even though there are indefinitely many other possible channels available. Nor does the flexibility we stressed three paragraphs back eliminate the indeterminacy. There we noted that, if an original choice of quasi-universals led to overwhelming difficulties in constructing a grammar for some previously neglected language, the universals might be patched and the early grammars that suggested them might be abandoned. But the new choice of quasi-universals has no more claim to uniqueness than the old. For they too will be abstracted from *dags* that were selected over competitors largely by virtue of historical accident.

To the appropriately conditioned reader this indeterminacy will appear familiar enough. It bears strong analogy with Quine's thesis of the indeterminacy of translation.[16] Quine's analytical hypotheses, like the first *dags*, are underdetermined by the data. The selection of one *dag* or one set of analytical hypotheses is largely a matter of cultural bias or historical accident. But once a *dag* or a set of analytical hypotheses has been formulated, it has profound effects on the remainder

[16] Cf. 'Speaking of Objects', *Proceedings and Addresses of the American Philosophical Association*, 31 (1957/8), 5–22; 'Meaning and Translation', in Fodor and Katz, *The Structure of Language*, op. cit.; *Word and Object* (MIT Press, Cambridge, Mass., 1960), ch. 2; and 'Ontological Relativity', *The Journal of Philosophy*, 69, No. 7 (4 April 1968), 185–212, reprinted in *Ontological Relativity, and Other Essays* (Columbia, New York, 1969).

of the translation theory (for analytical hypotheses), or on the acquisition model and *dags* for other languages. Both analytical hypotheses
and early *dags* are susceptible to later tampering; but neither a patched
dag nor a patched analytical hypothesis has any more claim to uniqueness than the originals.

My departure from Quine comes on the score of the *implications*
of the indeterminacy. Were Quine to grant that grammars and translation manuals share a sort of indeterminacy,[17] he would presumably
conclude that for grammars, as for translations, modulo the indeterminacy, there is nothing to be right about. On this view there is no
saying that one *dag* of a language is more correct than another, except
relative to a given set of quasi-universals. Yet the selection of quasi-
universals, like the selection of analytical hypotheses, is in part quite
arbitrary. My dissent comes in the step that passes from recognition
of arbitrariness in quasi-universals or analytical hypotheses to the claim
that there is (modulo the indeterminacy) nothing to be right about.
For I think that, *pace* Quine, the same indeterminacy could be shown
lurking in the foundations of every empirical science. Grammar and
translation are not to be distinguished, in this quarter, from psychology
or biology or physics. If we are disinclined to say that in all science,
modulo the indeterminacy, there is nothing to be right about, it is
because the theories we are willing to allow as correct are those whose
arbitrary features have the sanction of tradition. But all this is to stake
out my dissent, not to defend it. The defence is a project I must post-
pone until another occasion.

4

Our sketch of the grammarian's doings is all but complete. We have
surveyed the data to which he attends and indicated the nature of
the theory he builds upon his data. It remains to say something of
the interest of the grammarian's theory and to set out the relation
between his theory and the speakers whose intuitions and behaviour
are his data.

As I have depicted it, a grammar is a modest portion of a psychological theory about the speaker. It describes certain language-specific
facts: facts about the acceptability of expressions to speakers and facts
about an ability or capacity speakers have for judging and classifying
expressions as having or lacking grammatical properties and relations.

The modesty of a grammar, on my account, stands in stark contrast

---

[17] There is evidence that he would. Cf. 'Methodological Reflections . . . '
op. cit.

to more flamboyant portraits. On Jerrold Katz's view, a grammar is a theory in physiological psychology whose components are strongly isomorphic to the fine structure of the brain. 'The linguistic description and the procedures of sentence production and recognition', according to Katz, 'must correspond to independent mechanisms in the brain. Componential distinctions between the syntactic, phonological, and semantic components must rest on relevant differences between three neural submechanisms of the mechanism which stores the linguistic description. The rules of each component must have their psychological reality in the input-output operations of the computing machinery of this mechanism'.[18] Though Katz's claims about grammar are more expansive than those I have made, the evidence he uses to confirm a grammar is of a piece with the evidence indicated in my account. Thus it remains something of a mystery how the grammarian has learned as much as Katz would have him know about the structure of the brain, having left the skulls of his subjects intact.

Less imaginative than Katz's view, but still not so sparse as mine, is a story about grammar put forward by Chomsky.[19] On this account a grammar describes the speaker's 'competence'—his knowledge of his language. The speaker is held to have a large and complex fund of knowledge of the rules of his grammar. The grammarian's theory mirrors or describes the knowledge that the speaker has 'internalized' and 'internally represented'. Chomsky's view is intriguing, though an explicit unpacking of the metaphors of 'internalization', 'representation', and the rest can prove an exasperating task. My own view is that the notion of competence is explanatorily vacuous and that attributing knowledge of a grammar to a speaker is little more plausible than attributing knowledge of the laws of physics to a projectile whose behaviour they predict. But the issues are complex, and I have aired my views at length elsewhere.[20] I will not rehash them here. What is important to our present project is the observation that, on the account of grammar and acquisition models we have constructed, no knowledge claim is *needed*. A grammar is a theory describing the facts of acceptability and intuition; a grammar-acquisition model is a theory specifying a grammar which comes to be true of a child, as a function of the linguistic environment in which he is placed. Grammar and the theory of grammar acquisition are bits of psychological theory.

[18] 'Mentalism in Linguistics', *Language*, 40 No. 2 (April/June 1964), 124–37, p. 133.
[19] In *Aspects of the Theory of Syntax*, op. cit., and elsewhere.
[20] 'What Every Speaker Knows', *Philosophical Review*, 80, No. 4 (Oct. 1971), 476–96, and 'What Every Grammar Does', *Philosophia*, 3, No. 1 (Jan. 1973), 85–96.

If our account of the grammarian's activity is accurate, then it is perhaps misleading to describe him as constructing a theory of the language of his subjects. Rather he is building a description of the facts of acceptability and linguistic intuition. A theory of a language seriously worthy of the name would provide some insight into what it is to *understand* a sentence, how sentences can be used to communicate and to deal more effectively with the world, and into a host of related questions that we have yet to learn to ask in illuminating ways. But a grammar does none of this. Indeed, it is logically possible that there be a person whose linguistic intuitions matched up near enough with our own, but who could neither speak nor understand English. Such a person would serve almost as well as an English speaker as an informant for constructing a grammar of English, provided only that we shared a metalanguage in which we could question him about the sequences of sounds he did not understand. What is important about this bit of fiction is that it is *only* fiction. It is an empirical fact that comprehension and intuition run in tandem. And this fact provides the beginning of the answer to a question that will likely have begun to trouble the reader: Of what interest is a grammar? If a grammar is not, in any exciting sense, a theory of a language, why bother constructing it?

The answer is twofold. First, there is substantial correspondence between the grammatical sentences and the sentences we do in fact use for thought and communication; grammatically related sentences are understood in similar ways[21] (though in our present state of ignorance we have no serious understanding of what it is to 'understand sentences in similar ways'); the ability to speak and understand a language is an empirically necessary condition for the possession of linguistic intuitions about the expressions of the language. So one reason for studying grammar is the hope that these overlaps and correlations can be exploited to yield deeper insight into the exciting phenomena of comprehension and communication. Once we have the sort of description of acceptability and linguistic intuition provided by a grammar we can begin to seek an explanation of these facts. We can ask what psychological mechanisms underlie the speaker's ability to judge and relate sentences as he does. The parallels between linguistic intuition and other language-related phenomena make it reasonable to hope that

---

[21] Cf. Chomsky, *Syntactic Structures* (Mouton, The Hague, 1957), p. 86: 'the sentences (i) *John played tennis* [and] (ii) *my friend likes music* are quite distinct on phonemic and morphemic levels. But on the level of phrase structure they are both represented as *NP-Verb-NP; correspondingly, it is evident that in some sense they are similarly understood.*' [Last emphasis added.]

insight into the mechanisms underlying intuition will explain much else about language as well. But hope is not to be confused with accomplishment. If we fail to recognize how modest a theory a grammar is, we can expect only to obscure the extent of our ignorance about language, communication, and understanding.

A second reason for doing grammar is that it is something to do. In grammar, at least we have a coherent set of data that we know how to study, intelligible questions to ask, and some clear indication as to how we can go about answering them. Acceptability and grammatical intuitions are language-related phenomena about which we have the beginnings of an empirical theory. Few other approaches to the phenomena of natural language fare as well. Thus grammar is a natural focus of attention for the investigator concerned with language. It is an entering wedge to a theory of a language, and, for the present at least, there are few competitors.

7

SOME NOTES ON WHAT LINGUISTICS IS ABOUT

J. A. FODOR

ALL THE chapters in this part are about what it is for a linguistic theory to be true. The question what it is for a linguistic theory to be true is an *interesting* question and should be sharply distinguished from the question what it is for a true theory to be linguistic. The question what it is for a true theory to be linguistic is a *boring* question. Very often, in these chapters, the authors appear to be discussing the first. This is quite a standard tactic in philosophical argument. Philosophers like to appear to be discussing boring questions (such as how the word 'good' is used) when they are in fact discussing interesting questions (such as what it is for something to be good). Heaven knows *why* philosophers like to do this, but they do and the reader is hereby forewarned. The question at issue in these papers is *not*: who gets to call his research real linguistics (as opposed to mere psychology or mere mathematics)? The question at issue is: what is it for a linguistic theory to be true?

Truth is (of course) correspondence to the facts. So, if we want to know what it is for a linguistic theory to be true, we have to know (*a*) which facts a true linguistic theory corresponds to and (*b*) what relations to these facts are constitutive of the correspondence. Most of the discussion in these chapters centres on (*a*) since, presumably, whatever correspondence is, it's the same wherever truth claims are at issue. It might be that linguistic theories, when they are true, correspond to the facts in a different way than, say, physical theories do when *they* are true. But, so far, no one has suggested that this is so, and there is reason to hope that no one is about to.

So the question is: what facts are such that the truth of a linguistic theory consists in its correspondence to *those* facts, whatever correspondence may itself consist in? There are, as it turns out, really only

Reprinted by permission of the publishers from pp. 197–207 of *Readings in the Philosophy of Psychology*, vol. II, edited by N. Block, Cambridge, Mass.: Harvard University Press, Copyright © 1981 by Ned Block.

two schools of thought on this question, though it may be a little hard to see that this is so, partly because other issues keep getting in the way, and partly because some of the players keep changing sides. One school (roughly, the forces of darkness) holds that the question is susceptible of a priori settlement; in fact, that we can even now specify a priori some set of facts such that the truth of a linguistic theory consists in its correspondence to *them*. The other school (roughly, the forces of light) holds that the question what facts a true linguistic theory corresponds to is answerable only a posteriori; in fact, only after adequate linguistic theories have been developed. The borders between these two positions are slightly vague, as, indeed, the borders between light and darkness are forever wont to be. But, to a first approximation, the two accounts are exclusive and exhaustive. Moreover, how you choose between them will determine your views on most of the rest of the methodological issues in the field.

The idea that it is possible to enumerate a priori the kinds of facts a scientific theory is required to account for has a considerable provenance in the history of philosophical discussions of scientific methodology. So, in the positivist tradition, it used to be believed that the truth of a scientific theory consists in its correspondence to those facts that constitute its *data*. This idea amounted to more than a triviality since the notion of data was proprietary. For example, the data might consist of just those facts that can be reported in a *data language*, where a data language, in turn, is one whose predicates subsume only 'directly observable' objects, or only middle-sized objects, or any qualia, or whatever. The motives for holding this sort of view were usually epistemological (a desire to confine inductive risk to some level of theory distinct from its data sentences) and they need not concern us in detail. Suffice it to remark upon two tenets of positivist philosophy of science that appear to have survived the positivist's epistemology: that the data base for a theory can be delimited antecedent to the construction of theory, and that the truth claims a theory makes are exhausted by what it says about its data base. (All theories that entail the same data sentences are therefore equivalent unless they are distinguishable in respect of simplicity.)

Linguistics since 1957 has been busy rewriting its history in the approved Kuhnian fashion, and I make no claims about what real 'taxonomic' linguists really thought that they were doing. But there is a taxonomic straw man with whom we are all acquainted and he, at least, was a positivist in the sense just specified. That is, he thought (*a*) that there is a specifiable data base for linguistic theories; (*b*) that this data base can be specified antecedent to theory construction;

(*c*) that the empirical content of linguistic theories consists of what they say about the data base; and (*d*) that the data base for linguistics consists of the corpora of utterances that informants produce (or, in some versions, would produce given specified forms of prompting). Forget the epistemology and alter (*d*) to read 'the data base for linguistics consists of the intuitions (about grammaticality, ambiguity, and so on) that informants produce (or would produce . . .)' and you get the view that seems to be common to Stephen P. Stich in 'Grammar, Psychology, and Indeterminacy',[1] and Jerry Katz in 'The Real Status of Semantic Representations', *Linguistic Inquiry*, Vol. 8, No. 3, 1977, pp. 559-84. I need a name for this view. I shall call it the Wrong View.

Thus, the Wrong View and Positivist View are in pretty fair agreement that the question what linguists is about is one that can be settled a priori. But it is essential to bear in mind that the arguments currently being advanced for the Wrong View are really quite different from the ones that used to be advanced for the Positivist View. If positivists thought themselves warranted in identifying the empirical content of a theory with the data sentences that it entails, that was often because they thought that meaningfulness is a matter of verifiability, or that theoretical entities are fictions, or that theoretical terms must be definable in an observation vocabulary, and so on. There may be those who hold the Wrong View for these sorts of reasons, but you will not find their writings in this volume.[2] I think (if I may momentarily abandon the posture of perfect neutrality that I have thus far assumed) that the Wrong View is certainly wrong. But the standard antiverificationist arguments aren't what one has against it.

I want to discuss the arguments against the Wrong View at some length. First, however, let me set out, quite briefly, the alternative position (which I shall call the Right View). The Right View is the one enunciated in Noam Chomsky and Jerry Katz's 'What the Linguist is Talking About', *Journal of Philosophy*, Vol. 71, No. 12, 1974, pp. 347-67, and assumed in Janet D. Fodor, Jerry A. Fodor, and Merrill F. Garrett's 'The Psychological Unreality of Semantic Representations', *Linguistic Inquiry*, Vol. 6, No. 4, 1975, pp. 515-31.[3] What it amounts to is the following claims. (*a*) Linguistic theories are

[1] [Reprinted as Essay 6 in the present volume.]

[2] *Readings in the Philosophy of Psychology*, ed. N. Block, Harvard University Press, Cambridge, 1981, Volume II.

[3] Katz thinks that Garrett and I once held the Wrong View (in the passage he cites from our *Some Reflections on Competence and Performance*), but he is wrong to think so. What we said was that 'the internal evidence in favor of the structural descriptions modern grammars generate is so strong that it is difficult to imagine them succumbing to any purely experimental disconfirmation.' NB.:

descriptions of grammars. (*b*) It is nomologically necessary that learning one's native language involves learning its grammar, so a theory of how grammars are learned is *de facto* a (partial [?]) theory of how languages are learned. (*c*) It is nomologically necessary that the grammar of a language is internally represented by speaker/hearers of that language; up to dialectical variants, the grammar of a language is what its speaker/hearers have in common by virtue of which they are speaker/hearers of the *same* language. (*d*) It is nomologically necessary that the internal representation of the grammar (or, equivalently for these purposes, the internally represented grammar) is causally implicated in communication exchange between speakers and hearers in so far as these exchanges are mediated by their use of the language that they share; talking and understanding the language normally involve exploiting the internally represented grammar.[4]

'hard to imagine', not 'methodologically inconceivable'. What we try to show in *The Psychological Unreality of Semantic Representations* (ch. 12) is that all of the internal evidence (all the evidence that linguists have thus far alleged) favouring lexical decomposition can be met equally well by using meaning postulates; and, moreover, that the latter approach can cope with the available experimental data.

I wouldn't fuss about these exegetical details except that I have changed my mind, at one time or another, about almost everything *but* the Right View, and I do claim credit for this little island of consistency. I suspect that what caused the confusion is that Katz takes such distinctions as 'internal' versus 'experimental' evidence to be principled, whereas it would never have occurred to Garrett or to me to view them as other than heuristic. This sort of point will loom large below.

[4] A word about these nomological necessities. For all we now know, it is nomologically possible that there should be organisms (chimps? Martians? machines?) that could learn and use English without learning or exploiting its grammar. So, for all we now know, these nomological necessities hold at most for *our* species (or for species with our sort of nervous system). Linguistics is certainly part of human psychology, according to the Right View; the rest is an empirical issue currently up for grabs.

This is not, of course, an *objection* to the Right View. Sciences often leave unspecified the domain of the nomological necessities they articulate. A biologist who says that respiration is necessary for (our kind of) life is not thereby denying the possibility of life forms *very* different from us. And some cosmologists think that even fundamental laws of nature may have restricted applicability: that they may not hold at very remote times or in very extreme states of matter.

A fortiori, it does not follow from these nomological necessities that 'it would be logically absurd to claim that creatures with sufficiently different information processing mechanisms from ours also speak English' (Katz, ch. 13). The identification of the grammar of *L* as that system that is nomologically necessary for *us* to learn if we are to learn *L* is quite compatible with the assumption that that grammar plays *no* role in the use of *L* by other (nomologically possible but very different) kinds of creatures. Should it be proposed that the grammar of *L* is that system that is neutral between the ways in which *L* might be represented by any

Never mind, for the moment, whether the Right View is right. My present purpose is to emphasize a glaring difference between the Right View and its antagonist. According to the latter, as we have seen, there is a proprietary body of data (the speaker/hearer's linguistic intuitions according to the most popular version) such that, a priori, the facts that a true linguistic theory corresponds to are exhausted by those data, and such that any theories that predict the same such data are *ipso facto* 'empirically equivalent'.[5] Whereas, according to the Right View, *any* facts about the use of language, or about how it is learned, or about the neurology of speaker/hearers, or, for that matter, about the weather on Mars, could, in principle, be relevant to the choice between competing linguistic theories. This is because, according to the Right View, linguistics is embedded in psychology (it offers a partial theory of the capacities and behaviours of speaker/hearers) and is thus sensitive to whatever information about the psychology of speaker/hearers we are able to bring to bear. Moreover, *sensitive* to is, in this respect, a transitive relation: if we get our neurology (or our astronomy) to bear on some part of our psychology, then if that part of our psychology bears on our linguistics, then so too do our neurology and our astronomy.

It is thus a consequence of the Right View that there is no a priori distinction between linguistic data and psychological data (or, indeed, between linguistic data and data of *any* other kind). Such distinctions as we *are* able to draw are a posteriori; we find out more and more about how grammars function in the mental processes of speaker/hearers. This seems to me to be precisely as it ought to be; it accords with our intuitions about how scientific practice should proceed. Suppose that, tomorrow, some very clever astro-linguist were to devise an argument that runs from observations of the Martian climate to some or other constraint on theories of human psychology and thence to the proper formulation of the English pseudocleft. *Surely* we would say, 'Bravo and, well done', not 'Ingenious but not pertinent'.

The alternative view is that the scientist gets to *stipulate* what data

nomologically possible *L*-speakers, we would require arguments to show that there *is* a unique such system—or, indeed, that there are *any* such systems. I know of no such arguments.

[5] 'Empirically equivalent' theories cannot, in point of logic, compete in respect of truth. For (*a*) truth is correspondence to the facts; (*b*) the facts linguistic theories correspond to are, by assumption, the linguistic data; and (*c*) linguistic theories are empirically equivalent if they correspond to the same data in the same way. Hence, in particular, simplicity is not a truth criterion according to the Wrong View (though one may, of course, prefer the simplest set of empirically equivalent theories on grounds *other than* truth—for instance, on aesthetic grounds).

are to count as relevant to the (dis)confirmation of his theories, and my point is that that view simply isn't plausible given the way that real science is conducted. I take this to be a point of utmost methodological seriousness since it implies that either the Wrong View misdescribes linguistics or what linguists do is somehow an exception to the methodological principles that other sciences endorse. Here is one way that (barring the anachronisms) the argument between Ptolemy and Galileo might have gone:

GALILEO. I have these telescopic observations, and they seem to show that Venus has phases. It's going to be awfully hard to square that with Venus and the Sun revolving around the Earth, so I think you guys have got trouble.

PTOLEMY. Ingenious but not pertinent. The data of astronomy are [i.e. are exhausted by] observations of the positions of the stars and planets. Astronomy *is* [i.e. = *df*] the science that predicts such observations. It follows that any two theories that make the same such predictions are *ipso facto* (barring simplicity) equivalent theories. That one but not the other predicts phases for Venus *could not* be relevant to a choice between them. For: Nothing but astronomical data can be relevant to a choice between astronomical theories, and OBSERVATIONS OF THE PHASES OF VENUS DO NOT CONSTITUTE ASTRONOMICAL DATA. They constitute, to coin a phrase, *performance data*. There is a great deal that we do not know about telescopes.

The point is that the argument didn't go that way. If Ptolemy *had* tried stipulating a proprietary data base for astronomy, his problem would have been to make the stipulation stick; and, stipulation notwithstanding, anybody rational prefers a theory that predicts both the observed locations of the planets *and* the phases of Venus to a theory that predicts only the former.

Indeed, a stronger—and rather less familiar—point appears to be germane. It's not just that the observation of planetary positions has no *stipulated* position as the data par excellence of astronomy; it is also true that one requires a posteriori justification for the claim that such observations are relevant *at all*. This is not, of course, an idiosyncrasy of astronomy. Any science is under the obligation to explain why *what it takes to be* data relevant to the confirmation of its theories *are* data relevant to the confirmation of its theories. Typically one meets this condition by exhibiting a causal chain that runs from the entities that the theory posits, via the instruments of observation, to the psychological states of the observer. (So, the astronomer can argue, if there are such things as planets, and if they are at least roughly the sorts of things that his theories suppose them to be, then given the way that terrestrial astronomers are situated, and given the way that telescopes work, telescopic observations of the apparent positions of the planets *should* bear upon the confirmation of theories about how the planets are arranged in space.) Whereas, if there is reason to suppose that such a causal chain does *not* connect the observations to the postulated entities, the scientist has no warrant to appeal to those observations as data in support of his theories, however much tradition may sanction such appeals.

This all applies, *mutatis mutandis*, to linguistics, or so one would have thought. In particular, an adequate linguistics *should explain why it is that the intuitions of speaker/hearers constitute data relevant to the confirmation of grammars*. The Right View meets this condition. It says 'We can use intuitions to confirm grammars because grammars are internally represented and actually contribute to the etiology of the speaker/hearer's intuitive judgements.' The Wrong View says only: 'We do it because we have always done it', or 'We do it by stipulation'.

So far, I've been running the discussion on the assumption that linguistics works the way that science does, and of course that assumption might be false. I now want to look at some of the arguments that allege that linguistics is special in a way that exempts the linguist from adherence to the usual canons of scientific methodology; in particular, that because of the kind of discipline that linguistics is, linguists can (as Ptolemy could not) specify a priori what data are to bear on the confirmation of their theories.

The easiest of these arguments to understand (and to sympathize with) is one that I take to underlie much of Stich's chapter. Stich sees very clearly that the Right View is tenable only if sense can be made of the notion of internal representation. After all, the Right View construes learning a language as a process that eventuates in the internal representation of a grammar, and it construes the production/perception of speech as causally mediated by the grammar that the speaker/hearer learns. On both grounds, it is committed to a Realistic construal of the notion of internal representation; what isn't there has no effects or causes.

It is thus only because it allows itself free use of 'the internally represented grammar (the internal representation of the grammar)' that the Right View can define truth-for-a-linguistic-theory in the way that it does: as correspondence between the grammar that the theory postulates and the grammar that the speaker/hearer learns. If, then, the notion of internal representation is *not* coherent, the only thing left for a linguistic theory to be true of is the linguist's observations (*de facto*, the intuitions of the speaker/hearer as extrapolated by the formally simplest grammar). Take the notion of internal representation away from linguistic metatheory and you get positivism by subtraction.

Of course, this would constitute a serious argument for the Wrong View only if no sense could be made of the notion of internal representation, and that is a moot question. Some philosophers think that there exists a distinguishable intellectual enterprise called 'conceptual analysis'. The idea is that, if a question should arise as to whether a notion can be made clear, you can answer the question by getting a philosopher to do some of this conceptual analysing. When he is finished analysing, the philosopher will tell you whether or not you are allowed to use the notion to do science with.

I do not think that this is how things work. Philosophers don't get to tell you what counts as permissible scientific construct, any more than scientists get to tell you what counts as relevant scientific data. What determines which constructs are permissible (and which data are relevant) is: how the world turns out to be. We will find out whether we can make sense of 'mental representation' *as we go along*. (The prospects look rather better now than they did a decade or two ago.)

I think that Stich thinks that claims about internal representations suffer from an inherent resistance to (dis)confirmation, and that this flaw irremediably infects theories that entail such claims. In particular, I take it to be Stich's view that (*a*) you can make sense of choosing among descriptively adequate grammars (*dags*)[6] only given a reputable notion of internal representation; but (*b*) no merely empirical result could licence a choice among descriptively adequate grammars (so that no such result could require us to embrace the internal representation construct). I think that (*a*) is probably correct, but it is easy to imagine cases contrary to (*b*).

Indeed, such cases arise again and again in the actual practice of validating linguistic theories. For example, nobody is interested in grammars that *demonstrably could not be learned*, though there is no reason why some such grammars shouldn't be *dags* in Stich's sense. Or, consider the following unsubtle example. Suppose it turned out that, among the equally simple extrapolations of the adult's intuitions, there existed one (*G3*) that contained precisely three rules. And suppose it were also to turn out that, in learning English, a child goes

---

[6] A *dag* is any adequately simple extrapolation of the adult corpus of intuitions that is compatible with the data in the corpus.

through three distinguishable stages. In stage 1, he produces precisely the sorts of utterances (or intuitions) that he would produce if he knew only rule 1 of *G3*; in stage 2 he produces precisely the ones he would produce if he knew only rules 1 and 2 of *G3*; and in stage 3 he produces the typical adult corpus. It would surely be mad, under such circumstances, not to prefer *G3* to other *dags*, all other things being equal, for it could be claimed of *G3*—but, by assumption, not of any other *dag*—that it is learned *rule by rule*. This is to say that it would be mad, under these circumstances, not to do precisely what (according to Stich) requires you to embrace a notion of internal representation: namely, choose among descriptively adequate grammars. But it is conceptually possible that such circumstances might obtain; the world *could* turn out that way. So, it looks as though the world could turn out so as to license the use of the notion of internal representation, and could do so even if philosophers hadn't finished analysing it at the time.

There are two arguments for the Wrong View that do not depend upon agnosticism about internal representations. These need to be looked at now. I'll move fairly quickly, since many of the relevant points have already been made.

It is sometimes suggested that the Wrong View can be defended by appeal to the competence/performance distinction. (This is a proposal that Katz appears to endorse in his discussion of 'Competencism.') My own view is that there is a competence/performance distinction but that it has been much abused by some of its devotees. I often wish that it would go away. Still, at a minimum, something has to be said by way of showing that making the distinction in a defensible form doesn't commit one to the Wrong View of linguistic theories.

At heart, the competence/performance distinction is a distinction between *kinds of explanations*. 'Competence theories' account for facts about the behaviours and capacities of a speaker/hearer by reference to properties of his internalized grammar, whereas 'performance theories' account for facts about the behaviours and capacities of a speaker/hearer by reference to interactions between the internally represented grammar and other aspects of the speaker/hearer's psychology. So, to cite the classical example, we explain the speaker/hearer's ability to understand and produce novel linguistic forms by reference to the productivity of the grammar he has learned, but we explain the speaker/hearer's *in*ability to understand multiply center-embedded sentences by reference to the interactions between the mentally represented grammar and the (short-term) memory he employs in parsing the sentences that the grammar generates.

Notice that, so construed, the competence/performance distinction is clearly to be drawn a posteriori; we discover which aspects of the speaker/hearer's behaviour/capacity are in the domain of theories of competence, and which are not, by discovering which explanations of the speaker/hearer's behaviour/capacity are *true*. Notice also that the competence/performance distinction, so construed, is not a very *interesting* distinction. Its primary use is to explain (for example) why hiccoughs aren't part of English even though they *do* occur, from time to time, in the corpus of English utterances. The explanation goes: hiccoughs that occur during speech are produced by the interaction of the language mechanisms with the hiccough mechanisms. An adequate theory must, therefore, treat utterances that contain hiccoughs as inter-action effects. It must not, in particular, attribute them to the function-ing of the language mechanisms per se; were it to do so, the theory would not be *true*. It should be emphasized that, according to this analysis, it is the notion of truth, and not the performance/competence distinction, that is actually doing the work in constraining the linguist's theories. Similarly, in cases where we appeal to the competence/performance distinction to correct an informant's linguistic intuitions: What's wrong with the intuition that a multiply self-embedded sentence is ungrammatical is not that it somehow flouts the competence/performance distinctions; it's simply that the intuition is false. The competence/performance distinction isn't, in short, a methodological constraint imposed upon linguistic theories over and above the demand for correspondence to the facts. On the contrary, we honour the performance/competence distinction when—and only when—we get the facts right.

A sensible discussion of the competence/performance distinction might well stop here. Beyond this point there are monsters, however.

You can, if you like, use the competence/performance distinction to introduce a notion of *Ideal Speaker/Hearer*. You do so as follows. Imagine what a real speaker/hearer would be like if his behaviour did *not* exhibit certain effects that are consequences of interactions between the language mechanisms and other psychological states and processes. For example, if speaker/hearers had infinite short-term memories, then (assuming our current theories are true) they would be able to construe arbitrarily self-embedded sentences. And, perhaps, they would always be able to tell whether a string in their language was grammatical (though this is by no means obviously so). Well, then, an Ideal Speaker/Hearer is just like a real speaker/hearer except that, in explaining the behaviour/capacities of the former, we do not need to refer to the effects of these interactions; we define the behaviours characteristic of Ideal Speaker/Hearers by abstracting from such effects. We can even add this: grammars per se are theories about Ideal Speakers/Hearers. This sounds wildly deep and ontological and sexy, but actually it is trivial and harmless. All it means is that grammars are not, per se, theories of the interaction effects. (Of course, there *is* a question of fact here, and it's not a small one: namely, which is the *correct* parsing of the speaker/hearer's psychology into 'linguistic mechanisms' and 'others'. Only a characterization of the Ideal Speaker/Hearer that gets this parsing right will be of use for purposes of empirical theory construction.)

Finally, having gone this far, we can take the rest of the plunge and characterize a proprietary notion of 'linguistic data'. Linguistic data, in this proprietary sense, are those that, *de facto*, are explicable by reference to just the theoretical constructs appealed to in theories of the Ideal Speaker/Hearer. Since the grammar *is*, by assumption, a theory of the Ideal Speaker/Hearer, it will follow that linguistic data are relevant to the confirmation of the grammar.

There are now two mistakes just aching to be made. One is to ignore the '*de facto*' and assume that you can somehow determine a priori *which* aspects of the behaviour/capacities of the speaker/hearer are preserved under idealization (hence which data are linguistic in the proprietary sense). The other is to suppose that the linguistic data *exhaust* the facts that bear on the confirmation of a grammar. I take it that the first of these is *obviously* a mistake. The kinds of observations that linguists have thus far taken to bear on their theories about grammars are, almost certainly, a heterogeneous and fragmentary sample of the data that God would consider relevant. As our theories and techniques of observation get better, we will surely revise our views about which observations are germane; in what science is this not the case? The point is: because we know very little about the grammar and practically nothing about the way it interacts with other psychological faculties, *we do not know which capacities an Ideal Speaker/Hearer has qua Ideal Speaker/Hearer*. Moreover, we aren't allowed to *stipulate* these capacities on pain of introducing a notion of Ideal Speaker/Hearer that is, *de facto*, useless for theory construction. (PTOLEMY. The Sun *does* revolve around the Earth in an *Ideal* Solar System.) Again What the capacities of the Ideal Speaker/Hearer are depends on which theory of real speaker/hearers is *true*.

But suppose we *did* know, a posteriori, what capacities an Ideal Speaker/Hearer has qua Ideal Speaker/Hearer. Couldn't we then say that the simplest grammar that accounts for *those* capacities is *ipso facto* true? For example, suppose that it turned out, in light of the best theories we can devise, that the ability to formulate intuitions of grammaticality is the only such capacity. Couldn't we then say: the true grammar is the (simplest) one that predicts the grammaticality intuitions of the speaker/hearer?

Patently not. For, suppose we had two equally simple grammars, G and G', which gave the same account of the grammaticality intuitions of speaker/hearers. And suppose we had a theory M of the organization of memory in human adults, such that M is independently highly confirmed. Finally, suppose that the conjunction of M and G predicted that multiply self-embedded sentences are not construable by human adults, whereas the conjunction of M and G' predicted the contrary. It would then be mad to deny that we had evidence for preferring G to G', even despite the fact that they make the same predictions about those behaviours/capacities that Ideal Speaker/Hearers have qua Ideal Speaker/Hearers. Here, then, is another moral from the general philosophy of science: the data relevant to the confirmation of T include the data predicted by *the conjunction of T with any other theory that is independently well confirmed*.[7] In particular, they are *not* exhausted by the entailments of T taken alone. From the assumption that grammars are theories of the capacities of Ideal Speaker/Hearers, it does *not* follow that the confirmation base for a grammar is exhausted by the claims about the capacities of Ideal Speaker/Hearers that the grammar makes.

The short form of this discussion goes like this: there are no such things as 'competence data' or 'performance data' (just as there are no such things as 'linguistic data' or 'psychological data' or 'astronomical data'). I mean that none of these classifications is *principled*. In principle, there are just the facts, on the one hand, and the totality of the available scientific theories, on the other. It is probably a historical accident that, so far, the best field of data for the confirmation of grammars has been the well-formedness intuitions of speaker/hearers. It is to be hoped (and, for once, optimism is rational) that new fields of data will become increasingly available as we learn more about how to use facts about the interactions between internally represented grammars and other psychological mechanisms to constrain both the theory of the grammar and the theory of the interactions.[8]

[7] Assuming, of course, that the conjunction is consistent.

[8] Just as the distinction between 'linguistic' and 'psychological' data is not principled, so, too, the distinction between collecting intuitions and running experiments (or between 'on-line' and 'off-line' mental processes) is heuristic from the point of view of specifying the data relevant to the confirmation of a linguistic theory. Of course, it *could* turn out a posteriori (that is, in light of a true theory of language processing) that only a specifiable class of observations (such as collecting intuitions, or collecting responses that it takes more than six minutes

There is, however, one version of the Wrong View that does seem to me to be, in a certain sense, unassailable; it's the position that Katz calls Platonism. In effect, the Platonist is unmoved by any of the methodological morals that I have been drawing from general scientific practice because he doesn't think that linguistics is (empirical) science. What he thinks is that linguistics is a part of mathematics, and (I suppose) in mathematics you can stipulate whenever you are so inclined.

Hence, a possible position in this: 'I am interested in the mathematical problem of formally specifying a grammar that predicts certain of the intuitions of speakers/hearers; more precisely, I am interested in this project in so far as such intuitions are not artefacts of memory limitations, mortality, lapses of attention and other "performance factors." I stipulate that any pair of equally simple theories that make the same such predictions are to count as equivalent for these purposes. There is therefore nothing that, for these purposes, could decide between two such theories.' (Note that what counts as a 'performance factor' in this view is itself determined by stipulation, and not, as previously, by reference to which etiology of the behaviour of the speaker/hearer is true. Thus there is no particular reason why, in choosing a domain for his theory, the Platonist needs to attend to those of the speaker/hearer's capacities that are left when you eliminate contamination from memory limitations and the like. In principle, he might just as well attend to the construction of grammars that predict only intuitions about sentences with more than seven vowels, or sentences whose twelfth word is 'grandmother', or sentences that happen to be uttered on Tuesdays. Once you start to stipulate, it's Liberty Hall.)

It is worth emphasizing that Platonism, so construed, isn't incompatible with the Right View. It doesn't deny that some grammars are learned (and thus internally represented) or that the grammar that is learned causally mediates the production/perception of speech. Indeed, a reasonable Platonist might well want to endorse these claims since he would presumably want *some* story about the etiology of the speaker/hearer's linguistic intuitions, and the internal representation story seems to be the only one in town. But while he denies none of this qua, as it were, mildly interested observer, he officially doesn't care one

for the subject to produce, or, for that matter, weighing your grandmother) in fact bear on which grammar is true. But this would be a *discovery*, not part of a stipulative definition of 'linguistic data'. You don't get to stipulate what counts as construct validity for an experiment, any more than you get to stipulate which data are relevant to the truth of a theory.

way or the other qua Platonist. Qua Platonist, he isn't interested in the empirical truth of linguistic theories any more than the geometer (qua geometer) is interested in the empirical truth of Euclidean theory (in whether physical space is Euclidean). Indeed, strictly speaking, the Platonist has no use for distinguishing among grammars in respect of *truth* at all, so long as they make the same predictions about the speaker/hearer's intuitions. Formal simplicity, for example, is not a truth criterion in Platonistic linguistics any more than it is in number theory.[9]

The only thing against Platonism, so construed, is that, deep down, nobody is remotely interested in it.[10] Mathematical linguistics aren't, because what *they* care about is the formal properties of those grammars that are current or foreseeable candidates for theories of what the speaker/hearer learns when he learns his language (namely, for theories of internal representation). There isn't, after all, the remotest reason to believe that the class of generative sources that have in common *only* the ability to predict the intuitions of speaker/hearers has any mathematical interest whatever. (Indeed, there is some a posteriori reason to believe that it does not, since, so far at least, the intuitive data have failed to yield clear decisions among types of grammars of very different formal structure.)

A fortiori, practising empirical linguists aren't Platonists, for the good and sufficient reason that Platonism is so much less interesting than the Right View. Suppose that we grant the Platonist proprietary use of the term 'linguistics'. So, by stipulation, linguistics is part of mathematics. But then, just down the road, there must be another science *just like linguistics* except that it *does* care about empirical truth because it cares about how the mind works. Suppose we call this other science 'psycho-linguistics'. Psycho-linguistics, so construed, is part of the theory of internal representation. If, as we now suppose, intuitions have construct validity for the theory of (internally represented) grammars, then we are guaranteed that the psycho-linguist's grammar will turn out to be one of the grammars that the Platonist is interested in. Like the Platonistic linguist, the psycho-linguist is interested in predicting the intuitions of speaker/hearers because he believes (*believes*, not *stipulates*) that intuitions are relevant to the

---

[9] See n. 3 above.

[10] I provisionally except certain 'Montague grammarians', who do appear to have achieved the requisite detachment from the claims of mere fact. See, for example, Richmond Thomason's remarks in his introduction to R. Montague's *Formal Philosophy* (Yale University Press, New Haven, 1974) (which, however, are perhaps more enigmatic and less univocal than they may at first appear.)

confirmation of grammars. But, unlike the Platonistic linguist, the psycho-linguist thinks that other kinds of data can constrain the choice of grammars too. He is therefore professionally interested in how languages are learned, how utterances are understood, whether there are linguistic universals, whether transformations are innate, how cognition affects language, how language affects cognition, aphasic speech, schizophrenic speech, metaphorical speech, telegraphic speech, dolphin speech, chimp speech, speech production, speech acts, and, in short, all that stuff that got people interested in studying languages in the first place. Go ahead, be a Platonist if you like. But the action is all at the other end of town.

I shall now once more relax the attitude of strict impartiality that I have hitherto assumed. The Right View is the right view *so far as we can now make out*. The italics are not, however, intended to be taken lightly. The Right View defines the goals of linguistics *ex post facto* in light of the theories now in the field. It's certain that these theories aren't true in detail, and it's entirely possible that they are false root and branch. In that case, there will be a residual philosophical question whether we ought to say that linguistics was misconstrued by the Right View or that there is no such science as linguistics. I, for one, won't much care.

C. REALIST FOUNDATIONS

8

STRUCTURAL ANALYSIS OF LANGUAGE

L. HJELMSLEV

FERDINAND DE SAUSSURE may in many respects be considered the founder of the modern science of language. He too was the first to call for a structural approach to language, i.e. a scientific description of language in terms of relations between units, irrespective of any properties which may be displayed by these units but which are not relevant to the relations or deducible from the relations. Thus, Saussure would have it that the sounds of a spoken language, or the characters of a written language, should be described, not primarily in terms of phonetics or of graphiology, respectively, but in terms of mutual relations only, and similarly, the units of the linguistic content (the units of meaning) should be described primarily not in terms of semantics but in terms of mutual relations only. According to Saussure, it would be erroneous to consider philology as a mere aggregate of physical, physiological and acoustic descriptions of speech sounds, and of investigations into the meanings of words, and, we may add, of psychological interpretations of such sounds and meanings. On the contrary, the real units of language are not sounds, or written characters, or meanings: the real units of language are the relata which these sounds, characters, and meanings represent. The main thing is not the sounds, characters, and meanings as such, but their mutual relations within the chain of speech and within the paradigms of grammar. These relations make up the system of a language, and it is this interior system which is characteristic of one language as opposed to other languages, whereas the representation by sounds, characters, and meanings is irrelevant to the system and may be changed without affecting the system. It may be added, incidentally, that this view of Saussure's, which meant nothing short of a revolution to conventional philology, conventional philology having been concerned with sounds and meanings only, is in perfect

From *Studia Linguistica*, Année I·(1947), Numero 2, pp. 69–78.

accordance with everyday usage, and covers exactly what the man in the street would suppose a language to be. It is nothing but a mere commonplace to state that, e.g. Danish when spoken, Danish when written, Danish when telegraphed by means of the morse code, Danish when signalized by means of the international flag code of the navies, is, in all these cases, essentially one and the same language, and not essentially four different languages. The units of which it is composed differ from one of these cases to another, but the framework of relations between these units remains the same and this is what makes us identify the language; accordingly, this framework must be the main object and the chief concern of philology, whereas the actual representations or manifestations of this framework are immaterial to the language in this stricter sense of the word. We should not fail to observe, however, that Saussure did not mean to discard phonetics and semantics altogether; but he meant them to be subordinate to the study of the relational system, and he assigned to phonetics and semantics the modest role of ancillary sciences. For sounds and meanings he would substitute linguistic values, defined by the relative positions of the units within the system. He compared these values with the values of economics: just as a coin, a bank note, and a check may be different representations or manifestations of one and the same value, and this value, say e.g. a pound or a shilling, remains the same whatever the manifestation, in the same way the units of the linguistic expression remain the same irrespective of the sounds representing them, and the units of the linguistic content remain the same irrespective of the meanings representing them. Saussure's favourite comparison was that of the language system with a game of chess: a chessman is defined exclusively by its relations to the other chessmen and by its relative positions on the chessboard, whereas the external shape of the chessmen, and the substance of which they are made (whether ivory or wood or whatever it may be) is immaterial to the game. A chessman, say e.g. a knight, which usually has the shape of a horse's head, might be replaced by any other piece which by convention might be adopted for the same purpose: if during the game of chess a knight is by accident dropped on the floor and goes to pieces, we can take any conceivable object of a convenient size, and assign to that object the value of a knight. In the same way, one sound can be replaced by another sound, or a sound by a letter, or by other conventional signals, and, in both cases, the game, the system, remains the same. I think we may add, in consequence of Saussure's statements, that during the historical evolution of a language, sounds may undergo changes which are material to the system, and others which are not; thus we would arrive at a fundamental distinction between changes of language structure, on one hand, and mere sound changes not affecting the system, on the other. A mere sound change might be comparable to the pawn in chess which, when arriving at the opposite end of the chessboard, according to the rules of the game, assumes the value of a queen and takes over the functions of a queen; in this case, the value of the queen is taken over by a piece of a quite different external shape; but irrespective of this external change, a queen remains a queen within the system.

At the outset, Saussure arrived at this view through a consideration of the Indo-European vowel system. As early as 1879, the analysis undertaken by Saussure of that system in his famous *Mémoire* had shown him that in some cases the so-called long vowels can be conveniently reduced to combinations of a simple vowel plus a particular unit which by Saussure was symbolized by $*A$. The advantage of such an analysis over the classical one is that of furnishing a simpler solution, the so-called long vowels being discarded as such from the system, and of revealing a striking analogy between ablaut series which had been considered up till then as radically different. By interpreting, e.g. τίθημι: θωμός: θετός as $*dheA$: $*dhoA$: $*dhA$, this ablaut series reveals itself as fundamentally the same as that of δέρχομαι δέδορχα ἔδραχον, which is equal to $*derk_1$: $*dork_1$: $*drk_1$. Thus, $*eA$ is to $*oA$ what $*er$ is to $*or$ and $*A$ plays the same role in the ablaut series as the $*r$ of $*drk_1$. This analysis was carried out for internal reasons only in order to gain a profounder insight in the fundamental system; it was not based on any evidence available in the languages compared; it was an internal operation within the Indo-European system. Direct evidence for the existence of $*A$ has later on been furnished by Hittite, but not until after Saussure's death.[1] The unit $*A$ has been interpreted from the phonetical point of view, as a laryngeal. But it is well worth noting that Saussure himself would never have ventured any such phonetic interpretation. To him the $*A$ was not a sound, and he took care not to define it by any phonetic properties, this being immaterial to his argument: his concern was the *system* only, and in this system $*A$ was defined by its definite relations to the other units of the system, and by its faculty of taking up definite positions within the syllable. This is stated expressly by Saussure himself and this is the famous point where he introduces the term *phoneme* to designate a unit which is not a sound but which may be represented or manifested by a sound.[2]

---

[1] Cf. Hans Hendriksen, *Untersuchungen über die bedeutung des hethitischen für die laryngaltheorie* (Copenhagen, 1941) = *Det Kgl. Danske Videnskaberness Selskah Historisk-filologiske Meddelelser* xxviii. 2, particularly p. 19.

[2] Cf. *Bulletin du Cercle linguistique de Copenhague*, 7, pp. 9–10, and

The theoretical consequences of this view were worked out by Saussure in his *Cours de linguistique générale*. This is where we find expounded the theoretical background which has been summarized in the beginning of the present paper. But it should be kept in mind that Saussure's theory, as expounded in these lectures on various occasions and with certain intervals, is not completely homogenous. Saussure's discoveries meant an entirely new departure within the field of language study, and it is no wonder that Saussure himself had to fight against conventional ideas; his lectures on general linguistics are the outcome of his struggle to gain a foothold on the new ground he had disclosed, and not an ultimate statement of his final views. There are discrepancies between some of the statements found in this book. Saussure makes the fundamental distinctions between form and substance, between language, in the narrower sense of the word, French *langue* and speech, French *parole*, which, by the way, includes writing, as explicitly stated by Saussure.[3] Saussure declares in explicit terms that language, *langue*, is form, not substance, and this of course is in accordance with his general outlook. But the distinction is not carried out in a completely clearcut way in all parts of the book, and the term *langue* actually has more than one sense. In a previous paper[4] I have endeavoured to disentangle, as far as it goes, the various layers or strata which can be observed in Saussure's meditations, and to lay bare what to my mind is the entirely new and really profitable idea in his work. This is, if I am not mistaken, the conception of language as a purely relational structure, as a pattern, as opposed to the usage (phonetic, semantic, etc.) in which this pattern is accidentally manifested.[5]

It is obvious, on the other hand, that, provided that I am right in my interpretation of Saussure's theory, this theory could hardly have been understood by the majority of his contemporaries and successors, trained as they were in the fundamentally different tradition of conventional philology. What is mainly taken up by them, then, are those

Mélanges linguistiques offerts à M. Holger Pedersen (Aarhus, 1937) = *Acta Jutlandica* ix 1), pp. 39–40. The term *phoneme* has been introduced by Saussure independently of N. Kruszewski, and in the same year (see J. Baudouin de Courtenay, *Versuch einer theorie phonetischer alternationen* (Strassburg, 1895), pp. 4–7). The sense in which it was used by him op. cit., p. 7, n., and. later, by Baudouin de Courtenay op. cit., p. 91, is entirely different from that of Saussure. The tradition of the Prague Linguistic Circle goes back to the above-mentioned Polish authors.

[3] Cf. Alan H. Gardiner, *The Theory of Speech and Language*, Oxford, 1932.

[4] 'Langue et parole', in *Cahiers Ferdinand de Saussure* 2, pp. 29–44.

[5] To readers who know Danish, a reference may be added to my account in *Videnskaben i dag*, Copenhagen, 1944, pp. 419–43.

parts of Saussure's work where *langue* is not identified with pure form, but where language is conceived as a form within the substance, and not independent of the substance. This is, e.g. the way in which Saussure's ideas came to be utilized, or, as it may perhaps be legitimate to say, appropriated by the Prague school of phonology, where the 'phoneme' is a phonetic abstraction, but definitely a phonetic one, and radically different from what, to my mind, Saussure's phomeme must have been. This is why the structural approach to language, in the real sense of the word, conceived as a purely relational approach to the language pattern independently of the manifestation in the linguistic usage, has not been taken up by philologists before the present day.

If talking of one's own efforts would not be considered too pretentious, I should like to state, modestly but emphatically, that such a structural approach to language, considered merely as a pattern of mutual relations, has been and still will be my chief concern in all my endeavours within this field of study. In contradistinction to conventional philology, I have proposed the name *glossematics* (derived from γλῶσσα 'language') to denote this purely structural kind of linguistic research. I am convinced that such a new departure will yield highly valuable information about the very intimate nature of language, and is likely not only to provide a useful supplement to older studies, but to throw an entirely new light on old ideas. As far as I am concerned, my endeavour is on the side of *langue* studied and conceived as a mere form, as a pattern independently of the usage. Saussure summarizes in the following words what he himself considers as the fundamental idea of his lecture: *la linguistique a pour unique et véritable objet la langue envisagée en elle-même et pour elle-même.* This is the last sentence of his lectures.[6] The late Professor Charles Bally, who was the successor of Saussure in the chair of linguistics in the University of Geneva, wrote a letter to me some few months before his death in which he said: 'Vous poursuivez avec . . . constance l'idéal formulé par F. de Saussure dans la phrase finale de son Cours de linguistique générale.' Indeed, it is an astonishing fact that this has never been done up to recent times.

On the other hand, I should like to emphasize that the theory of glossematics should not be identified with that of Saussure. It is difficult to know what were in detail the conceptions in Saussure's mind, and my own theoretical approach had begun to take shape, many years ago, before I even knew of Saussure's theory. Reading and rereading Saussure's lectures has given me confirmation in regard to many of my

---

[6] *Cours de linguistique générale*, p. 317 (2nd edn. Paris, 1922).

views; but I am necessarily looking at his theory from my own angle, and I should not like to go too far in my interpretations of his theory. I have mentioned him here in order to emphasize my profound indebtedness to his work.

The structural approach to language has certain intimate relations with a scientific trend which has taken shape in complete independence of philology, and which has not yet been very much noticed by philologists, namely the logistic language theory, which at the outset emerged from mathematical considerations, and which was carried out particularly by Whitehead and Bertrand Russell and by the Vienna School of logicians, especially by Professor Carnap, of the University of Chicago, whose recent works on syntax and semantics have certain undeniable bearings upon the philological study of language. A certain contact has been established recently between logicians and philologists in the *International Encyclopedia of Unified Science*.[7] In an earlier work by Professor Carnap, *structure* is defined in a way which agrees completely with the views I have here been advocating, namely, as a purely formal and purely relational fact. According to Professor Carnap, all scientific statements must be structural statements in this sense of the word: according to him, a scientific statement must always be a statement about relations without involving a knowledge or a description of the relata themselves.[8] This view of Carnap's confirms completely the results which have been gained in recent years within philology itself. It is obvious that the description of a language must begin by stating relations between relevant units, and these statements cannot involve a statement about the inherent nature, essence or substance of these units themselves. This must be left to phonetics and semantics, which accordingly presuppose that structural analysis of the language pattern. But it is obvious too that phonetics and semantics will have to proceed in exactly the same way and along the same lines: phonetic and semantic statements must, in their turn, be structural statements, e.g. physical statements about sound waves which form part of the units which have been previously found through the analysis of the language pattern. This too will have to be stated in terms of relations, in terms of form and not of substance: I hope I shall be right in stating that physical theory in itself would never speak of substance, or matter, if not in a critical sense. We can wind up this discussion by stating that linguistics describes the relational pattern of language without knowing what the relata are, and that phonetics and semantics do

---

[7] Chicago, 1938 sqq.
[8] R. Carnap, *Der logische aufbau der welt*, Berlin, 1928, p. 15.

tell what those relata are, but only by means of describing the relations between their parts and parts of their parts. This would mean, in logistic terms, that linguistics is a metalanguage of the first degree, whereas phonetics and semantics are metalanguages of the second degree. I have developed this idea at some length in a recent book[9] and I shall not go further into this now, since my only concern in the present paper is the language pattern.

I have pointed out certain obvious relations between the logistic language theory and the philological one. But unfortunately these relations soon come to an end. Logistic language theory has been carried out without any regard to philology, and it is obvious that logicians, while constantly talking about language, are neglecting in a somewhat indefensible way the results of the philological approach to language. This has had a detrimental effect on logistic language theory. In particular, the sign concept advocated by these scholars has considerable shortcomings and is unmistakably inferior to that of Saussure; it is not understood by logicians that the linguistic sign is two-sided, comprising a content and an expression, both of which can be submitted to a purely structural analysis. And logicians are therefore neglecting the *commutation*, the fundamental relation which is the very clue to the understanding of languages in the philological sense of the word.[10]

When conceived as a mere structure, language cannot be defined in terms of sound and meaning, as has constantly been done by conventional philology. Saussure realized clearly that a structural definition of language must lead us to recognize as languages certain structures which have not been regarded as such by conventional philology, and that the languages in the conventional philological sense constitute only one particular case of languages in general. Saussure would have it, consequently, that philology, or in French *linguistique*, should form a subdivision of a larger science of sign systems in general, which would be the real theory of language in the structural sense of the word. This larger science was called by him *semiology*.

But, for the reasons which have been indicated, this side of Saussure's theory did not appeal to philologists, and, as a matter of fact, semiology has never been carried out from a philological point of view. Quite

---

[9] *Omkring sprogteoriens grundlæggelse*, Copenhagen, 1943. A french edition of this book is forthcoming. A critical summary has been given by A. Martinet in *Bulletin de la Société de linguistique de Paris*, 42, pp. 19–42 and, in Danish, by Eli Fischer-Jorgensen in *Nordisk tidsskrift for tale og stemme*, 7, pp. 81–96.

[10] *Omkring sprogteoriens grundlæggelse*, pp. 44–68. Martinet, op. cit., pp. 27–31.

recently, a book published by the Belgian philologist E. Buyssens[11] is something of a first approach to semiology, though it is only to be regarded as a provisional attempt.

Language structures which are not languages in the conventional philological sense of the word have been studied to some extent by logistics, but, for the reasons I have indicated, these contributions are not likely to bring about results which will prove useful to philological research.

On the other hand, it would be highly interesting to study such structures by means of a strictly philological method, particularly because such structures would provide us with simple models in which the basic structure of language is laid bare without the complications due to the superstructures of ordinary language.

In the aforementioned work from 1943 I have attempted a structural definition of language[12] which should account for the basic structure of any language in the conventional philological sense. I have, later on, taken up a glossematic analysis of some very simple structures from everyday life, which are not languages in the conventional philological sense of the word, but which fulfil, partly or totally, the definition of the basic structure of language. Such border-line cases which I have studied from this theoretical point of view are: traffic lights, such as exist in most large towns where two streets intercross, and where a succession of *red, yellow, green, yellow* on the plane of expression corresponds to a succession of 'stop', 'attention', 'proceed', 'attention' on the plane of content. Further, the telephone dial employed in towns with automatic telephone service. Third, the chime of a tower-clock striking quarters and hours. Still simpler examples have been adduced in these studies, such as the morse alphabet, the prisoner's rapping code, and the ordinary clock, striking hours only. I have developed these examples in a series of lectures I have been giving recently in the University of London,[13] not merely for the fun of the thing, and not to serve purely pedagogical purposes only, but in order to gain a deeper insight in the basic structure of language and of systems similar to language; in comparing them with ordinary language in the conventional sense, I have used them to throw light upon the five fundamental features which, according to my definition, are involved in the basic structure of any language in the conventional sense namely the following:

[11] *Les langages et le discours*, Brussels, 1943.
[12] Op. cit., p. 94. Martinet, p. 33.
[13] I hope to publish these lectures under the title *Structural Analysis of Language*.

1. A language consists of a content and an expression.
2. A language consists of a succession, or a text, and a system.
3. Content and expression are bound up with each other through communication.
4. There are certain definite relations within the succession and within the system.
5. There is not a one-to-one correspondence between content and expression, but the signs are decomposable in minor components. Such sign components are, e.g. the so-called phonemes, which I should prefer to call taxemes of expression, and which in themselves have no content, but which can build up units provided with a content, e.g. words.

9

AN OUTLINE OF PLATONIST GRAMMAR[1]

J. J. KATZ

I WANT to raise and answer a question that it will appear strange to be asking in the first place and whose answer will seem obvious to almost everyone. The question is, *What is a grammar, a scientific theory of a natural language, a theory of?*

The considerable progress in formal grammar that has taken place in linguistics over the last three decades makes it seem strange to be asking what a grammar is a theory of. We couldn't, it is felt, have gotten all this far without knowing what we were doing. This is true in some sense of 'know', but the real question concerns our explicit knowledge of what we were doing it to. It is not uncommon in science for theories to develop rapidly while an understanding of their foundations remains at a standstill. Quine once observed that 'Ancient astronomers knew the movements of the planets remarkably well without knowing what sorts of things the planets were.' He added that, although such a situation is not untenable, 'it is a theoretically unsatisfactory situation'.[2]

The answer to the question will seem obvious to the vast majority of linguists, philosophers of language, psycholinguists, and computer scientists familiar with the Chomskyan revolution. The seemingly obvious answer is that a grammar is a theory of something psychological. There are disagreements about what kind of psychological theory a grammar is, but almost everyone agrees that it is some kind of psychological theory. But, despite its seeming obviousness, this answer is

Pages 1–33 from *Talking Minds: the Study of Language in Cognitive Science*, edited by T. Bever, J. M. Carroll, and L. A. Miller, MIT Press, Cambridge, Mass., 1984. Copyright © 1984 by the Massachusetts Institute of Technology. Reprinted by permission of The MIT Press.

[1] The Platonist conception of language outlined here is developed more fully in Katz, *Languages and Other Abstract Objects*, Rowman and Littlefield, Totowa, 1981.

[2] W. V. O. Quine, *From a Logical Point of View*, Harper & Row, New York, 1953, p. 47.

mistaken. In this paper I will try to show why, and present the answer I think correct.

All scientific concepts that have significantly shaped their field seem obvious for some time after. It is well to recall that this is even true of concepts that are then superseded. Einstein once wrote:

> Concepts that have proved useful for ordering things easily assume so great an authority over us that we forget their terrestrial origin and accept them as unalterable facts. They then become labelled as 'conceptual necessities'. The road of scientific progress is frequently blocked for long periods by such errors. It is therefore not just an idle game to exercise our ability to analyse familiar concepts, and to demonstrate the conditions on which their justification and usefulness depend.[3]

The concept of grammars as psychological theories had a central place in the thinking that brought about the Chomskyan revolution in linguistics. This concept was an enormous improvement over American structuralism's concept of grammars as theories of disturbances in the air produced in speaking. Chomsky demonstrated that the psychologistic concept has impressive advantages over its predecessor in leading to more comprehensive, abstract, and precise theories of natural languages. After the revolution, as the psychological concept of grammars was handed down to new generations of linguists, this one revolutionary doctrine attained the obviousness of orthodoxy.

The absence of an alternative to the psychological concept was another significant factor responsible for its seeming obvious. The discredited structuralist concept could hardly be expected to make a comeback so soon after being overthrown, and no other concept of what grammars are theories of was available. But the absence of an alternative to the concept of grammars as psychological theories was only a matter of historical accident. Logically, an alternative concept of what grammars are theories of, one that does not take the discredited position of American structuralism, was always around. On this concept, grammars are theories of the structure of sentences, conceived of as abstract objects in the way that Platonists in the philosophy of mathematics conceive of numbers. Sentences, on this view, are not taken to be located here or there in physical space like sound waves or deposits of ink, and they are not taken to occur either at one time or another or in one subjectivity or another in the manner of mental events and states. Rather, sentences are taken to be abstract and objective. They

[3] G. Holton, *Thematic Origins of Scientific Thought*, Harvard University Press, Cambridge, Mass., 1973, p. 5.

are entities whose structure we discover by intuition and reason, not by perception and induction.

Given the possibility of a Platonist position, the situation at this point is as follows. Chomsky's choice of a psychological concept with which to replace the physical concept of the structuralists may have been the only reasonable choice in the circumstances, but there is nothing necessary about this choice. Platonism exists as a real, if undeveloped, alternative. Whatever defects Platonism may have, they are surely not those that made the structuralist's concept of grammars subject to Chomsky's criticisms. The structuralist concept of grammars as theories of sound waves and marks represents grammars as insufficiently abstract to account adequately for the grammatical properties and relations of sentences in natural languages.[4] Since the Platonist concept allows grammars a maximum of abstractness, Platonism cannot be faulted on the same grounds as the structuralist concept. New and independent reasons have to be found if a psychological concept is to be justified.

While Chomsky launched his attack on American structuralism and developed his new theory of generative grammar with its psychological ontology, he showed no sign of recognizing the necessity for such further justification. Recently, however, under the prompting of Montague grammarians,[5] Chomsky[6] has presented an argument against the possibility of a Platonist alternative. He claims that a theory of universal grammar in such a purely mathematical sense—one that 'attempts to capture those properties of language that are logically or conceptually necessary'—is merely 'an inquiry into the concept "language"', and that such an enterprise is 'unlikely to prove more interesting than an inquiry into the concept "vision" or "locomotion".'[7]

Is this argument good enough to provide a reason for rejecting not specifically the approach of Montague grammarians but any approach on which linguistics is a branch of mathematics? The argument has a defect that makes it useless against Platonism generally: there is no reason to restrict the Platonist approach to the study of the concept 'language' in Chomsky's narrow sense. There are *two notions* of 'concept of'. On the one that figures in Chomsky's formulation of the

    [4] N. Chomsky, *The Logical Structure of Linguistic Theory*, Plenum Press, New York, 1975, pp. 30-3.

    [5] R. Montague, *Formal Philosophy*, Yale University Press, New Haven, Conn., 1974, pp. 1-69.

    [6] N. Chomsky, *Rules and Representations*, Columbia University Press, New York, 1980, 29-30.

    [7] Ibid., pp. 29-30.

Platonist position, 'concept of' means 'lexical definition of'. Thus, the concept of 'vision' is something like 'the power to form mental images of objects of sight', and the concept of 'locomotion' is something like 'movement from place to place'. On this sense of 'concept of', what Chomsky says about the triviality of the view that linguistics is realist mathematics is certainly true, but use of this sense of 'concept of' in his formulation of the Platonist position is surely unfair, because Platonists would not use it in their formulation. On its other sense, which is the one that I, and I expect other Platonists, would use in the formulation of the Platonist position 'concept of' means 'concept of the nature of the thing itself.'[8] Here one is referring to the thing rather than the meaning of the word that names it. An inquiry into the concept of vision, locomotion, number, language, or natural language in *this* sense is no trivial matter of everyday lexicography, but a highly interesting theoretical enterprise. Granted that, on the Platonist view, the enterprise will not be empirical, still—judging just on intellectual interest, which is the basis of Chomsky's argument—this ought not matter in the slightest. Pure mathematics is surely not devoid of intellectual interest. The interest of an inquiry into the structure of the sentences of a language and into the invariants of all languages comes from the richness of structure revealed by the principles that account for the structure of the sentences, in the one case, and the invariants in the other. Chomsky's arguments, although successful against the Platonist position he sets up, fail against real Platonism.

A recent set of criticisms of Platonism by Fodor elaborates on this theme of Chomsky's that Platonism is uninteresting. Fodor writes: 'The only thing against Platonism, so construed, is that, deep down, nobody is remotely interested in it.'[9] On one way of taking Fodor's remarks, he is simply saying: 'Go ahead, be a Platonist if you like. But the action is all at the other end of the town.'[10]

If this is the claim, the reply is straightforward. The issue of what a grammar is a theory of, or what linguistics is about, does not turn on what Fodor or anyone else thinks is interesting. It turns on the ontological status of languages. Even if everyone were to share Fodor's relish for the science of psychology and exhibit the same disinterest in the

---

[8] This is the distinction between narrow and broad concepts in J. J. Katz, *Semantic Theory*. Harper & Row, New York, 1972, pp. 450–62.

[9] J. A. Fodor, 'Some Notes on What Linguistics is About', in *Readings in Philosophy of Psychology*, ed. N. Block, Harvard University Press, Cambridge, Mass., 1981, p. 159. [Reprinted as Essay 7 in the present volume. Page references are to the present volume.]   [10] Ibid., p. 160.

question of whether linguistics is mathematics or psychology, this would not make the question itself any the less a question, any the less interesting inherently, or any the less linguistically or philosophically important. Disinterest in mathematics itself coupled with a widespread craze for the psychology of human mathematical ability would have not the slightest bearing on the issue of what mathematical theories are theories of, or what mathematics is about, or whether Gödel's Platonism is important.

There is, however, another way of taking Fodor's remarks. This way results from the manner in which he construes Platonism. On this way, he is quite right about nobody being interested, and would have been right had he gone further to claim that nobody ought to be. But the Platonism that he is right about is only Platonism as Fodor-construes-it, which has no serious relation to Platonism as actually held.

Fodor's misconstrual of Platonism begins when he says that the position I call Platonism is unassailable in the unflattering sense that it says that anything goes in linguistics. He writes: 'What [Katz] thinks is that linguistics is part of mathematics, and (I suppose) in mathematics you can stipulate whenever you are so inclined.'[11] This is, in the first place, a bizarre view of mathematics. Try stipulating your way out of trouble when you are caught dividing by zero or stipulating your way into a complete and consistent formalization of arithmetic.

It is also a bizarre view of the philosophy of mathematics. While it may be that Wittgenstein[12] and the logical empiricists hold something like the view of mathematics that Fodor has in mind, Platonists don't. Ascribing this view to Platonists is like ascribing the verifiability principle to metaphysicians. Those in the philosophy of mathematics who advanced this conventionalist view introduced stipulation in the hope of thereby obviating the Platonist view. Platonists in the philosophy of mathematics have no need for stipulation in their account of the nature of mathematics, since they hold that numbers and systems of numbers are part of what is real and that mathematical truth is correspondence between mathematical statements and these abstract objects. Platonists in the philosophy of linguistics likewise have no need for stipulation, since they hold that sentences and systems of sentences (languages) are part of what is real and that truth in linguistics is correspondence between linguistic statements and these abstract objects. On the Platonist account, mathematicians and linguists neither

[11] Fodor, op. cit., p. 158.
[12] L. Wittgenstein, *Wittgenstein's Lectures on the Foundations of Mathematics*, ed. E. Diamond, Harvester Press, Hassocks, 1976.

invent such objects, nor stipulate truths about them; mathematicians and linguists merely discover and describe them.

Fodor says

there is no particular reason why, in choosing a domain for his theory, the Platonist needs to attend to those of the speaker/hearer's capacities that are left when you eliminate contamination from memory limitations and the like. In principle, he might just as well attend to the construction of grammars that predict only intuitions about sentences with more than seven vowels, or sentences whose twelfth word is 'grandmother', or sentences that happen to be uttered on Tuesday. Once you start to stipulate, it's Liberty Hall.[13]

Fodor *assumes* that there is some compelling reason why linguists ought to give their professional attention to competence and that it is to the discredit of Platonism that it does not endorse this reason. But this assumption is just what is at issue! Platonists in linguistics deny that such a reason exists—just as Platonists in mathematics deny that mathematicians ought to give their professional attention to human arithmetic capacities. Platonists contend that grammars are theories of abstract objects (sentences, languages). Hence, the implication that it is to the discredit of Platonists that they do not endorse the view that the linguist *qua* linguist ought to pay special attention to the 'speaker/hearer's capacities' begs the question. It can no more be to the discredit of Platonism that it doesn't pay attention to psychological capacities than it can be to the discredit of Fodor's psychologism that it doesn't pay attention to abstract objects.

Fodor equates Platonism with absolute freedom of choice in what can be studied in linguistics, which is almost true, but he suggests that adopting Platonism will inaugurate an era of licentiousness in linguistics, which is false. First, since Platonists constrain the choice of what can be studied in linguistics only in the minimal way that they constrain the choice of what can be studied in mathematics, any possible language *may* be taken as an object of study in linguistics, just as any possible system of numbers *may* be taken as an object of study in mathematics. This rules out the counterparts of systems with division by zero but leaves quite a lot. This seems to be a worrying prospect for some, but it is not clear why. It does not impose any priority on what is studied when or any restriction on how much. It does not preclude the linguist from emphasizing the study of natural languages any more

---

[13] Fodor, op. cit., p. 158. Note Fodor's equivocation on 'truth' in saying 'the Platonist has no use for distinguishing truth' (p. 159) and then saying '[the psycholinguist] cares about empirical truth' (p. 159). Being indifferent to empirical truth is not the same as being indifferent to truth.

than it has precluded mathematicians from emphasizing the study of natural numbers. Moreover, given that things that look at one time to be not worth study often turn out to be highly important in unexpected ways, one would have thought that freedom of the kind Platonism offers is a virtue rather than a vice. Thus, Fodor's idea that there is benefit in limiting the linguist's freedom of inquiry has little to recommend it to those who are not already convinced that linguistics is a psychological science.

Second, Fodor's insistence on restricting the domain of linguistics to a psychological reality is, in fact, insistence on a policy whose acceptance would, depending on contingent and presently unforeseeable circumstances, *commit* linguists to just the absurd grammars (e.g. ones with sentences whose twelfth word is 'grandmother') that Platonism merely *allows*. For, since it's an empirical question, it could turn out that the mental or neural structures responsible for the 'speaker/hearer's capacities' instantiate grammatical principles that do indeed introduce 'grandmother' into the deep structure of every English sentence (deleting it at various derived syntactic levels). As I shall argue in more detail below, this is merely one of an indefinitely large number of absurd possibilities that linguists let themselves in for in adopting the view that grammars are psychological theories.

The irony is that Fodor should raise the spectre of such absurd grammars when it is *his* position that is haunted by the prospect of embracing them. If the human mind or brain turns out to contain such absurd grammatical structures, Fodor's doctrine about the subject matter of linguistics would force linguists to adopt absurd grammars, and hence it would be Fodor's position that deserves the blame. If the doctrine that linguistics is psychology would saddle linguistics with absurd grammars in a myriad of contingent cases, it ought to be regarded as far less attractive, other things being equal, than a doctrine that runs no such risks.

It should also be mentioned that Fodor is wrong in suggesting that only his view 'defines the goals of linguistics *ex post facto*, in the light of the theories now in the field'. Platonism, too, does this. Theories can be viewed, within the Platonist framework, as explications in the sense of Chomsky:[14] grammars projected from early intuitions are revisable in the light of later intuitions and canons of theory construction; goals are refined, added, and dropped in the process.[15]

It must now be clear that Fodor's claim that 'the Right View [Fodor's

[14] N. Chomsky, *Syntactic Structures*. Mouton & Co. The Hague, Holland, 1957, pp. 13–17.

[15] J. J. Katz, 'The Real Status of Semantic Representations', *Linguistic Inquiry*, 8 (1977), 571–4.

euphemism for his own view] is the right view *so far as we can now make out*[16] is supported solely by arguments that either assume Fodor's view or replace Platonism with Platonism-as-Fodor-construes-it.

One final point. Consider Fodor's comment on the prospect of present (he supposes) psychologically inspired attempts to construct grammars turning out to have been totally on the wrong track:

> In that case, there will be a residual philosophical question whether we ought to say that linguistics was misconstrued by the Right View or that there is no such science as linguistics. I, for one, won't much care.[17]

The 'residual philosophical question' that arises in the event of a theoretical disaster is a facet of the perennial question at issue between conceptualists and Platonists from at least the time of Plato. The question of the ontological status of theories in linguistics is merely a special case of the classical philosophical question.[18] For Platonism is

---

[16] Fodor, op. cit., p. 160.

[17] Ibid., p. 160.

[18] Another example of the failure to appreciate the philosophical nature of the question that linguistic Platonism raises is found in J. Higginbotham, 'Is Grammar Psychological?' in *How Many Questions?*, L. S. Cauman, I. Levi, C. Parsons, and R. Schwartz, eds., Hackett Publishing Co., Indianapolis, 1983, pp. 170–9. Higginbotham is replying explicitly to *Language and Other Abstract Objects*. He accuses it of merely stipulating that linguistics is not psychology (pp. 172–4). What is peculiar about the accusation is that Higgenbotham ignores the argument that the book gives for this thesis, while his own case for the opposite thesis itself rests on nothing more than a stipulation. Higgenbotham says, 'Defense of this thesis Katz appears to take as entirely straightforward, once we distinguish between theories of the domain D and theories of the *knowledge* of D' (p. 172). He seems not to have looked beyond the first section of Chapter III, particularly, the next section of that chapter and Chapters V and VII, which contain the fuller form of the arguments at the end of the present essay.

Higginbotham's stipulation that linguistics is 'an empirical inquiry into the identity of human languages' begins with the quite true statement that 'one may also be interested in questions like (1): For which (S, S') is Jones's language = (S, S'), and why?' (p. 172). This is no more objectionable than saying that one may be interested in questions about the identity of human systems for arithmetic calculation. But then the unobjectionable statement is superseded by a full-blooded stipulation when Higginbotham claims that 'it is only by seeing the consequences of the attribution of such systems [(S, S')] to persons that linguistic theory can be tested' (p. 174). This only makes sense if we assume already that the principles being tested are principles about 'the identity of human languages'. If not, then it is a flat *non sequitur*. Could one sensibly claim against a Platonist in the philosophy of mathematics that it is only by seeing the consequences of the attribution of mathematical theories to person that mathematical theory can be tested? Neither mathematical intuition nor linguistic

an existential claim: it asserts that there are abstract objects. Hence, until the case of linguistics is settled, the classical philosophical question cannot be decided against Platonism. Fodor's 'I, for one, don't care' is the declaration of a philosopher who has hung around psychologists so long that he's gone native.

Chomsky also has taken the position that a Platonist linguistics is not a study of anything. This is because, as he puts it ' "language" is no well-defined concept of linguistic science.'[19] Chomsky's grounds for this position are that no clear principles have yet been formulated to distinguish languages from one another. But this is no support for his claim about Platonist linguistics. The absence of clear principles distinguishing virtue and vice is not grounds for abandoning ethics, but only reason to make more of an effort to define such principles. Indeed, conceptualist linguistics has yet to provide us with clear principles to distinguish linguistically relevant mental states from linguistically irrelevant ones. This, however, does not lead Chomsky to say that conceptualist linguistics is not about anything. Surely, Chomsky would take the position that specifying the linguistically relevant states (competence) is not something we can expect to have handed to us at the outset, but something that our inquiry aims at achieving in the long run. But, then, the same thing can be said about specifying languages.

The arguments of conceptualists against Platonism in linguistics have little force. If Platonism in its turn can mount a successful argument against the psychological concept of grammars, then, coupling this argument with Chomsky's argument against the structuralist concept, we obtain a strong case for the Platonist view that grammars are theories of abstract objects. The reason is that nominalism, conceptualism, and Platonism exhaust the ontological possibilities. One can take the objects of a theory to be concrete, physical particulars,

intuition presuppose that mathematical or linguistic theories are attributable to people in the sense required for claiming that linguistics is empirical. (See *Language and Other Abstract Objects*, Chapter VI.)

The confusion that runs through Higgenbotham's reply is between the sense of abstractness in which we speak of the objects in an empirical idealization being reached by abstracting away from certain aspects of real situations and the sense of abstractness in which Platonists speak of abstract objects. The former depends on empirical reality while the latter does not. Here, I think, is the reason for the failure to appreciate the nature of the question that the linguistic Platonist is raising: confusing these two notions of abstractness makes Higgenbotham and others think that they can do justice to the Platonist's stress on the abstractness of linguistic theories while still maintaining that linguistic theories are empirical.

[19] Chomsky, *Rules and Representations*, p. 217.

as the nominalist does, or take them to be psychological, mental, or biological particulars, as the conceptualist does, or deny they are particulars at all and take them to be atemporal, aspatial objective entities, as the Platonist does.

We might dwell for a moment on the special interest of our question for the disciplines concerned: linguistics, philosophy, psychology, and computer science. In linguistics, the question 'What is a grammar a theory of?' is pivotal. Any answer to this question is also an answer to others:

'What is linguistic theory a theory of?'
'What kind of science is linguistics?'
'What is a natural language?'
'What sort of object is a sentence?'
'What is the object of study in linguistics, and what are proper methods for studying it?'

If it can be shown that theories of natural languages are about abstract objects, then linguistic theory, being about natural languages collectively, is also about abstract objects, linguistics is a mathematical science, and its objects of study, sentences, are abstract objects.

Even practically minded linguists will have to face the fact that ontological questions are relevant to decisions they have to make between grammars and linguistic theories. I give two examples of how the ontological issue bears on the concerns of a working linguist. The first illustration comes from the controversy between Chomsky[20] and Postal[21] over whether Chomsky's Extended Standard Theory or Postal's version of Generative Semantics is 'the best theory'. The controversy is slightly dated, since Chomsky has moved on to his Revised Extended Standard Theory and Postal to his and Johnson's Arc-Pair Grammar, but it is a well-known controversy and the underlying issues are anything but resolved.

Postal argued that Generative Semantics, at least in his version, is the best theory because, in stating grammatical rules in the form of derivational constraints, it provides a completely 'homogeneous' statement of them. Postal argued that a more homogeneous grammar is preferable on standard methodological grounds in science (Occam's razor) because, in requiring less apparatus to explain the same facts,

[20] N. Chomsky, 'Some Empirical Issues in the Theory of Transformational Grammar', in *Goals of Linguistic Theory*, ed. S. Peters, Prentice-Hall, Inc., Englewood Cliffs, 1972, pp. 63–130. N. Chomsky, 'Chomsky' in *Discussing Language*, ed. H. Parret, Mouton & Co., The Hague, Holland, 1974, pp. 47–9.
[21] P. Postal, 'The Best Theory', in Peters, ed., op. cit., pp. 131–70.

it is a more parsimonious account. Chomsky replied that Postal might be right if the issue were as simple as Postal assumes. But Chomsky argued that the issue is not merely a matter of parsimony. Chomsky saw the issue as going beyond the question of whether a linguistic theory makes descriptively adequate grammars available for each language. From Chomsky's viewpoint, the issue also encompasses the question of selecting descriptively adequate grammars on the basis of primary linguistic data. Given that a linguistic theory concerns how a speaker acquires grammatical competence, Chomsky is correct in claiming that

the matter is considerably more complex. Given two theories T and T′, we will be concerned not merely with their simplicity or homogeneity, but also with their *restrictiveness*. If T and T′ both meet the condition of descriptive adequacy but T permits only a proper subset of the grammars permitted by T′, then we may well prefer T to T′ even if it is more complex, less homogeneous. Postal regards it as obvious that we would prefer T′ to T in this case, but this conclusion is plainly false in general, if our concern extends to explanatory adequacy.[22]

This is a big 'if'. Linguistic theory concerns questions of explanatory adequacy in Chomsky's technical sense only if Chomsky is correct that a linguistic theory is a psychological theory about the initial competence of a human language learner. Only then is restrictiveness relevant. Faced with the fact that a child learns an extremely complex and abstract system of rules rapidly, under difficult stimulus conditions and with little variation with respect to intelligence, it seems plausible, other things being equal, to prefer the theory that represents the child's choice as a selection from the narrowest set of possible grammars. Such a maximally restrictive theory best fits the facts of language acquisition as we know them. But if Chomsky's assumption about the psychological character of linguistic theory is incorrect, Chomsky's reply to Postal collapses.

Here is where Platonism bears directly on the concerns of the working linguist: it denies that linguistic theory is a psychological theory of the competence underlying human language learning. On the Platonist view, linguistic theory is no more than a theory of the common structure of the sentences in all natural languages,[23] and so an argument that we ought to severely restrict the class of grammars from which the child selects would belong to psychology rather than linguistics. Therefore,

---

[22] Chomsky, 'Chomsky', p. 48.
[23] This neglects the Platonist's conception of what the essence of language is, but the omission does not affect the argument in the text. See Katz, *Language and Other Abstract Objects*, pp. 221–40.

if Platonism can be shown to be preferable to conceptualism, Chomsky cannot claim that the issue between Postal and himself goes beyond the question of whether linguistic theory makes descriptively adequate grammars available for each language. Thus, even on Chomsky's account on the matter, Postal is right in preferring the most homogeneous theory. In short, Postal can exploit Platonism to claim that, although Chomsky's more restrictive theory may be better psychology, his less restrictive but more parsimonious theory is better linguistics.

The second illustration of the relevance of the ontological issue to the working linguist is more up-to-date. Langendoen and Postal[24] have recently argued that, if Platonism offers the best answer to what is a grammar a theory of, then every theory of grammar in which grammars have the form of constructive systems is wrong.

Langendoen and Postal argue that, ontological considerations to one side, there is no basis for imposing any size constraint on the sentences of natural languages and, as a consequence, the existence in natural languages of unbounded co-ordination subject to a natural closure principle entails that their sentences are more numerous than countable infinity. The argument against imposing any size constraint is a generalization of an argument showing that the sentences of a natural language cannot form a finite set as some linguists once claimed in connection with, for example, *very* long sentences and multiple center-embedded sentences.[25] The argument was that, for any upper limit on sentence length, there are strings exceeding the limit whose syntactic structure is exactly the same as strings that do not exceed the upper limit and these longer strings must *ipso facto* count as grammatical, since grammaticality is a matter of well-formed syntactic structure. No finite number of morphemes can determine that a string is too long to be a grammatical sentence. Langendoen and Postal generalize this argument by showing that nothing changes when the issue changes to strings of *any* size that exemplify a well-formed syntactic structure.

A linguist who wishes to resist Langendoen and Postal's argument might try to show that considerations outside of pure grammatical theory provide a basis for drawing the line to exclude non-finite sentences. Here the appeal might either be to nominalist scruples or to conceptualist ones. That is, either it is claimed that non-finite strings cannot be grammatical sentences because they cannot be realized

[24] D. T. Langendoen and P. M. Postal, *The Vastness of Natural Languages*, Basil Blackwell, Oxford, 1984.

[25] J. J. Katz, *The Philosophy of Language*, Harper & Row, New York, 1966, p. 122.

physically or because they cannot be generated even by the ideal speaker/hearer. But if Platonism can be shown to provide a better account of what grammars are theories of than either nominalism or conceptualism, then neither of these responses to Langendoen and Postal's argument is possible, and their conclusion about the non-constructiveness of grammars seems to go through. Their result would challenge Hockett's Finite Grammar, finite state grammars, Gazdar's Phase Structure Grammar, Bresnan's Lexical/Functional Grammar, Brame's Realistic Grammar, Lamb's Stratificational Grammar, Tagmemics, Partee and Dowty's form of Montague Grammar, Bartsch and Vennemann's Natural Generative Grammar, Chafe's Semantically Based Grammar, Dik's Functional Grammar, Daughter Dependency Grammar, Keenan's Phrasal Core Grammar, Chomsky's Generative Transformation Grammar, Kac's Corepresentational Grammar, Johnson's Relationally Based Grammar, Hays's Dependency Grammar, Lambek's Categorial Grammar, Lakoff and Thompson's Cognitive Grammar, Zellig Harris's Abstract Grammar, Langendoen's Neostructural Grammar, Woods's Augmented Transition Network Grammar, Joshi's String Adjunct Grammar, and Sanders's Equational Grammar.

The interest of our question for philosophers is straightforward. The realist's claim that there are abstract objects is the existential claim that there is at least one special science whose theories are about such objects. Thus, if it can be shown, as I shall argue here, that theories in the special science of linguistics are theories about abstract objects, then—given standard views of ontological commitment—quantifying over abstract objects in the pursuit of true theories in linguistics *ipso facto* commits one to the existence of such objects. Therefore, our question about grammars is relevant to the traditional philosophical controversy about universals: an answer showing that grammars are theories about abstract objects provides a basis for Platonic realism in ontology.

The interest of our question for psychologists and AI scientists has to do with the desirability of a clear-cut division of labour among the several disciplines that in one way or another concern themselves with language. I think many unfortunate quarrels are a consequence of confusion about where the line should be drawn between linguistics and cognitive science. I also think that this confusion exists largely because of a widespread acceptance of the view that linguistics is a branch of psychology. If, as the Platonist view of linguistics claims, linguistics is rather a branch of mathematics, as different from psychology of language as number theory is from the psychology of arithmetic reasoning, there is a clear boundary between linguistics and psychology that, one may reasonably expect, will provide as clear-cut a division of labour here as exists between mathematics and the psychology of mathematical reasoning.

Let me illustrate how a conception of linguistics as psychology gives rise to such boundary problems. Given this conception, the only thing to separate the linguist's task from that of psychological scientists is the distinction between competence and performance. But competence, as Chomsky has stressed, is a component of performance; it is the knowledge of the language applied in the use of language. 'A theory of performance (production or perception)', Chomsky writes, 'will have to incorporate the theory of competence—the generative grammar of a language—as an essential part'.[26] But, as psychologists and computer scientists have observed, it has hardly been proved beyond all reasonable doubt that the performance system underlying production and comprehension operates on linguistic knowledge *in the form it takes in grammars written in linguistics*. It might even be, as some claim, that no component in the performance system is modelled by standard transformational grammars. This is the line taken by Winograd[27] and by Wanner and Maratsos.[28] Dresher and Hornstein[29] accept the terms of the argument but respond that all that has been shown is that one account of the performance system is not constructed to incorporate the theory of transformational English syntax. Both ideas have enough of a point to keep the disputes going.[30] The anti-transformationalist side can press their point by claiming that the account in question is not just any account but the best account of the processing underlying production and comprehension. The transformational side can press theirs by producing internal evidence from grammatical intuitions to support the theory of transformational English syntax. Considering the strength of the evidence on each side, how different in nature such evidence is, how committed each side is to its

[26] N. Chomsky, 'The Formal Nature of Language', in *Biological Foundations of Language*, ed. E. Lenneberg, Wiley, New York, 1967, pp. 435–6.

[27] T. Winograd, *Understanding Natural Language*, Academic Press, New York, 1972.

[28] E. Wanner and M. Maratsos, 'An Augmented Transition Network Model of Relative Clause Comprehension', Harvard University Press, Cambridge, Mass., (unpublished manuscript).

[29] B. E. Dresher and N. Hornstein, 'On Some Supposed Contributions of Artificial Intelligence to the Scientific Study of Language', *Cognition*, 4 (1967), 321–98.

[30] An overview of this debate is found in V. V. Valian, 'The Wherefores and Therefores of the Competence–Performance Distinction', in *Sentence Processing*, eds. W. E. Cooper and E. Walker, Lawrence Erlbaum Associates, Hillsdale, 1979, pp. 17–19.

position, and how much weight each side puts on its own evidence, this controversy promises to go on interminably.

But why accept the terms of the argument? That is, why accept that grammars in linguistics, written as theories to explain evidence about the grammatical structure of sentences, are theories of the knowledge that underlies the speaker's use of the language? The only reason is that conceptualism says grammars are psychological theories. Thus, if Platonism is right in positing that grammars are not psychological theories, the two sides on this issue have been talking at cross purposes. Each side can be right and the issue dissolves. Therefore, for psychology AI, and the related cognitive sciences, the question of what a grammar is a theory of is important because its answer can resolve troublesome issues about where the linguist's work ends and the cognitive scientist's begins. A Platonist answer to this question would clearly divide linguistics and cognitive sciences so that the wasteful and unnecessary quarrels of the past can be put behind us.[31]

The major developments in linguistics over the last thirty or forty years have been concerned in large part with the question of what a grammar is a theory of. The most significant event of this period, the Chomskyan revolution, was basically a new answer to this question. The dominant view before this revolution was American structuralism. Under the influence of a neopositivist picture of science, it espoused a straightforward form of nominalism for linguistics.[32] The idea, as Bloomfield stresses in many places, is that a grammar is a theory of the physical disturbances in the air resulting from articulatory movements (secondarily, deposits of graphite, ink, etc.). Bloomfield wrote in one place, 'Non-linguists (unless they happen to be physicalists) constantly forget that a speaker is making noise, and credit him, instead with the possession of impalpable "ideas". It remains for linguists to show, in detail, that the speaker has no "ideas" and that the noise is sufficient'.[33] Linguists collect recordings or descriptions of such acoustic phenomena and classify distributional regularities in them. Taxonomic grammar was the structuralist theory of the proper type of classification of such regularities. The theory imposed constraints

---

[31] An attempt to exhibit the relevance of Platonism for language acquisition can be found in T. G. Bever, 'Some Implications of the Non-specific Basis of Languages', in *Language Acquisition State of the Art*, eds. L. Gleitman and E. Wanner, Cambridge University Press, Cambridge, 1982, pp. 429–49.

[32] L. Bloomfield, 'Linguistic Aspects of Science', in *International Encyclopedia of Unified Science*, 1, eds. O. Neurath, R. Carnap, and C. Morris, The University of Chicago Press, Chicago, 1938, pp. 219–32.

[33] L. Bloomfield, 'Languages or Ideas?' *Language*, 12 (1936), 93. [Reprinted as Essay 1 in the present volume.]

on grammatical description to ensure that there would be no back-sliding into mentalistic concepts or other concepts not reducible to constructions out of a material corpus.

The main thrust and most important consequence of Chomsky's revolution was to replace this nominalist scheme for interpreting grammars with a conceptualist scheme based on the idea that grammars are theories of competence—the idealized speaker/hearer's knowledge of the language. Chomsky's idea that grammars are theories of competence makes the object of study in grammar an idealized mental state; hence the nominalist view of the structuralists was replaced with the conceptualist view that grammars are psychological theories.

Popular culture has it that the Chomskyan revolution introduced transformational grammar into linguistics. However, although Chomsky convinced linguists of its superiority over phrase structure grammar, transformational grammar was invented by Zellig Harris[34] well before the Chomskyan revolution. Chomsky himself made this clear in his first paper on the transformational approach to syntax. He states that this approach

developed directly out of the attempts of Z. S. Harris to extend methods of linguistic analysis to the analysis of the structure of discourse. This research brought to light a serious inadequacy of modern linguistic theory, namely, its inability to account for such systematic relations between sentences as the active-passive relation. There had been no attempt in modern linguistics to reconstruct more precisely this chapter of traditional grammar, partly, perhaps, because it was thought that these relations were of a purely semantic character, hence outside the concern of formal, structural linguistics. This view was challenged by Harris, who has since devoted a good deal of research to showing that distributional methods of linguistic analysis can be broadened and developed in such a way as to include, in a rather natural manner, the study of formal relations between sentences, and that this extension yields much additional insight into linguistic structure.[35]

Transformational rules, on Harris's version of the theory, were a way of describing distributional regularities at the sentence level. Harris wrote:

Given a number of sentences in a kernel form, which have among them a particular acceptability ordering or differentiation . . . all

---

[34] Z. Harris, 'Discourse Analysis', *Language*, 28 (1952), 1–30.
[35] N. Chomsky, 'A Transformational Approach to Syntax', in *Proceedings of the Third Texas Conference on Problems of Linguistic Analysis in English, 1958*, ed. A. A. Hill, The University of Texas Press, Austin, Texas, 1962, pp. 124–58.

successions of transformations which are permitted, by the definition of their argument will produce sentences to preserve the same acceptability ordering. . . . If a sequence of words is not decomposable by transformation into one or more kernel sentences . . . then that sequence is ungrammatical. If it is so decomposable, then it has a certain kind and degree of acceptability as a sentence, which is some kind of reasonable sum of the acceptabilities of the component kernel sentences and the acceptability effects of the transformations that figure in the decomposition.[36]

The nominalist interpretation of transformational theory as an account of the distribution regularities that determine acceptability orderings greatly restricts the degree of abstractness with which grammatical transformations can be stated. Chomsky showed how Harris's transformational theory could be significantly improved if the formal theory of transformational structure is stripped of its nominalist interpretation and refitted with a conceptualist interpretation on which the theory represents the internalized tacit principles constituting a speaker's competence. By separating transformational theory from its nominalistic interpretation, Chomsky could make the theory abstract enough to overcome a wide range of explanatory problems that are essentially unsolvable within the structuralist framework.[37]

Except for the differences due to its generative form, Chomsky's early transformational theory is essentially the same mathematical theory of sentence structure as Harris's, only under a radically different ontological interpretation. Thus, the comparison of Harris's transformational theory with Chomsky's is of special interest here because it can give us a picture of how a formal mathematical theory of grammatical structure can be stripped of one ontological interpretation and refitted with another without its account of grammatical structure undergoing fundamental change. Such a picture will be useful to us in showing how the conceptualist interpretation of theories in current linguistics can be stripped off and replaced with a Platonist interpretation. Such a picture also enables us to see the Platonist proposal as in a direct line of development with earlier nominalist and conceptualist stages in American linguistics. The picture will enable us to construct

[36] Z. Harris, 'Transformational Theory', *Language*, 41: 3 (1965), 363–401. Reprinted in *Papers in Structural and Transformational Grammar*, D. Reidel Publishing Co., Dordrecht, Holland, 1970, p. 555.

[37] For further discussion, see Katz, *Language and Other Abstract Objects* (pp. 21–44), and also the earlier discussion in J. J. Katz and T. G. Bever, 'The Fall and Rise of Empiricism', in *An Integrated Theory of Linguistic Descriptions*, eds. T. G. Bever, J. J. Katz, and D. T. Langendoen, T. Y. Crowell, New York, 1976, pp. 11–64.

the argument in favour of replacing the conceptualist interpretive scheme with a Platonist one as a special case of a pattern of argument appropriate to determining the proper ontological interpretation for theories in a special science. Finally, it will enable us to see that, since the basic theory of sentence structure is preserved throughout changes of interpretation, accepting the argument for the new interpretive scheme sacrifices nothing essential in the theory of sentence structure.

Let me flesh out the claim that Harris's transformational theory is, in all essential respects, the same theory as the early version of Chomsky's transformational theory of syntactic competence. The parallels I shall draw clearly show that we have here the same formal theory of transformational structure which, from the different onto-logical perspectives of Harris and Chomsky, says different things about the nature of language. The version of Harris's theory in question is that in 'Discourse Analysis'[34] and 'Co-occurrence and Transformation in Linguistic Structure'.[38] The version of Chomsky's theory in question is that in *Syntactic Structures*[14] and 'A Transformational Approach to Syntax'.[35]

The principal parallels between Chomsky's theory and Harris's are these. First, both theories draw a fundamental distinction between *kernel* or *underlying sentence structures*, which serve as the base for the application of transformational rules, and the *derived sentence structures*, which constitute a transformational level superimposed on this base. Second, both theories use the same notion of 'transformational rule': a structure-dependent mapping of abstract representations of phrase structure on to abstract representations of phrase structure. True, Harris's transformational rules are less abstract, and even at that, their abstractness was an embarrassment to his structuralist principles; but structuralists have long been accustomed to invoking instrumentalist philosophy of science to explain away their embarrassing use of abstraction.[39]

Third, both theories classify transformational rules into *singulary transformations*, which take a single representation of phrase structure into a single representation of phrase structure and *generalized trans-fomations*, which take two or more representations of phrase structure, into a representation of compound phrase structure. Fourth, both

---

[38] Z. Harris, 'Co-occurrence and Transformation in Linguistic Structure', *Language*, 33 (1957), 283–340.

[39] Bloomfield saw the practical need to order grammatical rules, but such ordering was an embarrassment since ordering is too abstract to be *in* the corpus. Hence he claims that it is mere fiction. See L. Bloomfield, *Language*, Henry Holt & Co., New York, 1933, p. 213.

theories treat grammatical transformations as constructions out of *elementary transformations*, such formal operations on strings as deletion, permutation, copying, substitution for dummy elements, and insertion.

Fifth, in both theories, the transformational level is the place at which the variety of sentence types found in the language is introduced and also the place at which the indefinitely great syntactic complexity within sentences of a given type is produced. Sixth, even the particular types of transformations are largely the same. Harris had worked out, in the domain of singularies, the passive transformation, various question transformations, negation transformations, ellipsis (zeroing), and so on, and in the domain of the generalized transformations, the co-ordinating or conjunctive transformations, relative clause transformations, nominalization transformations, and so on.

Seventh, Harris's theory also takes the kernel or underlying level to be the place at which co-occurrence restrictions are stated, and transformations to be structure-preserving mappings. Thus, both theories enable the grammar to state such restrictions in the simplest way by putting them at the earliest point and having subsequent rules preserve structures that meet them. Finally, Harris's theory also contains ordering restrictions on the application of transformations in derivations, thus providing a form of the distinction between *obligatory* and *optional* rules.

Now, although there is this strong parallelism between Harris's formal theory of transformations and Chomsky's, Harris interpreted his formal theory as a device for predicting the relative acceptability of utterances. As a consequence, for Harris there is no sharp line between well-formed and ill-formed sentences, just a gradient of acceptability, determined distributionally. Furthermore, for him the generative capacity of grammatical rules has absolutely no psychological significance. Harris wrote:

Even when our structure can predict new utterances, we do not know that it always reflects a previously existing neural association in the speakers (different from the associations which do not, at a given time, produce new utterances). For example, before the word *analyticity* came to be used (in modern logic), our data on English may have contained *analytic, synthetic, periodic, periodicity, simplicity*, etc. On this basis, we would have made some statement about the distributional relation of -*ic* to -*ity*, and the new formation of *analyticity* may have conformed to this statement. But this means only that the pattern or habit existed in the speakers at the time of the new formation, not necessarily before: the 'habit'—the readiness to combine these elements productively—may have developed only when the need arose, by association of words that were partially similar as to composition and environment. . . . Aside from this, all we know about any particular language habit is the probability that new formations will be along certain lines rather than others, and this is no more than testing the success of our distributional structure in predicting new data or formulations.[40]

The contrast between nominalist and conceptualist interpretations of the same transformational theory is nowhere more striking than in the comparison between this remarkable claim of Harris's and the opposite claim that Chomsky made on behalf of generative capacity, namely, that the creative aspect of language use is *the* proof that speakers of a language have enduring neural structures that contain an infinite number of sentences in their generative potential. Chomsky stressed that

The normal use of language is innovative, in the sense that much of what we say in the course of normal language use is entirely new, not a repetition of anything that we have heard before and not even similar in pattern. . . . The number of sentences in one's native language that one will immediately understand with no feeling of difficulty or strangeness is astronomical.[41]

Indeed, Chomsky held that the

inadequacy of traditional grammars is [that] although it was well understood that linguistic processes are in some sense 'creative', the technical devices for expressing a system of recursive processes were simply not available until more recently. In fact, a real understanding of how a language can (in Humboldt's words) 'make infinite use of finite means' has developed only within the last thirty years. . . . Now that these insights are readily available it is possible to return to the problems that were raised, but not solved, in traditional linguistic theory, and to attempt an explicit formulation of the 'creative' processes of language.[42]

The heart of Chomsky's conceptualism is the idea that these new systems of recursive processes—particularly in their most linguistically sophisticated form, transformational grammar—account for 'the creative aspect of language use' when taken as a theory of the competence

---

[40] Z. Harris, 'Distributional Structure', *Word* (1954), 31. [Reprinted as Essay 2 in the present volume. The page reference is to the present volume.]

[41] N. Chomsky, *Language and Mind*, Harcourt Brace, & World, Inc., New York, 1968, p. 10.

[42] N. Chomsky, *Aspects of the Theory of Syntax*, The MIT Press, Cambridge, Mass., 1965, p. 85. [Pages 3–47 are reprinted as Essay 5 in the present volume. Page references are to the present volume.]

underlying such use. Creativity is formally modelled in the way that recursive rules of a transformational grammar 'make infinite use of finite means'. The understanding of novel sentences is reflected in the grammatical description that such rules assign the infinitely many sentences they generate.

The Chomskyan revolution also eliminated the nominalist interpretation of linguistic theory as a discovery procedure, that is, a procedure for mechanically producing taxonomic grammars when applied to a rich enough corpus, replacing it with a conceptualist interpretation on which linguistic theory is an evaluation procedure for 'selecting a descriptively adequate grammar on the basis of primary linguistic data'.[43] Linguistic theory is now seen as a theory of how children acquire the competence represented in grammars of natural languages.[44] Thus, linguistic theory

offers an explanation for the intuition of the native speaker on the basis of an empirical hypothesis concerning the innate predisposition of the child to develop a certain kind of theory to deal with the evidence presented to him.[45]

I want to argue that the conceptualist interpretation of grammars and linguistic theory should be replaced with an interpretation on which grammars are theories about abstract objects, sentences of a natural language, and linguistic theory is about invariances over all such abstract objects. We should note a few things before beginning this argument. First, although I have referred, and will refer, to Chomsky and to transformational grammar, my focus is *not* Chomsky *per se* and my concern is *not* with transformational grammar *per se*. I realize that Chomsky is far from being the only conceptualist in linguistics at present and that transformational grammar is far from being the choice of linguists everywhere. Rather, my focus is conceptualism of any stripe, and my concern is with the interpretation of any grammar that can lay claim to being a scientific theory. I have focused on Chomsky and transformational grammar because they have an overwhelming historical and systematic position in the field, but my argument is not restricted to them.

Second, Platonism denies that theories in linguistics are about psychological states, processes, etc., but does not deny the existence of such states, processes, etc., or the legitimacy of their study in psychology, computer science, neurophysiology, etc. The Platonist

---

[43] N. Chomsky, *Aspects of the Theory of Syntax*, p. 104.
[44] Ibid., pp. 97 ff.
[45] Ibid., p. 104.

in linguistics no more denies the existence of linguistic knowledge or the legitimacy of its study in empirical science than the Platonist in mathematics or logic denies the existence of mathematical or logical knowledge or the legitimacy of their study in empirical science. Thus, no one should object to Platonism on the grounds that it prevents us from making use of grammatical theories in the explanation of the human ability to acquire and use languages. The use of these theories in such explanations is like applied mathematics. The issue at hand is whether linguistics concerns a realm of grammatical objects beyond psychology.

Platonism draws a fundamental distinction between the *knowledge* speakers have of their language and the *languages* that speakers have knowledge of.[46] The distinction is simply a special case of the general distinction between knowledge and its object. No one confuses psychological theories of how people make inferences with logical theories of implication, or psychological theories of how people perform arithmetical calculations with mathematical theories of numbers. Yet, in the exactly parallel case of linguistics, conceptualists do not make the distinction, conflating a psychological theory of how people speak and understand speech with a theory of the language itself. Platonism is in part an attempt to be consistent in our treatment of the special sciences by drawing the same distinction between knowledge and its object in the case of linguistics that we draw, as a matter of course, in the parallel cases of logic and mathematics. Platonism claims that the subject-matter of linguistics is, in this sense, independent of psychological sciences—just as the subject-matter of logic and mathematics is independent of the sciences concerned with people's logical and mathematical ability.

The issue between Platonism and conceptualism (and also nominalism) is an a priori issue, and the competing claims of the Platonist and the conceptualist (and the nominalist) are a priori claims. It makes no sense to construe *these* claims as a posteriori claims about empirical matters, in so far as the issue between these ontological claims decides the logically prior question of whether empirical matters are relevant to linguistics at all. How could empirical evidence decide between the claim that a discipline is empirical and the claim that it is not? Because this is an a priori issue, it would make no difference if by some miracle the grammarian's theory of a natural language were to satisfy perfectly the empirical demands on a psychological model of the speaker's linguistic knowledge. Such an extraordinary coincidence would be a stroke of luck for cognitive scientists, whom it would provide with a

---

[46] See Katz, *Language and Other Abstract Objects*, pp. 76–93.

ready-made formal theory to serve as one component of their overall account of cognition; but it would not have the least relevance to the issue of whether the discipline from which the theory was borrowed is or is not a part of psychology. Such a hypothetical coincidence is comparable to the actual coincidence between the extension of 'creature with a kidney' and the extension of 'creature with a heart'. Just as the actual coincidence of the extensions of these expressions is compatible with an a priori, logical difference in their meaning, so the hypothetical coincidence of a grammar and a psychological model of competence is compatible with an a priori, logical difference between the domains of linguistics and psychology.

In its most general form, Chomsky's argument for conceptualism showed that a nominalist scheme for interpreting grammars and linguistic theory puts too low a ceiling on their abstractness for them to qualify as fully adequate by the traditional explanatory standards in the study of grammar. Taxonomic constraints on the admissibility of constructs—imposed to ensure that everything at higher grammatical levels can be reduced back down to the physical events at the lowest—precluded grammatical categories that are required to satisfy even minimal standards of grammatical explanation. Chomsky writes[47] that he tried for over five years to formulate explicit data-cataloguing procedures that, when applied to a corpus, mechanically produce the appropriate sets of phonological, morphological, and syntactic classes, but found it impossible to characterize the inductive step necessary for general phonological, morphological, and syntactic classes. He came to realize that there is no inductive basis on which such classes can be built out of the physical material in the corpus, and that the generality required for defining grammatical classes could be attained only if nominalist constraints were eliminated so that grammars, instead of having to be built up from a corpus, could be, as it were, dropped down from above. Chomsky thus conceived grammars, in analogy to formal deductive systems, as generative systems whose principles and categories are directly postulated. Although 'dropped down from above', grammars can be empirically justified on the basis of whether their predictions about sentences are confirmed by the judgements of fluent speakers.

Two features merit special attention in constructing a parallel argument for Platonism. One is that Chomsky's argument is basically a demonstration that the nominalist constraints ensuring a physical interpretation for taxonomic grammars are responsible for the inadequacy

---

[47] Chomsky, *The Logical Structure of Linguistic Theory*, pp. 30-3.

of these grammars as theories of natural languages. The other feature is that the standard of adequacy Chomsky uses to judge taxonomic grammars is conformity to facts about the sound pattern of sentences, word-formation processes, well-formedness, ambiguity, ellipsis, sentence types, agreement, and so on, as reported in speaker's intuitions.[48] Chomsky can presuppose such a standard because these formal features of sentences determine the domain of grammar.

Now, in the light of this standard, we can identify one direction to look in for an argument against conceptualism in linguistics. Although the psychological constraints that conceptualism imposes on theories in linguistics are tame by comparison with the physical constraints that nominalism imposes, the conceptualist's constraints are not negligible. In requiring conformity to a concrete reality, psychological reality conditions impose constraints of a kind different from the requirement that grammars correctly describe the sound pattern, well-formedness, ambiguity, and other structural features of sentences. Psychological reality conditions in linguistics do not concern the grammatical structure of sentences but concern particulars of subjective experience or human biology. Since conceptualism imposes constraints requiring grammars to reflect some concrete reality, it could, in principle, prevent grammars from achieving the degree of abstraction necessary for satisfying traditional descriptive and explanatory standards.

Thus, with conceptualism, as with nominalism, there is a possibility of conflict between a demand that grammars satisfy an extrinsic, ideologically inspired constraint and the traditional demand that grammars meet intrinsic constraints concerning the successful description and explanation of the grammatical structure. If such conflicts can exist, then linguists cannot adopt extrinsic, psychological constraints. Linguists, like other scientists, must always try to choose the best available theories, and hence cannot adopt an ontological policy that would select worse theories of natural languages over better ones.

These conflicts can arise on a conceptualist metatheory but not on a Platonist one because the latter imposes *no* restriction on the degree of abstraction in grammars. Conceptualists have to construct grammars as theories of the *knowledge* an ideal speaker has of the language, whereas Platonists construct grammars as theories of the *language* that such knowledge is knowledge of. Therefore, the conceptualist's theories address themselves to the *internal cognitive representation* that humans have of such things as well-formedness, ambiguity, word-formation,

---

[48] In *Language and Other Abstract Objects* (pp. 64-73), I develop this observation into a conception of a neutral framework for evaluating competing ontological positions.

ellipsis, and synonomy whereas a theory of the language should address itself to well-formedness, ambiguity, word-formation, ellipsis, and synonymy themselves. Because the mental medium in which human knowledge is internally represented can materially influence the character of the representation, there can be a significant divergence between what a theory of such an internal representation says and what is true of the language. Hence, only in the case of conceptualism is there the possibility of conflicts between ideologically inspired, extrinsic constraints and intrinsic constraints.

I now give a number of such conflicts. The first class of such conflicts contains cases in which the character of human cognitive representation makes the speaker's tacit linguistic knowledge take the form of one rather than another set of strongly equivalent rules. The character of human cognitive representation might make the speaker's tacit linguistic rules take a form differing from other possible forms just in the way that a propositional calculus with only conjunction and negation as primitive connectives differs from an equivalent one with only disjunction and negation. This is surely a possibility. But now conceptualism would have to say that the psychologically real version of these explanatorily equivalent theories is *the* true theory of the language because it is the psychologically real one. This seems obviously wrong: the theories are equally simple, equally adequate from a descriptive and explanatory viewpoint. Since the theories make exactly the same prediction about the grammatical properties and relations of every sentence in the language, they are just different ways of expressing the same claims about the language. Since the theories are equally simple, neither has an edge in how the claims are expressed.[49]

Consider a slightly different case involving notational variants instead of different but strongly equivalent systems. We are now talking about a case in which the character of human cognitive representation causes the speaker's tacit linguistic rules to have a form that differs from other possible forms in only the way that a system of propositional calculus expressed in Polish notations differs from one expressed in *Principia* notation (e.g. 'KCpqCqp' versus 'p ⊃ q · q ⊃ p'). Here

---

[49] Someone might object that it makes a difference what the primitives of a theory are in so far as the primitives express a theory's conception of the fundamental notions in the domain. But the objection begs the question because in the present case such a difference can only be significant from a psychological viewpoint. From a mathematical viewpoint, which sets of notions from equivalent sets is chosen as primitives matters no more than which of the true statements of a deductive system are chose as postulates. Asking which states should rank as postulates, as Quine once said, is 'as meaningless as asking which points in Ohio are starting points', *From a Logical Point of View*, p. 35.

there can be no linguistically relevant difference between the theory that conceptualism prescribes and the theory it forbids. Therefore, if one accepts conceptualism, one could be committed to claiming that, say, a grammatical counterpart to the calculus in Polish notation *is* the true theory of the language and a grammatical counterpart in *Principia* notation is not, even though they are mere notational variants, since the human mind could be constructed in such a way as to represent its grammatical knowledge in the one form rather than in the other. This is comparable to claiming that a Polish notation propositional calculus is preferable *as a theory of propositional logic* to a *Principia* notation propositional calculus when both express the same theory.[50]

Things get even worse. The psychologically preferable theory might not only be on all fours with theories disallowed by conceptualism, but it might even be outright inferior to them on either methodological or explanatory grounds. A methodological difference would exist if, say, the psychologically preferable theory is less parsimonious than some disallowed theories but otherwise the same. It is surely possible that the human mind is so constructed that its representations of grammatical knowledge use more theoretical apparatus than is necessary to formulate the grammatical rules of a language. For example, let us suppose that the grammar of English is transformational and that there are transformations in English, such as the passive or dative movement, in which lexical material is moved from one position to another. Transformations are formulated out of a fixed class of formal operations on strings like deletion, permutation, copying, substitution for dummy elements, etc. One can imagine a grammar of English, Gi, in which some movement transformations are constructed out of an operation of permutation that, as it were, picks up a constituent and puts it somewhere else, whereas other movement transformations are constructed out of an initial operation of copying a constituent into the new position and then an operation of erasing the copied occurrence. We can also imagine another grammar of English, Gj, without permutation, in which all movement is accomplished by copying and deletion, but which is otherwise identical with Gi. Since the effect of permutation can be obtained by a combination of copying and deletion, and both these operations are in both grammars, Gi is less parsimonious because it uses more theoretical apparatus to do a job that can be done with less (with a proper subset of the apparatus in Gi). Hence, by Occam's razor, the preferable scientific theory of the language

---

[50] Given Fodor's claims (Fodor, op. cit., p. 204), he must say here that logicians are "mad" not to prefer Polish logic over *Principia* logic on grounds of truth!

is clearly the more parsimonious grammar, Gj. But it could certainly happen that the child is genetically programmed for knowledge of a language in which formal operations are overdetermined with respect to the construction of movement rules. Accordingly, speakers acquire a competence system corresponding to Gi. Therefore, in the situation in question, conceptualism requires linguistics to prefer the more complicated grammar, Gi, over the simpler but otherwise identical grammar, Gj. Whereas in the preceding case conceptualism would force us to make a completely arbitrary choice among linguistically indistinguishable theories, in the present case it would force us to choose the less scientifically desirable theory over the more scientifically desirable one. Surely, abandoning conceptualism is preferable to committing ourselves to such methodologically perverse choices.

Not only could conceptualism in linguistics force us to make choices that run counter to sound methodological practice in science, but it could force us to choose false theories where true ones are available, and known, and nothing else stands in the way of their acceptance. Let me make the point by way of an analogy. Major calculator companies, such as Texas Instruments and Hewlett-Packard, construct some calculators on the basis of principles that incorrectly determine the values of a function for a range of arguments that, for empirical reasons, can never be inputs to the device. Companies do this because such 'incorrect principles' are either less complicated to build into the device, hence less expensive for the company, or more efficient in on-line computation, hence less costly to the customer. Since computations that produce the incorrect values of the function will never take place, these savings are free and clear. Now, it is plainly absurd to suppose that God, Nature, or Evolution would find it impossible to do what Texas Instruments and Hewlett-Packard can do. Hence we may imagine that, for essentially similar reasons, such heuristic principles have been built into the human brain as internalized competence rules for language processing, that is, as its knowledge of the language. In this best of all possible worlds, we have been provided with a language mechanism that requires less brain utilization and is more efficient in on-line processing. But for all such benefits, and not withstanding the fact that these internalized rules give the correct results for all sentences that can occur in performance, the rules *falsely* predict grammatical facts about sentences that can never occur in performance (because they are, say, too incredibly long or complex). For example, the internalized rules might convert all strings of words above a certain very great length, *n*, into word-salad, so that the best theory of the speaker's competence falsely predicts that strings of English words exceeding length *n* are ungrammatical. Or, the internalized rules might turn out to be nothing but a huge, finite list of *n* sentences, each of which is paired with a structural description. If this is what turns out to be in our heads, a psychologically real grammar must falsely predict that English contains only finitely many sentences, and only *n* of them at that. Given that no acceptable metatheory for grammars ought to allow us to be committed, even contingently, to false theories of natural languages when they are avoidable, it follows that, in committing us to these and indefinitely many further potentially psychologically real but linguistically false grammars of natural languages, conceptualism is unacceptable.

Finally, some grammatical properties of sentences are not explainable in grammars taken as psychological theories. Sentences like (1)-(4) have the property that Kant called 'analytic':

(1) Nightmares are dreams.
(2) People convinced of the truth of Platonism believe Platonism to be true.
(3) Flawed gems are imperfect.
(4) Genuine coin of the realm is not counterfeit.

The meanings of the words in these sentences and their syntactic arrangement guarantee the satisfaction of their truth conditions.[51] Two things are clear. First, analyticity is a semantic property, since it is determined by meaning, and hence it must be accounted for at the semantic level of grammars. Second, analyticity is a species of necessary truth. Sentences (1) through (4) express propositions that are true *no matter what*, unlike the synthetic sentences (5)-(8) which, though in fact true, could be false if circumstances were different:

(5) Nightmares usually take place at night.
(6) Few are convinced of the truth of Platonism.
(7) Flawed gems would be more valuable with less flaws.
(8) Genuine coin of the realm exists.

Theories of natural languages ought not preclude explanation of the grammatical properties of their sentences. At the very least, a theory of natural language ought not rule out the possibility of accounting for necessary truths like (1)-(4) which owe their necessity to the language. But this is exactly what conceptualist theories of natural language do in treating grammars as theories of psychological principles and in treating linguistic theory as a theory of the innate basis for internalizing such principles. Conceptualist theories are limited to

[51] Katz, *Semantic Theory*, pp. 171-200.

accounting for necessary truths like those expressed by (1)–(4) as nothing more than consequences of principles that human beings, by virtue of their psychological or biological make-up, cannot take to be false. Such necessary truths come out on the conceptualist's account as merely what human beings are psychologically or biologically forced to conceive to be true no matter what. But this is a far cry from what *is* true no matter what. On the conceptualist's account, impossible objects like *genuine coin of the realm which is counterfeit* are nothing more than something humans cannot conceive. Conceptualists must treat such *impossible* objects as four-dimensional space was once treated, inconceivable by us but for all we know quite possible.

If we raise the prospect of beings different from us whose psychology makes them take (1)–(4) to be false, the conceptualist must embrace relativism. The conceptualist must say, 'We have our logic, they have theirs.' The Platonist is the only one who can say, as Frege said in a similar connection, 'We have here a hitherto unknown type of madness.'[52] Only Platonism enables us to say that such necessary truths are true no matter what—no matter even if we discover that *human* cognitive apparatus is built to take (1)–(4) to be false.

I have described a number of ways in which theories of the competence underlying human linguistic ability are not abstract enough to be adequate theories of the grammatical structure of a natural language Linguists, like other scientists, are obliged to prefer the best available theory. Thus, linguists cannot adopt a general policy for interpreting their theories that would lead to their preferring worse theories over better ones. Hence, linguists cannot adopt the conceptualist policy.

The psychological view of linguistics has been so prevalent that even the present attempt simply to outline an alternative must consider some of the questions that will undoubtedly arise concerning whether we stand to lose anything valuable in relinquishing conceptualism. One such question is whether, in eliminating constraints on the psychological reality of grammars, we are dropping constraints that we need in order to choose among theories. Pointing to the proliferation of theories in recent linguistics and the trouble linguists have had in obtaining consensus on which theory is closest to the truth, some conceptualists say we ought to welcome the introduction of new constraints that narrow the range of theories, and they will surely complain that, in rejecting psychological constraints, the Platonist

---

[52] G. Frege, *The Basic Laws of Arithmetic*, trans. and ed. G. Furth, University of California Press, Berkeley, California, 1967, p. 14. Also, Katz, *Language and Other Abstract Objects*, pp. 160–73.

is looking a gift horse in the mouth. But it makes no sense to insist on constraints *just* because they narrow the range of theories. After all, constraining the range of theories about a natural language by requiring them to be theories of hiccups or the origin of life does a pretty good job of narrowing. There is the prior question of establishing that the constraints are the right kind. This is the question begged when Platonism is criticized on these grounds.

Underlying the conceptualist's demand for psychological constraints to narrow the range of theories of a language is the further assumption that it is desirable to narrow it so drastically. Why ought we welcome such new constraints solely because they reduce the number of theories that have survived confrontation with the grammatical evidence? It is a common fact of scientific life that evidence underdetermines the choice of a theory, even given methodological criteria like simplicity. Presumably, then, the conceptualist wishes to say something stronger, namely, that, even assuming we had *all* the evidence about the grammatical properties and relations of sentences in the language, there would still be a choice remaining between equally simple (and otherwise methodologically equal) theories for which the new constraints are needed. But why suppose that such a further choice is substantive? Theories that are equivalent in grammatical description, and on all methodological grounds, are completely equivalent theories of *grammatical* structure. So at least the Platonist claims. One question that divides Platonists and conceptualists is thus whether there is a *linguistically significant* choice between theories of a language that do not reflect a difference either in what grammatical properties and relations they predict or in how methodologically well they predict them.

All such equivalent theories of a language can be taken as optimal grammars of the language because, on the most natural definition, an 'optimal grammar' is a *system of rules that predicts each grammatical property and relation of every sentence in the language and for which there is no simpler (or otherwise methodologically better) such predictively successful theory*. The fact that more than one theory of a language will count as an optimal grammar just puts the situation in linguistics on a par with the one familiar in logic and mathematics.

Platonism also offers a natural conception of the notion 'correct linguistic theory'. Linguistic theory, on the Platonist view, is a theory of the invariances in the grammatical structures of all natural languages: the relation between linguistic theory and grammars of natural languages is like the relation between topology and the geometries whose invariances it studies.[53] A 'correct linguistic theory' states all invariances and essential properties of natural language in the simplest way.

Another question concerning whether we stand to lose anything in replacing conceptualism arises in connection with the three fields that came into existence with the Chomskyan revolution: linguistic semantics, formal properties of grammars, and cognitively oriented psycholinguistics. These have become important research fields, and no one would suggest giving up any of them. But there is no risk of that. Though they came in with conceptualist ideology, they would not go out with it since none of these fields depends on conceptualism.

Linguistic semantics did not exist within structuralism, because concepts in the theory of meaning are not reducible to features of the acoustic material in a corpus. But, in so far as Platonism does not replace the extrinsic constraints it removes, the liberalization that brought linguistic semantics into existence is not jeopardized by Platonism.

The field of formal properties of grammars came into existence with the Chomskyan revolution because the revolution provided the stimulus for various new kinds of grammar and because of the special attention Chomsky gave to the study of formal properties. But since the field of formal properties of grammars never concerned itself with more than the mathematical structure of grammars, it has no investment in the conceptualist ideology.

Finally, cognitively oriented psycholinguistics, too, would continue without alteration under Platonism. Platonism makes no criticism of the new psycholinguistics. Platonism leaves this discipline in its proper place, namely, in psychology.

Nothing of value is lost in Platonist linguistics and much is gained.

---

[53] For further discussion, see Katz, *Language and Other Abstract Objects*, pp. 221–40. Platonist linguistic theory formulates an account of the nature (or essence) of natural language in logical rather than in psychological terms. Chomsky and Halle [*The Sound Pattern of English*, Harper and Row, New York, 1968, p. 4] give a psychological account in which the essential properties of natural language are those contributed to all competences by the child's innate endowment for language acquisition. Such an account will, of course, contain the same problems noted above with a psychological account of grammars because, on conceptualist theory, universal grammatical structures must reflect the mental characteristics of the medium of representation. Such problems are eliminated when the conceptualist interpretation of linguistic theory is abandoned and a psychological account of the essential properties of natural language replaced with a logical one. One such account is that the essential properties of natural language are the invariants of the sentence/meaning correlations in particular natural languages that are necessary in order for natural languages to be expressively unrestricted, that is, effable.

Linguistics proper gains a conception of what its theories are theories of that is free of inherent conflicts between ideology and its commitment to descriptive and explanatory aims. On the Platonist conception, theories in linguistics are subject only to traditional descriptive and explanatory aims and the methodology of science generally. Grammars thus are under no constraint that force linguists to choose arbitrarily between equivalent theories or notational variants, to settle for uneconomical theories, or, worst of all, to accept false theories when true ones can be had. Nor is linguistics forced to rule out the possibility of explaining necessary truths in natural languages. In fact, Platonism in linguistics offers an explanation of the necessary truths like (1)–(4) in terms of its conception of sentences and their senses as abstract objects.[54]

Philosophy gains a new approach to the long-standing issue over the existence of abstract objects.[55] Moreover, in coming at the issue from the perspective of the ontological status of languages, the approach is particularly timely in the light of recent nominalist contributions to the issue which assume that a nominalist reconstruction simply can take the status of language for granted.[56]

Psychology, artificial intelligence, neurophysiology, etc., gain a clear, sharp boundary between where the work of the linguist ends and the work of the cognitive scientist begins. This boundary makes the division of labour between the linguist and the psychologist, artificial intelligence scientist, and neurophysiologist as clear as that between the mathematician and the empirical scientist.

One final thought. The conceptualist criticized the nominalist for confusing competence and performance: the speaker/listener's *knowledge* of the language with the *speech* resulting from the exercise of this knowledge. The Platonist criticizes the conceptualist for confusing the speaker/listener's *knowledge* of the language with the *language* that the speaker/listener has knowledge of. The nominalist's constraints require faithfulness to the facts of speech; the conceptualist's require faithfulness to the facts of knowledge. Only Platonist constraints require faithfulness to just the facts of language.

---

[54] Katz, *Language and Other Abstract Objects*, pp. 179–86. Furthermore, it offers an explanation of a priori knowledge of analyticity and other grammatical properties and relations of sentences in terms of a new theory of intuition. Ibid., pp. 192–216.

[55] And a more comprehensive and viable Platonist position; see Katz, *Language and Other Abstract Objects*, pp. 12–17, 192–220.

[56] For example, H. Field, *Science Without Numbers*. Oxford University Press, Oxford, 1981.

10

SEMANTICS AND PSYCHOLOGY*

S. SOAMES

1. INTRODUCTION

RECENT years have seen a significant convergence of interest among philosophers and linguists in constructing semantic theories of natural languages. This convergence has led to a growing acceptance of two major views:

(1) An adequate semantics for a natural language must contain a theory of truth conditions that characterizes logical properties and relations such as logical truth, contradiction, entailment, and consistency.

(2) An adequate grammar for a natural language must integrate a semantics with both a syntax and phonology for the language.

(1) represents a traditional philosophical view that a theory of meaning ought to include, though not necessarily be limited to, a theory of truth conditions. (2) represents the generative grammarian's insistence on a unified theory of language in which semantic, syntactic, and phonological issues interact.

The acceptance of (1) and (2) has led to an impressive and growing body of interdisciplinary research. Nevertheless, fundamental questions

* Early versions of this article were presented to the Cognitive Science Groups at Stanford University and the University of California at Irvine in May of 1979, as well as to the philosophy department of the State University of New York at Albany in December 1979, and the philosophy department of the University of Washington in May 1981. I would like to thank the participants at those sessions, and also Noam Chomsky, Robin Cooper, Barbara von Eckardt, Jerry Fodor, Robert M. Harnish, Jerrold Katz, Julius Moravcsik, Jeff Poland, and Tom Wasow for their useful comments on earlier drafts. This work was supported in part by a Fellowship for Independent Study and Research from the National Endowment for the Humanities.

about the nature and ultimate goals of the enterprise remain. One of the most important of these has to do with the relationship between linguistic theories of natural languages and psychological theories of natural language users.

The received view among generative grammarians has been that

(3) linguistics is a branch of cognitive psychology; and
(4) the rules and representations that make up linguists' grammars are psychologically real mechanisms which are causally responsible for (some significant portion of) the linguistic behaviour of competent speakers.

Together, the psychological interpretation of linguistics and the truth conditional conception of semantics entail that theories of truth conditions must themselves be psychological.

(5) Truth conditional semantics for natural languages (in the sense of (1)) are theories of the cognitive structures and processes underlying linguistic competence.
(6) The rules and representations that make up truth conditional semantics are psychologically real mechanisms which are causally responsible for some portion of the linguistic behaviour of speakers.

Although these conclusions may seem surprising, they are not altogether without attraction. Part of their attraction comes from the widespread acceptance of (1)–(4). However, they also have deeper, more perplexing motivations.

For example, consider the use of theories of truth in connection with the artificial languages of symbolic logic. Typically, the specification of these languages consists of two parts—a syntax and a semantics. The syntax consists of rules defining the well-formedness of various classes of expressions—including formulas and sentences. If the language is used to express a formal theory, the syntax may be extended by labelling certain sentences as 'axioms' and certain mechanical operations as 'rules of inference'. However, unless an interpretation is added, the language remains a collection of meaningless expressions and the 'proof procedure' represents nothing more than a formal device for deriving one set of uninterpreted expressions from another.

Standardly, theories of truth are used to give interpretations by which sentences come to be used to make statements that bear various logical properties and relations. In this connection, truth theories can be seen as playing two related roles.

(7) They are the means employed by those using the language to *endow* sentences with truth conditions.

(8) They are theories which can be used by anyone to *describe* the truth conditions that speakers of the language have established.

In the case of artificial languages of logic, truth conditional theories are used as devices both for giving meaning initially and for describing meaning once it has been given.

Now consider English. English sentences are not just strings of uninterpreted symbols. Rather, they are meaningful expressions which are used to make claims about the world that bear logical properties and relations. It would seem, then, that it must be possible to construct a theory which *describes* the truth conditions of these sentences in the manner of (8). It may also be tempting to think that native speakers have some internalized theory that is used to *establish* these truth conditions in the manner of (7). After all, it might be argued, speakers' internal cognitive processes determine the way sentences are used, which, in turn, gives rise to their truth conditions. If this is correct, then cognitive processes causally responsible for linguistic competence determine the truth conditions of natural language sentences. And how, it might be asked, can they do this unless they include internalized truth theories?

There are, then, reasons which might make (5) and (6) seem plausible. Nevertheless, I believe they are false. If I am right, then truth conditional semantics are not themselves psychological. However, this does not mean that they have no psychological significance. After specifying the ways in which they must be distinguished from psychological theories of language acquisition and use, I will indicate the respects in which truth conditional semantics are potentially relevant to such theories.

2. TRUTH CONDITIONS AND PSYCHOLOGICAL DETERMINATION

The specification of truth conditions can be roughly divided into two parts.[1]

(9) A specification of the semantic values (intensions/extensions) of lexical items.

---

[1] I am ignoring here the semantics of indexicals, which requires the specification not of intensions/extensions but of functions from contexts to intensions/extensions (i.e. what David Kaplan (1977) calls 'character'). Although this is an important part of semantics, a discussion of it is not needed for the points I wish to make here.

(10) A specification of recursive principles that assign semantic values (intensions/extensions) to compound expressions as a function of the semantic values of their parts.

To show that the assignment of truth conditions to sentences of a natural language is a non-psychological task it is sufficient to show that (9) is non-psychological. The strongest arguments for this are given by Kripke and Putnam.[2] These arguments indicate that the semantic values (intensions/extensions) of proper names and many general terms are determined not by descriptions speakers associate with them, but rather by socio-historical chains connecting speakers to one another and, ultimately, to entities in the non-linguistic world. Putnam's Twin-Earth example[3] extends these arguments to show that identical expressions used by speakers who are psychologically (and physiologically) indistinguishable could nevertheless have different semantic values. If this is correct, then the semantic values of these expressions, and of sentences containing them, are not (wholly) determined by psychological facts. Thus, specification of these values, including specification of the truth conditions of sentences, is not a (purely) psychological task.[4]

The status of (10) is not as clear. Many existing semantic theories (e.g. many versions of possible world semantics) ignore the semantic values of lexical items and concentrate exclusively on recursive aspects of the determination of truth conditions.[5] Such theories do not specify the intensions/extensions of expressions or the truth conditions of sentences. However, they do define *truth-in-a-model* (or truth at an index in a model) and use this notion to characterize logical properties and relations like entailment, logical truth, and contradiction. One

---

[2] Kripke (1971), (1972), and Putnam (1970), (1975).

[3] Putnam (1975).

[4] The specification of the intensions/extensions of lexical items is a proper task for lexical semantics. For example, if Putnam is right about natural kind terms like 'water' and 'H_2O', then a complete semantics for English must entail ⌜'Water' refers to T_1 (in English)⌝ and ⌜'H_2O' refers to T_2 (in English)⌝. In order for the semantics to be correct, T_1 and T_2 must be coreferential. However, the semantics does not have the job of telling us that they are. If it did, then semantics would have to include chemistry and, indeed, all of science, which of course it does not. For a contrary view in which proper names don't have definite semantic extensions see Katz (1979). In the case of natural kind terms, Katz holds that Twin-Earth type examples can be handled using Donnellan's notion of reference under a false description. Replies to this latter point can be found in Putnam (1975), Donnellan (1977), and Kripke (1979).

[5] See Richmond Thomason, 'Introduction' to Montague (1974).

might wonder whether these theories (or recursive components of full truth conditional accounts) are psychological in nature.[6]

It is useful to break this question into three related parts.

Q_1 Are recursive theories of truth conditions theories of psychologically real rules and representations that are causally responsible for semantic competence?

Q_2 Are the (recursive) clauses of such theories mentally represented?

Q_3 Do truth conditional theories (of the above sort) have psychological import?

The answer to the first of these questions is clearly 'no'. If truth conditional semantics were theories of mental rules and representations, their theorems would consist in claims of the form (11).

(11) Recursive apparatus R is (unconsciously) represented in the minds of speakers of L.

But this is absurd. The recursive elements in truth conditional semantics are what the theories use to make predictions, not what the predictions are about.

This point can be illustrated with the help of an analogy. Mathematical formalizations of elementary number theory use axioms and rules to make claims about natural numbers. Psychological theories of arithmetical reasoning make claims about the rules and representations people employ in drawing arithmetical conclusions. Since the arithmetical truths are compatible with a wide variety of hypotheses about the psychological processes involved in trying to grasp them, the two kinds of theories must be distinguished. The same is true of truth conditional semantics and psychological theories of semantic competence.

It is important to recognize that this sort of difference between theories is compatible with any degree of similarity between their formal structures. For example, suppose one's formalized number theory consisted of a standard first order language L, together with a set A of arithmetical axioms, plus some proof procedure P. Suppose also that the correct cognitive theory of ordinary arithmetical reasoning turned out to be one which claimed that reasoners unconsciously translated arithmetical sentences of natural language into L and applied

<hr/>

[6] Barbara Partee (1979) agrees that lexical semantics cannot be wholly psychological. However, she believes that the recursive components of truth conditional accounts may be psychologically real. ' . . . the rules for combining interpretations of parts to make interpretations of wholes are finitely representable and correspond as far as one can tell with the intuitions of native speakers, and, in principle, there seems to be no difficulty in saying that the speakers of a language "know" these rules as part of their competence.' (p. 197.)

A and P. This would be a miraculous instance of complete convergence between the structures utilized by a mathematical theory of the natural numbers and the structures posited by a cognitive theory of arithmetical reasoning.[7]

Although this imagined convergence would justify the claim that the mathematician's formalization was psychologically real, it would not change the fact that the mathematical enterprise of constructing a theory of the natural numbers is conceptually distinct from the psychological enterprise of constructing a theory of the arithmetical reasoning of certain organisms. The two theories would still make different claims and be established by different means. Truth conditional semantics and psychological theories of semantic competence are conceptually distinct in this sense—no matter how much, or how little, their formal structures may converge.

This being so, the psychological status of truth conditional semantics naturally focuses on Q_2 and Q_3. Since a positive answer to the latter is a necessary, but not sufficient, condition for a positive answer to the former, the first thing to do is to determine whether truth conditional theories have any psychological significance.

I believe they do. The reason they do is brought out by the fact that one apparently cannot construct a Twin-Earth argument regarding (10) paralleling the one constructed by Putnam regarding (9). For example, let X and Y be two groups of psychologically and physiologically indistinguishable speakers whose native languages, Lx and Ly, are syntactically identical. It seems implausible that these languages could differ in truth theoretically defined logical properties and relations—i.e. it seems implausible that S_1 could entail S_2 in Lx but not Ly, or that S_3 could be logically true in Ly, but not in Lx. Thus it may well be that psychological (and physiological) truths about speakers determine the logical properties and relations of sentences of their language.[8] If this is right, then semantic theories specifying such

---

[7] Even in this imagined case there would be some differences in the respective proof procedures. For the arithmetical theory one doesn't really have a proof *procedure*, but rather a characterization of proof in terms of logical axioms and rules of inference. For the psychological theory it would be necessary to add a heuristic strategy for constructing proofs in accord with these axioms and rules.

[8] This claim can be understood in two different ways, depending on one's metaphysical views about language. *View 1.* The properties of languages are wholly dependent on empirical facts about language users and their environment. In particular, *psychological* facts about speakers determine the logical properties of the language (e.g. English) that they, in fact, speak. *View 2.* Languages are abstract objects whose semantic properties are not dependent on empirical facts. What is empirically determined is which language a group of

properties constrain psychological theories of competent speakers. In this sense, truth conditional theories have psychological import.

However, this does not guarantee that the recursive apparatus of such theories is mentally represented. Roughly speaking, to say that the set P of psychological (and physiological) truths about speakers in a population Q determines the logical properties and relations of sentences of their language is to say that semantic truths of the type illustrated in (12) are supervenient on P.

(12) a. S_1 is logically true in the language of Q.
   b. S_2 is contradictory in the language of Q.
   c. S_3 entails S_4 in the language of Q.

Although this ensures that variations in (12) will be accompanied by variations in the psychology (and physiology) of speakers, it does not tell us what in the psychology (and physiology) must vary, or what fixes the logical properties and relations of sentences. Thus, determination of logical properties and relations does not guarantee that any semantic characterization of truth (in-a-model) will be psychologically real.

3. THE DIVERGENCE OF PSYCHOLOGICAL AND TRUTH CONDITIONAL STRUCTURES

3.1. *The Basic Argument*

The divergence of psychological and truth conditional structures is based on a requirement that theories in cognitive psychology face. These theories attempt to explain a subject's intellectual capacities by positing internal computational routines that are causally responsible for his abilities. In order to be non-question-begging, these theories must not presuppose the very intelligence they try to explain. Thus, if all intellectual capacities are to be accounted for, the internal computational routines posited by cognitive theories must not themselves require intelligence to follow; that is, they must be effective, or mechanical, procedures in the mathematical sense.[9] This means that if

people speak. In particular, it is *psychologically* determined that they speak a language the sentences of which bear various specified logical properties and relations. On View 1, truth conditional theories have potential psychological import. On View 2, the claim that a population speaks the language characterized by such a theory has psychological significance. Although I prefer to think about these issues in the seond way (see Soames (1984b)), the arguments given above are independent of the choice between these alternatives. I am indebted to Jeff Poland for a discussion of this point.

   [9] See Dennett (1978) chs. 4 and 5 for a discussion of this point.

the recursive clauses of a truth conditional semantics are mentally represented, they must constitute an effective procedure for accomplishing some task that speakers are able to perform. The problem is that there seems to be no task that speakers can perform for which an internally represented semantic theory would constitute both a plausible and an effective procedure.

I will illustrate this by considering three things that speakers can do.

(i) Recognize entailments (and other logical characteristics of sentences).

(ii) Recover semantic representations in the process of sentence comprehension (in general, connect surface structures with representations of meaning).

(iii) Evaluate sentences given information about the semantic values of their parts.

For each task, I will argue that a truth conditional semantics is either not an effective procedure for accomplishing the task, or only one of many such procedures. In effect, I will argue that there is not much work for a mentally represented semantic theory to do; and, moreover, that the jobs that could, in principle, be done by such a theory can be accomplished more plausibly in other ways.

3.2. *Recognizing the Logical Characteristics of Sentences*

Speakers of a natural language are able to recognize various entailments and logical truths. Presumably, a mentalistic theory will attempt to explain this ability by positing an internalized computational procedure for determining which sentences bear these logical properties and relations (e.g. an internalized procedure for drawing inferences). However, semantic theories are not such procedures.

What is distinctive about truth conditional semantics is that they allow one to define logical properties and relations in terms of a recursive account of the connection between language and the world. Given the appropriate semantic definitions, one can ask which sentences are instances of the various properties and relations. For some languages, it is possible to devise effective procedures that correctly recognize all semantically defined entailments, logical truths, and so on; for other languages, this is not possible. However in *none* of these cases is the semantic theory itself such a procedure.

The point can be made more graphic by considering a case of conscious rule following. Let S be a student who has been studying the predicate calculus. Suppose one wanted to know which logical truths S could recognize and how he went about determining whether a sentence was logically true. For the purpose of finding this out, it would not help to be told that S had mastered the characterization of truth-in-a-model and the accompanying semantic definition of logical truth. Since such knowledge is neither necessary nor sufficient for recognizing individual logical truths, neither the hypothesis that S knew the model theory, nor the hypothesis that he didn't, would allow one to predict which sentences he would judge to be logically true.[10] To make these predictions one would need to know what system of proof S accepted and what procedure he used to construct proofs in that system. In effect, one would have to know not what model theory was psychologically real, but what proof theory was.

The same is true in the case of native speakers of English. To claim that speakers recognize entailments by recognizing that they fall under the relevant internalized truth-theoretic definition would be to fail to explain how this latter recognition was accomplished, and to fail to predict which sentences speakers would judge to entail which others. These defects are avoided if cognitive psychology posits not an internalized truth conditional semantics, but rather an internalized proof procedure or other effective test for logical properties and relations.

If a proof procedure is both sound and complete, it will, of course, characterize the same classes of logical truths and entailments as the relevant semantic definitions do. However, this does not mean that there will be a close, point by point, correspondence between the two. In some cases there will be and in some cases there won't. For example, the 'tree method' for first order logic is a sound and complete negative test for consistency, which, in effect, consists of a method for constructing a model for the sentences being tested.[11] Other proof procedures (that characterize the same classes of logical truths and entailments) do not bear this close connection with semantic (model theoretic) ideas. Thus, even if it could be shown that speakers of a language had mastered a sound and complete proof procedure, it would remain an open question whether that computational routine was closely related to any semantic theory.

For many languages, it cannot be assumed that speakers do possess a sound and complete proof procedure. One can understand a language without being able to recognize (even under idealized conditions) all entailments formulated within it. This is particularly evident in the case of higher order languages, or those with branching quantifiers. The lack of sound and complete positive tests for entailment in these

---

[10] I assume the subject has some pretheoretic grasp of what a logical truth is (whether or not he knows any precise definition).

[11] See Jeffrey (1981).

languages does not make it impossible to understand them. Since there is no guarantee that English is not itself such a language,[12] there is no guarantee that it is even possible for one to possess a competence which, under idealized conditions, would allow one to recognize all entailments in English.

A similar point holds even if entailment in English should turn out to be fully formalizable. The existence of sound and complete positive tests for entailment in a language does not guarantee that speakers must have internalized at least one of them. In fact, there is a speculative, but not implausible, line of reasoning which suggests that systems of linguistic competence do *not* include sound and complete proof procedures. It is based on the fact that the set of logically valid arguments in English includes many which are not routinely recognized by ordinary speakers. The identification of these arguments as valid often requires intelligence, practice, or explicit instruction. Moreover, the process of drawing the relevant inferences is typically slow, laborious, and fully conscious. This contrasts with the mental operations posited by psychological theories of sentence perception and comprehension. Although quite complex, such operations are typically rapid, unconscious, and not the result of explicit instruction.

The approach to psychological theories of language growing out of the work of Noam Chomsky takes differences like these to be potentially significant. For example, in setting the task of theories of language acquisition, Chomsky requires that they characterize not the class of languages learnable by any means—including explicit instruction, drill, etc.—but rather the class of languages learnable in the normal, rapid, and largely unreflective way. This is part of his overall modular approach to the study of human capacities. General, conscious, problem-solving abilities constitute one domain of psychological states and processes. Implicit unconscious abilities constitute another. There is no reason to expect the same kinds of mental operations to apply in both domains.

This approach suggests that speakers' judgements about logical properties and relations may not be due entirely to their systems of linguistic competence, but rather may result, at least in part, from their general ability to reason. If so, these judgements can be expected to vary with the intelligence and experience of the individual. Hence,

[12] For arguments that there are no sound, complete, positive tests for entailment and logical truth in English, see Hintikka (1974), Gabbay and Moravcsik (1974), Barwise (1979), and Boolos (1981).

not all speakers can be expected to recognize all instances of logical properties and relations (even under idealization).[13]

There is, then, a considerable difference between truth theoretic characterizations of logical properties and relations and psychological theories of how speakers come to recognize that various sentences bear those properties and relations. It can be argued that speakers of a natural language have internal procedures for drawing inferences. However, since truth conditional semantics are not such procedures, they cannot be *identified* with the computational routines employed by speakers. Nor is there any a priori reason to expect these routines to be *related* to semantic theories in a close or direct way. Since speakers' proof procedures may either fail to be sound and complete, or fail to bear a close, point by point, correspondence with characterizations of truth-in-a-model, the psychological mechanisms underlying speakers' semantic judgements are apt to differ considerably from truth conditional semantics for their language.[14]

3.3. *Recovering Semantic Representations*

I have just argued that the job of explaining how speakers recognize instances of logical properties and relations is one that internally represented truth conditional semantics cannot, in principle, perform.

---

[13] ' . . . some intellectual achievements, such as language learning, fall strictly within biologically determined cognitive capacity. For these tasks, we have "special design", so that cognitive structures of great complexity and interest develop fairly rapidly and with little if any conscious effort. There are other tasks, no more "complex" along any absolute scale (assuming that it is possible even to make sense of this notion), which will be utterly baffling because they fall beyond cognitive capacity. Consider problems that lie at the borderline of cognitive capacity. These will provide opportunity for intriguing intellectual play. Chess, for example, is not so remote from cognitive capacity as to be merely a source of insoluble puzzles, but is at the same time sufficiently beyond our natural abilities so that it is challenging and intriguing. Here we would expect to find that the slight differences between individuals are magnified to striking divergence of aptitude.' Chomsky (1975), p. 27.

[14] It is reasonable to take truth conditional semantics for natural languages to be (parts of) linguistic theories for those languages. This is not the case for the proof procedures used by speakers. Unlike the logical properties and relations characterized by truth conditional semantics, the procedures speakers use to draw inferences are not constitutive of the language they speak. Thus, two groups of language users, X and Y, may speak the same language even though they employ computationally different theorem proving techniques. These procedures need not even be extensionally equivalent so long as the X and Y expressions correspond completely with respect to all linguistically significant properties and relations. The use of non-equivalent proof procedures by speakers of the same language would indicate differences in their ability to exploit the logical features of their common language.

Thus, if such semantics are to be so much as candidates for psychological reality, some other psychological function must be found that they are capable of fulfilling. One such function is that of explaining how languages are learned and understood.

Sometimes people learn artificial languages by learning truth theories for them. This happens when a person knows the metalanguage of the theory and understands the truth characterization stated in that language. In such cases, the *pedagogical* role of the theory of truth is to allow the learner to pair metalanguage sentences, which he understands, with object language sentences, which he does not.

The theory establishes this pairing by providing recursive means for deriving instances of Tarski's schema T.

Schema T: X is true in L iff P.
(Instances are obtained by replacing 'X' with the quote name of a sentence S of L and replacing 'P' with the metalanguage counterpart of S.)

It should be noted that the *semantic* purpose of a theory of truth is not to pair sentences; neither it nor the T-sentences derivable from it assert anything about sentence pairs, or mention the metalanguage at all. Nevertheless, the *pedagogical* value of such a theory to someone learning the object language is essentially the same as that of a translation manual which explicitly pairs the relevant sentences for each instance of schema T.

In this way, a theory of truth can be used to learn a language. Conceivably, such an account could also be extended to psychological theories of sentence comprehension for native speakers of natural languages. To make this extension would be to make the following claims:

(13) Understanding a natural language involves the ability to pair its expressions with psycho-semantic representations in an already understood 'language of thought'.

(14) This pairing is accomplished by a formalized, but internally represented theory of truth which makes possible the mechanical derivation of the relevant T-sentences.

On this view, psycho-semantic representations are not themselves interpreted by a psychologically real theory of truth, but are understood directly.

Although the conjunction of (13) and (14) seems to be a logically possible view, it isn't very plausible. One potential problem is that it presupposes the existence of an internal 'language of thought'. Although many psycholinguists accept the view that understanding a natural language involves the ability to pair its expressions with psychologically real semantic representations, some investigators doubt that these representations should be thought of as sentence-like. If the doubters are right, it is hard to see how the generation of T-sentences by a recursive theory of truth could be a psychologically real procedure connecting natural language sentences with internal representations of their meanings.

However, putting this issue aside, one finds that there is still another serious difficulty to contend with. (14)'s assertion about the nature of the mapping between natural language and psycho-semantic representations is arbitrary—i.e. nothing now known would lead one to accept (14) as opposed to other alternatives. A translation manual relating the object language and the metalanguage would do the job, as would any process taking sentences in one language as input and yielding sentences in the other as output. Thus, there are many ways of using a language one knows to learn a new language. What (14) does is to arbitrarily select one of these ways and extend it to psychological theories of semantic competence for native speakers of natural languages.

To assume in advance that (14) must be correct is to confuse the indispensable role of characterizations of truth in truth conditional semantics with their merely potential status in psychological theories. The function of a definition of truth in truth conditional semantics is to specify the connection between language and the world in a way that provides the basis for an account of logical properties and relations. Theories of translation, or any other devices that merely pair sentences of one language with those in another, don't do this. Since this function is central to truth conditional accounts, such theories must include recursive characterizations of truth.

The status of theories of truth in psychology is quite different. If such theories are to be internally represented, they must accomplish some task that speakers of a language are capable of performing. One such task is that of mapping surface structures onto internal representations of their meanings. For certain languages, it is conceivable that an internalized theory of truth could do this. However, unlike the situation in semantics, any number of non-truth-theoretic devices could accomplish this task equally well.

In the absence of further linguistic or psycholinguistic evidence involving speakers' judgements, reaction times, error rates, learning, and so on, there simply are no grounds for preferring the truth theoretic (14) to these other alternatives. There is even some reason to expect (14) to prove to be untrue. In general, the derivations of T-sentences from characterizations of truth for natural languages are quite complicated and laborious, much more so than, for example, explicit translations of natural language sentences onto logical forms. Of course, this derivational complexity makes no more difference to semantics than the length of derivations of arithmetical equations makes to formalizations of elementary number theory. However, it does make a difference to psychology. It simply is not reasonable to suppose that the process of comprehending a sentence is inordinately complex, especially when the factors making for derivational complexity are avoidable and don't serve any further psychological function. Since recovery of semantic representations via an internalized characterization of truth would seem to have just this kind of gratuitous complexity, it seems quite unlikely that a psychological theory incorporating (14) will turn out to be correct.

3.4. *Evaluating Sentences Given Semantic Information about their Parts*

Perhaps there is another ability that could be used to establish the psychological reality of truth conditional semantics—e.g. the ability to evaluate the truth values of sentences given semantic information about their parts. One instance of this is the ability of English speakers to assign a truth value to a conjunction

(15) P and Q

given the truth values of both conjuncts. It might be thought that this is best explained by a mentally represented theory of truth for the language.

But what, exactly, is this ability of which the conjunction example is an instance? In answering this question, let us focus on a speaker of a language L of the first order predicate calculus whose competence in L parallels the competence of native speakers of natural languages. It is a fact about L that the recursive clauses in its truth definition determine the truth values of its sentences, relative to a domain of objects and an assignment of n-tuples of those objects to the predicates, function signs, and names of L. In short, the recursive structure of the truth definition fixes the truth values of sentences, given an interpretation of the lexical (i.e. non-logical) vocabulary of the language.

In light of this, it might be thought that someone who knew a truth definition for such a language would be able to determine the truth values of its sentences, when provided with an effective procedure for specifying exactly which objects were correlated with its non-logical vocabulary. The suggested analogy to natural language would then be this.

(16) *a.* Speakers have the ability to determine truth values of arbitrary sentences given an effective specification of a domain of discourse and extensions of all lexical items.

     b. This ability is explained by mental representations of the recursive clauses of a theory of truth.

The problem is that (16*a*) is false. This can be demonstrated when the language in question is first order, and contains elementary number theory (i.e. plus, times, successor, identity, and quantification over natural numbers). If speakers of such a language had the ability in (16*a*), then there would be an effective procedure P for deciding the truth value of any sentence, given an effective specification of the domain plus the assignment of objects to non-logical vocabulary. However, if there were such a P, then there would be an effective negative test N for logical truth. It would operate as follows: given a sentence S, generate all S′ formed from S by substituting open sentences for atomic formulas in S. For each S′ use procedure P to determine its truth value. It can be shown that one of these S′ will be false if and only if S is not a logical truth.[15] Thus, N will be a sound, complete, effective negative test for logical truth. But it is a metatheorem of first order logic that there is no such effective negative test for logical truth. Thus, the ability mentioned in (16*a*) does not exist. I suggest a similar conclusion for natural language.

Might there be some more restricted abilities of the same general type that speakers really do have? Of course; we have already seen one such example involving conjunction. However, even in this case there is little reason to suppose that the ability is due to a mentally represented truth theoretic clause for conjunction.

(17) ⌜P and Q⌝ is true in E iff P is true in E & Q is true in E

It should be noted that if such a mental representation is to provide the explanation of speakers' ability to evaluate conjunctions, then presumably it must also provide them with their understanding of 'and'. For if they understood 'and' independently, then their ability to assign truth values to conjunctions, given truth values of conjuncts, could be explained by appealing to that understanding, plus a recognition of the trivial fact that 'true' is disquotational.

Assuming, then, that (17) is the means by which speakers give 'and' a meaning, one must also assume that the metalanguage counterpart of 'and' (in this case '&') is not 'and' itself. Clearly, speakers cannot give 'and' meaning by saying to themselves,

---

[15] W. V. O. Quine (1970, chapter 4).

(18) $\ulcorner$P and Q$\urcorner$ is true in E iff P is true in E and Q is true in E

for that would presuppose that 'and' had already been given a meaning prior to the citation of the clause in the truth characterization. Thus, if such a clause is used, the metalanguage counterpart of 'and' must be distinct from 'and', and already understood by the speaker.

This points up the weakness of positing an internalized clause (17). Although it may be logically possible for such a postulation to be part of a causal explanation of how speakers fix the meaning of 'and', such a postulation could not be entirely satisfactory unless it were accompanied by an account of what is causally responsible for speakers' understanding of '&'; and here there is no internalized model theory to appeal to. Moreover, given a causal account of '&', one would have no reason to assume that the psychological mechanism that connects it to 'and' is (17). All that is required is that the logical properties and relations of English expressions be causally inherited from those of their psycho-semantic representations. Once the latter are accounted for (non-model theoretically), a variety of devices for connecting internal representations with natural language sentences could be used.[16] Thus, the ability (such as it is) to assign truth values to sentences given information about their parts doesn't provide any clear reason for posting mental representations of recursive clauses of theories of truth.

4. TWO WAYS IN WHICH TRUTH CONDITIONAL SEMANTICS ARE POTENTIALLY RELEVANT TO PSYCHOLOGY

4.1. *The Psychological Relevance of Semantics*

I have argued that truth conditional semantics are neither theories of cognitive states and processes, nor psychologically real procedures for accomplishing tasks that constitute semantic competence. However, there are two other ways in which semantics may have significance for cognitive psychology. The first involves the use of semantic ideas as possible sources for computational hypotheses. The second involves the significance of semantic universals for theories of language acquisition.

---

[16] Nothing in my argument precludes the possibility of giving a causal explanation of the logical characteristics of English expressions without positing psychologically real semantic representations at all. If there are no such representations, then, obviously, model theoretic characterizations of truth are not psychologically real mechanisms mediating between semantic representations and natural languages.

It is as important to recognize these legitimate areas of potential psychological significance as it is to acknowledge the various ways in which truth conditional semantics must be distinguished from cognitive psychology.

4.2. *Mental Models*

Consider the following highly schematized picture of an aspect of deductive reasoning.[17] Given a set of premises plus a potential conclusion C, one can imagine the following cognitive process for determining whether C follows from P.

(i) Construct a set of heuristic 'mental models' representing the information contained in P. For concreteness one might think of these on analogy with maps—with certain designated points representing the objects mentioned in P and certain geometrical relations among the points representing the properties and relations attributed to those objects by P.

(ii) Check all of the models in (i) to see if they are models of C. If they are, infer C from P.

I haven't said how 'models' are constructed for sentences, how many such 'models' are constructed in any given case, or how, given a 'model' M and a sentence S, one checks to see whether M is a 'model' for S. However, it is not implausible to suppose that some of these tasks might be accomplished by subprocesses corresponding to different sentential constructions. For example given a 'model' of A, and a 'model' of B, there might be some process for combining the two to form a 'model' of the conjunction, $\ulcorner$A and B$\urcorner$. Or again, given a disjunction, $\ulcorner$A or B$\urcorner$, plus a 'model' M, the process of checking to see whether M was a 'model' of the compound sentence might be, first, to see whether M was a 'model' of A, and then (if it wasn't) to see whether it was a 'model' of B. On this picture there would be no mental representations of clauses of a truth definition—there would be no internally represented truth theory in the 'language of thought'. However, there would be a rough correspondence between at least some of the clauses of a truth definition and mental operations on internal 'models'.

I am not sure whether any picture of this general sort will prove to

---

[17] The account that follows is modelled, very roughly, on a psychological theory of reasoning presented by P. N. Johnson-Laird in the 1983 Langfeld Lectures at Princeton University. I have not attempted to reconstruct the detailed hypothesis or experimental evidence presented by Johnson-Laird, but have instead tried to indicate the way in which model theoretic ideas might stimulate psychological hypotheses.

be psychologically correct; or, if it does, how closely it will parallel truth conditional semantics. For it to be at all plausible, the computational process should not be thought of as encompassing a sound and complete, positive test for entailment. Thus, the set of arguments it recognizes should be different from the set of arguments characterized as valid by the truth conditional semantics. It is not even clear the extent to which the envisioned process should be considered as a part of semantic competence, as opposed to the general ability to reason.

Still, the picture just sketched illustrates the way in which formal semantics can be used as a source of ideas for hypotheses in cognitive psychology. Doubtless, there are other sources as well, none of which enjoys an a priori advantage over the others. There is no obvious reason why there *must* be close parallels between formal semantics and computational psychology. However, there might be; and psychological hypotheses based on semantic ideas have as much claim to further investigation as any others.[18]

4.3. *Semantic Universals*

The second area of potential psychological import of truth conditional semantics is considerably less speculative than the first. As in the case of phonology and syntax, work in truth conditional semantics has resulted in a number of proposed linguistic universals.[19] In each case, the universal eliminates many coherent and abstractly possible languages from being candidates for humanly possible natural languages. This sort of restriction on the class of possible natural languages is important for theories of language acquisition; if, as Chomsky has emphasized, normal instances of acquisition require a radical limitation of the linguistic alternatives a child must consider. Many linguists regard the specification of the class of possible natural languages as both the central task in linguistics, and the main source of psychological import for their theories. There is no reason why work in truth

---

[18] The 'mental models' hypothesis is, in effect, a proof procedure inspired by semantic ideas. The point made about it complements one of the observations of section 3.2. There I noted that the ability of competent speakers to recognize entailments does not provide a reason for preferring semantically inspired proof procedures over others. Here I note that hypotheses positing such procedures deserve further empirical investigation on a par with alternative accounts. As with any proposal about computational procedures, that investigation will rely crucially on aspects of performance that go well beyond what is required for linguistic competence. (This point, touched on in n. 14, is discussed in Soames (1984a), and is implicit in the type of data used by Johnson-Laird to support his version of the 'mental models' hypothesis.)

[19] See, in particular, Barwise and Cooper (1981).

conditional semantics shouldn't contribute to this task as much as more traditional work in syntax and phonology.

In my opinion, the reason this fact has not been as widely recognized as it should be stems from a misconception regarding the kinds of universals that are the proper subject of linguistic theory. Following Wasow (1978), one may distinguish between constraints on the class of possible grammars and constraints on the class of possible languages. Wasow makes three main points about this distinction.

(i) Whereas constraints on the class of possible natural languages always implicitly limit the class of possible grammars, constraints on the class of possible grammars do not always limit the class of possible natural languages. (Since different grammars might generate the same languages.)

(ii) To construe linguistic universals as psychologically significant constraints on grammars (even when they don't restrict the class of possible languages) is to presuppose a closer correspondence between linguists' grammars and speakers' cognitive processes than is justified by available evidence.

(iii) One ought to construe linguistic universals as constraints on possible natural languages. To do this is to take them as specifying the scope of the cognitive capacity to learn languages, without speculating on the internal computational routines that implement this capacity.

I believe that Wasow is right about universals of all types—syntactic, phonological, and semantic. However, this analysis is especially important in the case of truth conditional semantics. Here, more than anywhere else, there is a clear gap between linguists' formal theories of grammatical properties, on the one hand, and the internal computational processes that are causally responsible for the appearance of those properties in observed languages, on the other. If one thought that linguistic universals had to be formulated directly in terms of causally efficacious cognitive structure, then it would be natural to be sceptical of truth conditional semantics as a source of such universals. However, that is not the way to think of universals.

Both truth conditional semantics for particular languages and semantic universals constrain psychological theories of language users. The reason they do involves a fact noted earlier. Logical properties and relations of the kind characterized by recursive, truth conditional theories are supervenient on psychological facts. Thus, restrictions on the former give rise to constraints on the latter.

5. SEMANTICS AND SEMANTIC COMPETENCE

The upshot of this discussion is that truth conditional semantics are not psychological theories (Observations 1 and 2); nor are they psychologically real procedures responsible for semantic competence (Observation 3); however, they are psychologically significant (Observation 4).

Observation 1
Semantic facts regarding certain lexical items are non-psychological as are the truth conditions of sentences containing those items.

Observation 2
Although recursive aspects of truth conditional semantics deal with facts that are supervenient on psychological facts, and hence constrain psychological theories, they do not specify or make predictions about cognitive structures and processes.

Observation 3
There is no task required for semantic competence that justifies postulation of an internally represented truth conditional semantics in 'the language of thought'.

Observation 4
Truth conditional semantics are sources both of linguistic universals and of hypotheses about psychological processing.

In short, the truth conditional approach to semantics is not a branch of cognitive psychology, but it has significance for cognitive psychology. If linguistic theories of natural languages include truth conditional semantics, then the same can be said of linguistics itself.

I have been assuming all along that the truth conditional approach is fundamental to linguistic semantics. Although I believe this to be essentially correct, I must acknowledge that the most familiar argument for this view is inadequate. A central premise in that argument is (19).

(19) To know the meaning of a sentence is to know the conditions under which it is true.

Since truth conditional semantics give the truth conditions of sentences, it is thought that they must qualify as theories of meaning. Unfortunately, on any straightforward rendering of what it is to know the truth conditions of a sentence, (19) is false.

Let us take the truth conditions of sentences to be given by instances of the following schema:

(20) 'S' is true in L ≡ P.

(Instances are formed by replacing 'P' with a sentence that means the same as the sentence replacing 'S'; '≡' can be taken to express either material or necessary equivalence.) Let us suppose that knowing the truth conditions for the sentences of a language L is knowing, for each sentence S of L, the proposition expressed by the relevant instance of (20). It can easily be seen that knowing the truth conditions of the sentences of L (in this sense) is neither a necessary, nor a sufficient, condition for knowing the meanings of those sentences. It is not necessary, since it is possible to understand the sentences of a language without possessing a metalinguistic concept of truth. It is not sufficient, since knowledge of truth conditions, of the sort illustrated by (21), is compatible with incorrect beliefs about the meanings of sentences, of the sort illustrated by (22).[20]

(21) 'Firenze é una bella città' is true in Italian ≡ Florence is a beautiful city.

(22) 'Firenze é una bella città' means in Italian that Florence is a beautiful city and arithmetic is incomplete.

There is no other account of what it is to know the truth conditions of a sentence, that I am aware of, which avoids this result.

How, then, should one think of truth conditional semantics? The most successful versions are intensional, or index, semantics. For simplicity's sake, we can think of indices as possible worlds and semantic theories as incorporating definitions of truth at a world. Such semantics implicitly associate a set of possible worlds with each sentence. These sets are supposed to constitute the information carried by sentences, and hence are called 'propositions'.

Semantic theories of this type do two things:

(i) They characterize the logical properties and relations (logical truth, entailment, etc.) of sentences.

(ii) They associate with each sentence a proposition, which is taken to be a non-linguistic entity constituting the information encoded by the sentence.

[20] It is possible to know the proposition which is expressed by (21) while consistently believing the proposition expressed by (22). All that is needed for this is for one to believe the disjunction: either Florence is a beautiful city and arithmetic is incomplete, or Florence isn't a beautiful city. Since it is theoretically possible to be in this situation with respect to every sentence of the object language, knowledge of truth conditions is not sufficient for understanding meaning. See Foster (1976) for relevant discussion.

In my opinion, any adequate semantics must accomplish both of these tasks. The weakness of standard truth conditional approaches is that they wrongly identify propositions with sets of possible worlds (indices), when more finely grained objects are needed. Although there are suggestions for remedying this defect within the truth conditional approach, the resolution of this issue remains open.[21] Fortunately, this difficulty shouldn't affect the conclusions drawn above about the relationship between semantics and psychology. Any adequate semantics will have to do so much that is already done by standard truth conditional accounts that essentially the same arguments regarding psychological significance should apply to both.

If this is right, then linguistic semantics must be regarded as psychologically significant without being a branch of psychology. It seems to me that the same should be said for other areas of linguistics as well, for example syntax. Although I haven't argued for this general conception of linguistics here, I hope that consideration of the special case of semantics has added plausibility to it.[22]

BIBLIOGRAPHY

Barwise, J. (1979) 'On Branching Quantifiers in English', *Journal of Philosophic Logic*, Vol. 8, No. 1.
— and Cooper, R. (1981) 'Generalized Quantifiers and Natural Language', *Linguistics and Philosophy*, Vol. 4, No. 2.
— and Perry, J. (1983) *Situations and Attitudes*, MIT/Bradford, Cambridge.
Bigelow, J. C. (1978) 'Believing in Semantics', *Linguistics and Philosophy*, Vol. 2, No. 1.
Boolos, G. (1981) 'For Every A There is a B', *Linguistic Inquiry*, Vol. 12.
Chomsky, N. (1975) *Reflections on Language*, Pantheon Books, New York.
Cresswell, M. J. (1973) *Logics and Languages*, Methuen and Co., London.
— (1975) 'Hyperintensional Logic', *Studia Logica*, Vol. 34.
Dennett, D. C. (1978) *Brainstorms*, Bradford Books, Cambridge.
Donnellan, K. S. (1977) 'Review of *Language, Mind, and Knowledge*', *Language*, Vol. 53.
Foster, J. A. (1976) 'Meaning and Truth Theory', in G. Evans and J. McDowell (eds.), *Truth and Meaning*, Clarendon Press, Oxford.
Gabbay, D., and Moravcsik, J. M. E. (1974) 'Branching Quantifiers, English, and Montague Grammar', *Theoretical Linguistics*, Vol. 1, No. 1.
Hintikka, J. (1974) 'Quantifiers vs. Quantification Theory', *Linguistic Inquiry*, Vol. 5, No. 2.
Jeffrey, R. C. (1981) *Formal Logic: Its Scope and Limits*, McGraw-Hill, New York, second edition.
Kaplan, D. (1977) 'Demonstratives', unpublished manuscript.
Katz, J. J. (1979) 'The Neoclassical Theory of Reference', in P. A. French,

---

[21] See, for example, David Lewis (1970) § v; Cresswell (1973), (1975); Bigelow (1978); and Barwise and Perry (1983).
[22] I do argue for this conception of linguistics in Soames (1984a).

T. E. Uehling, Jr. and H. K. Wettstein (eds.), *Contemporary Perspectives in the Philosophy of Language*, University of Minnesota Press, Minneapolis.

Kripke, S. A. (1971) 'Identity and Necessity', in M. K. Munitz (ed.), *Identity and Individuation*, New York University Press, New York.

— (1972) 'Naming and Necessity', in D. Davidson and G. Harman (eds.), *Semantics of Natural Language*, Reidel, Boston.

— (1979) 'Speaker's Reference and Semantic Reference', in P. A. French, T. E. Uehling, Jr. and H. K. Wettstein (eds.), *Contemporary Perspectives in the Philosophy of Language*, University of Minnesota Press, Minneapolis.

Lewis, D. K. (1970) 'General Semantics', *Synthese*, 22.

Montague, R. (1974) *Formal Philosophy*, R. H. Thomason (ed.), Yale University Press, New Haven.

Partee, B. H. (1979) 'Montague Grammar, Mental Representations, and Reality', in P. A. French, T. E. Uehling, Jr. and H. K. Wettstein (eds.), *Contemporary Perspectives in the Philosophy of Language*, University of Minnesota Press, Minneapolis.

Putnam, H. (1970) 'Is Semantics Possible?' in H. E. Kiefer and M. K. Munitz (eds.), *Language Belief and Metaphysics*, State University of New York Press.

— (1975) 'The Meaning of "Meaning" ', in K. Gunderson (ed.), *Language, Mind, and Knowledge*, University of Minnesota Press, Minneapolis.

Quine, W. V. O. (1974) *Philosophy of Logic*, Prentice-Hall, Englewood Cliffs.

Soames, S. (1984*a*) 'Linguistics and Psychology', *Linguistics and Philosophy*, Vol. 7, No. 3.

— (1984*b*) 'What is a Theory of Truth?', *Journal of Philosophy*, Vol. LXXXI, No. 8.

Wasow, T. (1978) 'On Constraining the Class of Possible Transformational Languages', *Synthese*, Vol. 39.

11
SETS AND SENTENCES
D. T. LANGENDOEN AND P. M. POSTAL

1. BACKGROUND AND GOALS

LINGUISTIC research over the past quarter century has been largely guided by two major assumptions introduced by Noam Chomsky: (i) that the best theory of a natural language (NL) is a grammar that generates its sentences and (ii) that human beings know an NL in virtue of knowing that grammar. These assumptions cannot be maintained. The collection of sentences comprising each individual NL is so vast that its magnitude is given by no number, finite or transfinite. This means that NLs cannot, as is currently almost universally assumed, be considered recursively enumerable, hence countable (or denumerable) collections of sentences. For if they were such, the magnitude of each would be no greater than the smallest transfinite cardinal number $\aleph_0$. It then follows that there can be no procedure, algorithm, Turing machine or grammar that constructs or generates all the members of an NL, since, by definition, such a grammar can construct or generate only recursively enumerable, hence countable, collections. A system which constructs *some* NL sentences must inevitably leave most NL sentences unconstructed.

2. THE ANALOGY WITH CANTOR'S RESULTS

2.1 *Co-ordination*

Our conclusion concerning the vastness of NLs is based on a demonstration of a strict parallelism between the collection of all sentences of an NL and the collection of all sets. The discovery around the turn of this century that the latter collection is not itself a set led to

Adapted by the authors from *The Vastness of Natural Languages*. Reprinted by permission of Basil Blackwell Publisher.

fundamental reforms in logic and the foundations of mathematics. The same reasoning that establishes that the collection of all sets cannot itself be a set (a collection with fixed magnitude, finite or transfinite) also establishes that the collection of all NL sentences cannot be a set. Consequently, fundamental revisions of currently standard views of NLs and grammars are required for reasons similar to those that operated in the foundations of logic and mathematics.

We assume that co-ordinating particles like English *and, or*, etc., have a structure in which, quoting Gazdar (1981, p. 158):

. . . the co-ordinating word forms a constituent with the immediately following node and is not simply a sister of all the conjuncts.

However, we generalize to eliminate reference to 'following' to cover NLs where the co-ordinating particle follows. For concreteness and ease of reference, we assume these particles belong to a grammatical category called Conj, whose elements have the properties in (1):

(1) If A is a Conj node, then there exist nodes B and C such that:
    (*a*) There is a grammatical category Q such that both B and C are Q nodes; and
    (*b*) A is a daughter of B and the unique sister of C.

In these terms, we say that nodes instantiating variable B in (1) are *conjuncts*, while those instantiating C are *subconjuncts*. Ignoring the order of sisters, every conjunct thus has the structure in (2):

(2)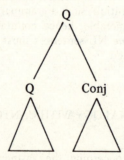

We allow a Conj terminal to be null for NLs without visible co-ordinating particles and for cases in NLs like English where one or more instances of Conj are not visible. Thus we take (3*a*) to have a structure like (3*b*), associating nodes with numbers for ease of reference:

(3) (*a*) Tom and Bill
    (*b*)

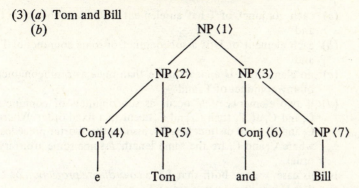

In this case, according to our definitions, nodes 2 and 3 are conjuncts, while nodes 5 and 7 are subconjuncts.

Nodes like 1 in (3*b*) will be referred to as *co-ordinate compound constituents (nodes)*, definable as in C (4):

(4) A constituent (node) Q is a co-ordinate compound of grammatical category C if and only if:

    (*a*) Q is of category C; and
    (*b*) Q has at least two immediate constituents; and
    (*c*) each of Q's immediate constituents is a conjunct.

Observe that nothing in the definition of 'co-ordinate compound' imposes any upper limit, finite or transfinite, on the number of immediate constituents in such structures. Co-ordinate compounds are evidently subject to the two fundamental lawful restrictions in (5):

(5) All sister conjuncts are of the same grammatical category as

    (*a*) each other; and
    (*b*) the co-ordinate compound constituent of which they are immediate constituents.

However, we take C in (4) to vary only over so-called 'major' categories, so as not to exclude the possibility of, e.g. compounds of the category Plural with exclusively singular immediate constituents, etc.

Co-ordinate compounding in NLs is, we claim, governed by a fundamental condition we refer to as *co-ordinate compound closure*. To characterize this principle it is convenient to introduce two more basic terms, *co-ordinate projection*, and *projection set* as in (6):

(6) Let U be a set of constituents all of category Q and of cardinality > 1 and let T be some co-ordinate compound of category Q. Furthermore, assume that:

(a) each conjunct of T has an element of U as a subconjunct; and

(b) each element of U is a subconjunct of some conjunct of T; and

(c) no element of U appears more than once as a subconjunct of any conjunct of T; and

(d) if two elements of U occur as subconjuncts of conjuncts C_i and C_j of T, then C_i and C_j occur in a fixed order. Where C_i and C_j are of distinct lengths, assume the shorter precedes; where C_i and C_j are the same length, assume some arbitrary order.

In this case, we say both that T is a *co-ordinate projection of U* and that U is *the projection set of T*.

(e) Example: Let U = {Laura, Maxine, Brooks}. Then one may choose T = *Laura, Maxine, and Brooks*.

(6a) demands that the subconjuncts for T be drawn exclusively from U, while (6b) demands that each element of U be used to form some subconjunct. (6c) prevents repetitions of elements from the projection set. (6b,c) together determine *inter alia* that the number of conjuncts in a co-ordinate projection is identical to the number of elements in its projection set. (6d) insures that different orders of conjuncts are irrelevant. Given the latter, co-ordinate projections of a set of constituents are unique *up to choice of element of Conj*. For simplicity, the discussion is henceforth limited to some unique element of the category Conj, thus determining a unique co-ordinate projection for any set of constituents, making it sensible to speak of *the* co-ordinate projection of such a set.

As stressed by E. Keenan (personal communication), it is important to show that every subset of a collection of constituents of category Q has a co-ordinate projection. But this is straightforward. For consider some such subset U. Take the cardinality of U to be k, with k indifferently finite or transfinite. Clearly, from the purely formal point of view, there is a co-ordinate compound W belonging to the category Q, hence having immediate constituents of the category Q. Moreover, each of these immediate constituents is a conjunct. Since there are no size restrictions on co-ordinate compounds, W can have any number, finite (> 1) or transfinite of immediate constituents. W can then, in particular have exactly k such constituents. Each of these (conjuncts) has one and only one subconjunct. The set of all such subconjuncts, call it V, obviously then also has exactly k members. To show that W is a co-ordinate projection of U, it then in effect suffices that there exist a one-to-one mapping from U to V. But this is trivial, since the two sets have the same number of elements. However, the conclusion that each subset U of constituents of category Q has a co-ordinate projection does not mean that the co-ordinate projection is necessarily well-formed in the NL from which U is drawn. The latter can only be determined by axioms to this effect, to which we now turn.

The notion of closure for co-ordinate compounding is stated in (7):

(7) The Closure Principle for Co-ordinate Compounding
    If U is a set of constituents each belonging to the collection, S_w, of (well-formed) constituents of category Q of any NL, then S_w, contains the co-ordinate projection of U.

Crucially, principle (7) has a 'recursive' property in that it also refers to cases where members of U are themselves co-ordinate compounds.

Although it is not entirely clear for what categories principle (7) holds universally, it is, we claim, at least valid for the one case of real concern here: where Q is the category S(entence). This yields (8), which we take as a truth about all NLs:

(8) Closure under Co-ordinate Compounding of Sentences
    (a) If U is a set of constituents each belonging to the collection, S_w, of (well-formed) constituents of the category S of any NL, then the co-ordinate projection of U belongs to S_w.
    More precisely, (8a) can be stated as in (8b):
    (b) Let L be the collection of all members of the category S of an NL and let CP(U) be the co-ordinate projection of the set of sentences U.
    Then:

$$(\forall U)(U \subset L \rightarrow CP(U) \in L)$$

Principle (8) is no doubt too general in one respect. Sentences (clauses) fall into types, declarative, interrogative, imperative, etc. And a co-ordinate compound is in general only freely permitted for members of a single type. One could amend (8) appropriately, by restricting the members of U to a single type. We ignore this complication in the wording of what follows.

The principle of closure for co-ordinate compounding of sentences formalizes the following observation about collections of attested NL sentences. Given any set of Ss (of the same type) of some NL L, there is a well-formed co-ordinate compound of those Ss in L, as illustrated in (9), where a double arrow means that the sentence on its right is the co-ordinate projection of the set of sentences on its left.

(9) (a) {Gregory is handsome; It is raining; Figs can kill} ⟹
     (b) Gregory is handsome, it is raining and figs can kill.
     (c) {Gregory is handsome; It is raining; Figs can kill;
          Gregory is handsome, it is raining, and figs can kill} ⟹
     (d) Gregory is handsome, it is raining, figs can kill and
          Gregory is handsome, it is raining and figs can kill.

We now show that the closure principle for co-ordinate compounding leads to the conclusion that there is no set of NL sentences just as the axiom of powers leads to the conclusion that there is no set of all sets.

2.2. *The Cantorian Analogue*

Let L be an NL whose ordinary vocabulary contains the name Z of a particular person or elephant. Assume L contains a denumerably infinite set, S_0, of *noncompound* sentences, each of which is about the entity Z, named by Z. This assumption seems uncontroversial, since, for many known NLs, it is easy to effectively specify such a set. For example, if L is English, S_0 could be the set in (10), where Z = Babar.

(10) {Babar is happy; I know that Babar is happy; I know that
      I know that Babar is happy; I know that I know that I know
      that Babar is happy . . . }

Assume that L is closed under co-ordinate compounding of clauses, that is, obeys (8). Then L also contains a set S_1 made up of all the sentences of S_0 together with all and only the co-ordinate projections of every subset of S_0 with at least two elements, that is, with a set containing one co-ordinate projection for each member of the power set of S_0 whose cardinality is at least 2. The clumsiness of this formulation arises from the fact that co-ordinate projections, given the nature of co-ordination, require by definition at least two subconjuncts, while power sets contain singletons as well as the null set. To simplify the discussion, we utilize the notation >1-*power set of X*, meaning that proper subset of the power set of the set X containing all and only the power set elements of cardinality 2 or greater. To illustrate, if S_o is as in (10), then S_1 can be taken as the set in (11):

(11) {Babar is happy; I know that Babar is happy; I know that
      I know that Babar is happy; . . . ; Babar is happy and I know
      that Babar is happy; Babar is happy and I know that I know
      that Babar is happy; . . . ; Babar is happy, I know that Babar
      is happy, and I know that I know that Babar is happy; . . . }

By assumption, the cardinality of S_0 is $\aleph_0$. To determine the cardinality of S_1, one can appeal directly to Cantor's theorem. Each member of S_1 can be put into one-to-one correspondence with a non-null member of the power set of S_0, determined as follows. Each non-compound sentence of S_1 corresponds to the singleton set whose unique element is the corresponding sentence of S_0. Each co-ordinate compound sentence of S_1 corresponds to its projection set. Hence each compound sentence of S_1 with two conjuncts corresponds to the set made up of the corresponding pair of sentences of S_0, each compound sentence of S_1 with three conjuncts corresponds to the set made up of the corresponding triple of sentences of S_0. Similarly, for each finite subset of S_0 of cardinality > 3, there is a corresponding compound sentence of S_1, namely, the co-ordinate projection of that subset of S_0. Finally, each *infinite* subset of S_0 also corresponds to a compound sentence of S_1, although, of course, each such co-ordinate projection *is of transfinite length*. Overall then, each co-ordinate compound sentence of S_1 corresponds to a member of the >1-power set of S_0. Since the cardinality of the power set of any denumerably infinite set, and hence of S_0, is of the order of the continuum, that is $\aleph_1$, the cardinality of S_1 is $\aleph_1$. Further, since L is closed under co-ordinate compounding, the sentences of S_1 are all contained in L, and therefore, if L has any determinate magnitude, this must be of *at least* the cardinality $\aleph_1$.

The set S_1 as a whole is characterizable as in (12), where '$\cup$' is the sign for set union.

(12) $S_1 = S_0 \cup K_0$,

where $K_0 = \{x : (\exists y)(y \subseteq S_0 \wedge x \text{ is the co-ordinate projection of } y)\}$

In other words, S_1 is the union of S_0 and the set K_0 consisting of all and only the co-ordinate projections of the >1-power set of S_0.

The cardinality of S_1 exceeds that of S_0 precisely because it contains sentences with transfinitely many co-ordinated constituents. The cardinality of the set S_0, made up of the union of S_0 with all those sentences of S_1 with at most finitely many conjuncts as immediate constituents is also $\aleph_0$. But the set S_1', the union of all of the sentences of S_0' together with the co-ordinate compound sentences of L whose immediate constituents are conjuncts with only sentences of S_0 as sub-conjuncts, is of the cardinality $\aleph_1$.

If English is governed by (8) and contains the sentences in S_0, then it also contains the sentences in S_1. That is, English contains at least as many sentences as the continuum.

But it evidently must contain even more. Consider the union of S_1 and a set containing the co-ordinate projection of every member of the >1-power set of S_1. That is, consider the set S_2, definable analogously to S_1 in (12), as in (13):

(13) $S_2 = S_1 \cup K_1$,

where $K_1 = \{x: (\exists y)(y \subseteq S_1 \wedge x$ is the co-ordinate projection of $y)\}$

Via the procedure outlined for S_1, the members of S_2 can be put into a one to one correspondence with the members of the power set of S_1, excluding the null set. Hence the cardinality of $S_2 = \aleph_2$. Futher, since L is closed under co-ordinate compounding, S_2 is also included within L. Consequently, the magnitude of L, if determinate, is at least of the cardinality $\aleph_2$.

Just as Cantor showed for power sets in general, the possibility of forming greater and greater sets of NL sentences always remains. For any set of sentences like S_1, S_2, etc., there is always a still bigger set *included in L*, given by the schematic characterization in (14):

(14) $S_i = S_{i-1} \cup K_{i-1}$, where $i > 0$ and where

$K_{i-1} = \{x: (\exists y)(y \subseteq S_{i-1} \wedge x$ is the co-ordinate projection of $y)\}$

At no point can a set of sentences be obtained that exhausts an NL having sentence co-ordination governed by the closure law (8). Naturally, this will not be less true if one begins, more realistically, with *all* of the finite sentences of that NL, not just an artificially small subset of these like (11) containing only expressions sharing a single name. To prove that no set of sentences can exhaust an NL, it suffices to construct an analogue of Cantor's Paradox *from the contrary assumption*, a construction which the previous remarks make directly possible. We call this result *the NL Vastness Theorem*, and state it as (15):

(15) *The NL Vastness Theorem*
      THEOREM: NLs are *not* sets (are megacollections)
      Proof:
            Let #X be the cardinality of an arbitrary set X and let L be the collection of all sentences of some NL.
      (a)   Assume to the contrary of the theorem that L is a set.
      (b)   Then L has a fixed cardinality, #L.
      (c)   Since L is closed under co-ordinate compounding, L contains a subset consisting of all and only the co-ordinate projections of the >1-power set of L. Moreover, each member of the >1-power set of L has a co-ordinate projection. Hence $(\exists Z)(Z \subseteq L)$, where:

$Z = \{x : (\exists y)(y \subseteq L \wedge x$ is the co-ordinate projection of $y)\}$

(d) Since many sentences in L, in particular, all those elements of L which are not co-ordinate compounds, are *not* in Z, Z is a *proper* subset of L. That is, not only $Z \subseteq L$ but in fact $Z \subset L$.

(e) Hence, $\#Z \leq \#L$.

(f) But $\#Z$ is, given the definition of Z in (15c), of the order of the power set of L.

(g) Hence, by Cantor's Theorem, $\#Z > \#L$.

(h) Since conclusion (15g) contradicts conclusion (15e), assumption (15a) is false.

The assumption that L is a set, hence a collection having a fixed cardinality, yields a contradiction and is thus necessarily false. Therefore, the collection L is not a set. But L in (15) was arbitrarily chosen. Just as Cantor's Paradox shows there is no single set containing all non-null sets, the NL Vastness Theorem shows that an NL can be identified with no fixed set of sentences at all, no matter how great its cardinality. Like the collection of all sets, an individual NL must be regarded as a megacollection.

2.3 *The Mathematical Argument as a Linguistic Argument*

Having constructed the central argument of this study, we now comment on its character. The demonstration in (15) that NLs are not sets but megacollections has, like any attempt to apply a mathematical result to some domain of facts, two distinguishable aspects. There must, first, be a proof of the relevant theorem, a question of formal mathematics, involving a purely demonstrative argument and, second, an argument, in general necessarily nondemonstrative, that the relevant domain of facts manifests all crucial properties of the mathematical assumptions underlying the proof of the theorem. In this case, the relevant theorem is the NL Vastness Theorem, whose proof corresponds closely to the proof of Cantor's Paradox. The second aspect, the consequence that this formal proof 'applies' to NLs, involves the claim that NLs do indeed model a system of mathematical objects having the properties which yield the NL Vastness Theorem. Only by confirming the second aspect of the argument can one avoid the problem properly noted by Hockett (1966, p. 186):

An ironclad conclusion about a certain set of 'languages' (in the formal sense) can be mistaken for a discovery about real human language.

There is another way to put the point. As with any proof from assumptions A to a conclusion Z, one can regard the NL Vastness Theorem as a proof of the conditional A $\Rightarrow$ Z. This proof does not require that A be true. But the detachment of Z as a true consequence then only follows via Modus Ponens, which requires that the antecedent of a conditional be true. Therefore, (15) is a proof of a conditional whose consequent is the conclusion that NLs are megacollections. But to derive the actual nonconditional conclusion, that is, the NL Vastness Theorem itself, via Modus Ponens requires that the antecedent to be true. In effect, this antecedent is the claim that NL co-ordination is governed by the closure principle (8). Surely, scepticism about the NL Vastness Theorem must focus on this axiom, which is not a traditionally or currently accepted linguistic principle.

Let us therefore briefly refocus attention on condition (8), the claim that NLs are closed under the co-ordinate compounding of sentences. Although not a familiar principle of past or present linguistics, (8) expresses, we claim, a profound truth about NLs. It says not only that the principles of grammatical theory and the rules of grammar directly relevant to characterizing co-ordinate structures must not themselves preclude closure, but that no other rules can have this effect either. No matter how one characterizes the collection of co-ordinate structures of English, closure would be violated if some *independent* English rule said, for example, that there was a maximum bound on number of conjuncts, or one which said that some particular pair of clauses of the same type could not form a co-ordinate compound, etc. Similarly, (8) would be violated if some rule of English required every co-ordinate compound to have *more* than k conjuncts for some fixed k, or if there were a rule ('filter') precluding, e.g. the sequence of English words *and+it*. But the known facts about co-ordinate compounding in NLs reveal the existence of no such constraints. Principle (8) claims that the lack of such is nonaccidental.

Closure principle (8) plays a role in the proof of the NL Vastness Theorem analogous to that played in set-theoretical discussions (in particular, the proof of Cantor's Paradox) by axioms which determine that every set does have a power set. Such axioms guarantee that the collection of sets is closed under power setting in essentially the way principle (8) guarantees that the collection of sentences of an NL is closed under co-ordinate compounding. It seems that there are exactly as good grounds for the latter as for the former.

Principle (8) mentions a set U of constituents but says nothing about its magnitude. Clearly, one obtains a variety of different closure laws by imposing differential magnitude requirements on U, as in (16):

(16) (a) U has less than k elements (k a positive integer).
    (b) U has less than $\aleph_0$ elements.
    (c) U has less than $\aleph_1$ elements.
    (d) U has less than $\aleph_2$ elements.

There are infinitely many possible magnitude restrictions on U, each limiting the collection of possible projection sets for co-ordinate compounds. If any of these are adopted *instead of (8)*, the argument that NLs are not sets will obviously not go through, because at some point in the definitions of sets S_3, S_4, etc., schematized in (14), the resulting co-ordinate compounds will not be determined to be included in the language.

More precisely, if one of the denumerably many restrictions in (16a) is chosen, the collection of co-ordinate compounds is not determined to be more than a finite set, while if (16b) is chosen, it is a countably infinite set. Consequently, it is critical for the conclusion that (8) rather than any element of (16) is the *correct* closure principle for co-ordinate compounding. In particular, it is critical to justify (8) against (16b).

First, (8) is simpler than any statement in (16), because, unlike those statements, (8) *says nothing at all about magnitude*. Hence (8) is, by Occam's Razor, theoretically preferable to any formulation covered by (16), since it is always simpler not to specify anything about the magnitude of some collection than to say something about its size. And this obviously holds for U in (8).

Second, one can regard grammars and grammatical theory as concerned with *projecting* from the properties of *attested* NL sentences, the basic data of grammatical investigation, to the maximal lawfully characterized collections of which these attested sentences are accidental examples. One wants, given a sample of English sentences, to characterize the collection of all English sentences, and, given a sample of NL sentences, the collection of NL sentences *per se*. General scientific principles demand that the projections from the small finite samples to the desired characterizations involve the maximally general (i.e. strong) laws (principles) projecting the regularities found in observed cases to the collections as wholes. One can never justifiably replace a stronger or more general projection by a weaker or less general one unless this is factually motivated, in particular, by the excess generality leading to some false entailment, e.g. a false claim about attested examples, some contradiction, etc.

For example, there is no basis for not projecting from attested sentences of various lengths to the maximally general view that sentences of any length whatever are possible, unless this yields some false entailment, which has never been shown. Therefore, there is no basis for not projecting from attested co-ordinate compounds of various lengths to the maximally general view, represented by (8), that co-ordinate compounds of any length whatever are possible, unless this yields some false entailment, which again has not been shown.

Thus, there are two reasons for choosing the closure principle (8) over any of the alternatives in (16): (8) is both simpler and stronger.

Obviously, the conclusion which (8) determines, that NLs are mega-collections, is itself no basis whatever for rejecting this principle, any more than the conclusion which the Axiom of Powers determines, that the collection of all sets is a megacollection, is a ground for rejecting that axiom. Essentially, principle (8) says that it makes no more sense to think that structures otherwise having the structural (linguistic) properties of co-ordinate compounds nonetheless fail to be co-ordinate compounds if they have more than some fixed number of conjuncts than it does to think that aggregates fail to be sets if they have more than some fixed number of elements. That is, it is as arbitrary to claim that some structures have too many conjuncts to be proper co-ordinate compound sentences as it is to claim that some aggregates have too many elements to be (power) sets.

To sum up, (8), the principle of closure under co-ordinate compounding, plays an absolutely crucial role in the argument that NLs are mega-collections. More precisely, it is the critical assumption guaranteeing that NLs are models of a system of objects for which all the mathematical assumptions underlying the proof of the NL Vastness Theorem hold.

The argument given in (15) involves the existence of sentences of transfinite length, the postulation of which, of course, clashes with standardly held but unmotivated and never justified views. The standard view is that while there is no longest sentence, every sentence is of finite length, that is, has a length less than $\aleph_0$. This amounts to imposition of what we will call *a length law* on NL sentences. Our claim is that no such length law is true of NL sentences. It is crucial, moreover, that the nonexistence of a length law is *not* a premise of the proof in (15) but, rather, is a corollary of the closure principle (8). This is shown in (17), which demonstrates the nonexistence of any length law for NL sentences, finite or transfinite. The proof utilizes a predicate Length, taken to be a measure of the number of words in a sentence. We also make use of the self-evident fact that the length of any co-ordinate projection is not less than the cardinality of its projection set. This is only to say that each member of a projection set T contributes at least one word to the co-ordinate projection of T.

(17)   *The No Upper Bound Theorem*
       THEOREM: Let L be the collection of all sentences of some NL. Then:

$$(\forall k)(\text{Cardinal }(k) \Rightarrow (\exists x)(x \in L \wedge \text{Length}(X) \geqslant k)).$$

Proof:

(a)   Assume to the contrary that j is a cardinal such that:

$$(\forall Y)(Y \in L \Rightarrow \text{Length}(Y) < j).$$

(b)   Every proper subset of L then has a cardinality $< j$. For the closure axiom (8) determines that every such subset is the projection set of some co-ordinate projection which is a sentence of L. And, as we have seen, the length of any co-ordinate projection is at least that of the cardinality of its projection set. Hence if some $C \subset L$ had $> j$ members, some $Z \in L$ would have a length $> j$, namely, for a Z equal to a co-ordinate projection of C.

(c)   We now show that if every proper subset of L has a cardinality $< j$, the maximal cardinality of L is j. There are two cases, since L is either finite or not finite.

       (i)   Case A. L is finite. Consider one member, M, of the set of *biggest* proper subsets of L. M will have one less member than L. Since M has, from (b), a cardinality $< j$, the maximum cardinality of L is j.

       (ii) Case B. L is transfinite. It follows from set theory that L is equipollent to some proper subset of L, call it D. Since, from (b), D has a cardinality $< j$, so does L.

(d)   It follows from (c) that L is a set with $\leqslant j$ members, contradicting the NL Vastness Theorem. Hence (a) is false.

The consequence that NLs are megacollections rather than recursively enumerable sets cannot be rationally avoided by a decision to adopt the finiteness limitation on sentence size or its analogue for the number of conjuncts even in the absence of substantively or logically motivated bases for such conditions. We are rejecting an argument which might go something like (18).

(18) The finiteness limitations are justified just because they subsume NLs within the realm of recursively enumerable sets and
Turing machine grammars, a mathematically well-understood
domain about which a rich, useful body of knowledge has
been accumulated.

The fallacy in such a defence of a closure principle like (16*b*) has
already in effect been uncovered by Chomsky several times in different
contexts. First, consider (19):

(19)   Chomsky (1957: 23):

We might arbitrarily decree that such processes of sentence formation in English as those we are discussing cannot be carried out more
than *n* times, for some fixed *n*. This would of course make English a
finite state language, as, for example, would a limitation of English
sentences to length of less than a million words. *Such arbitrary limitations serve no useful purpose, however.*' [Emphasis ours: DTL/PMP.]

While Chomsky's comment about 'fixed *n*' was intended only to cover
finite instantiations of *n*, the force of the remarks clearly carries over
to his own choice of length law and all others as well, since these are
nothing but instances where *n* varies over transfinite cardinals. The
same point applies to (16*b*).

Again, criticizing a certain argument which need not concern us,
Chomsky made the correct observation in (20):

(20)   Chomsky (1977*a*: 174):

In the first place, he is overlooking the fact that we have certain
antecedently clear cases of language as distinct from maze running,
basket weaving, topological orientation, recognition of faces or melodies,
use of maps, and so on. We cannot arbitrarily decide that 'language'
is whatever meets some canons we propose. Thus we cannot simply
stipulate that rules are structure-independent, . . .

Since NLs are independently given, they are not subject to arbitrary
decisions about sentence length or any other property. Just as one
cannot simply decide that rules are (or are not) structure-dependent,
one cannot just decide that sentences are (or are not) all finite, or
that the number of conjuncts in a co-ordinate compound is always
finite. In both cases, arguments based on the nature of the attested
part of the subject matter are required. Consequently, one can no
more decide that each sentence is finite in length than one can decide
that each is less than one thousand morphemes in length or that each

grammar is a finite state system. Unfortunately for linguistics, the sentence finiteness decision has been *arbitrarily* made and maintained for nearly thirty years. But this past mistake contains no justification for its continuation.

3. IMPLICATIONS

3.1 *Remarks*

So far we have established the two relatively simple substantive points about NLs in (1):

(1) (*a*) The NL Vastness Theorem; that is, the existence of un-bounded co-ordination subject to the closure principle (8) of Section 2 entails, via a Cantorian analogy, that the collection of sentences in NL is (i) bigger than countably infinite, and (ii), in fact, a megacollection.

    (*b*) The No Upper Bound Theorem, that is; there is no length law on NL sentences.

Moreover, we showed that (1*b*) is a logical consequence of the closure principle, which thus provides a principled reason for the nonexistence of NL length laws. Since the argument for (1*a*) was based exclusively on English data, it is more accurate to say that (1*a*) follows for any NL manifesting co-ordination with the essential properties characterized earlier.

However, we know of no NL ever described which has even been *claimed* to lack co-ordination of, *inter alia*, clauses, as expressed by Dik:

(2) Dik (1968: 1):

For a variety of reasons the so-called 'coordinative construction' is of special importance to linguistic theory. In the first place, this type of construction seems to be a universal feature of natural languages. Secondly, not only does its existence seem to be universal, but the way in which it is manifested in each particular language also shows a quite general, if not universal pattern.

Consequently, we hypothesize that both (1*a, b*) are proper universal truths about NLs.

3.2 *Linguistic Consequences*

(1) can be used, as earlier discerned facts about the nature of NLs have been, to falsify proposed grammatical theories on the grounds that

they are too weak. Just as certain facts about NLs were taken to show that finite state grammars, context-free grammars, etc., are too weak, the fact that NLs are megacollections shows that any conception of NL grammars under which they are Turing machines is inadequate. Put differently, (1*a*) entails that any theory which claims NLs are recursively enumerable sets is false. We formulate this consequence explicitly as a theorem referred to as *the NL Nonconstructivity Theorem*, given in (3):

(3) THEOREM: No NL has any constructive (= proof-theoretic, generative or Turing machine) grammar

Proof:

(*a*) Let L be an NL and let G be a constructive grammar.

(*b*) G specifies exactly some collection, call it C(G). From the definition of constructive systems, G recursively ｜enumerates C(G), which is hence a countably infinite or finite set.

(*c*) The NL Vastness Theorem shows that L is a megacollection.

(*d*) Thus (Eisenberg (1971: 304)) L > C(G); and hence C(G) ≠ L.

(*e*) Therefore, G is not a grammar of L.

Since G and L in (3) were arbitrarily chosen, it has been shown that *no* constructive system is a correct grammar of *any* NL.

Although the NL Nonconstructivity Theorem is straightfoward, its consequences are both extraordinarily broad and deep. For, as Chomsky observed in the passage in (4):

(4) Chomsky (1957: 34):

The strongest possible proof of the inadequacy of a linguistic theory is to show that it literally cannot apply to some natural language.

In Chomsky's terms then, the NL Nonconstructivity Theorem shows that every variant of every view taking NL grammars to be constructive devices is a *false* theory of NLs. This means that every logically possible variant (not only those *so far* described) of all the frameworks in (5) are false:

(5) *Frameworks Falsified as Theories of NLs by the NL Nonconstructivity Theorem*
  Finite Grammar (Hockett (1968))
  Finite State Grammar (Reich (1969))
  Phrase Structure Grammar (Harmon (1963); Gazdar (1981, 1982))

Lexical/Functional Grammar (Bresnan (1982))
Realistic Grammar (Brame (1979))
Stratificational Grammar (Lamb (1966); Lockwood (1972))
Tagmemics (Longacre (1964))
Montague Grammar (Partee (1975, 1976); Dowty (1978, 1982))
Natural Generative Grammar (Bartsch and Vennemann (1972))
Semantically Based Grammar (Chafe (1970*a*, 1970*b*))
Functional Grammar (Dik (1978, 1980))
Daughter Dependency Grammar (Hudson (1976); Schachter (1978))
Phrasal Core Grammar (Keenan (1980*a*, 1980*b*))
Transformational Grammar (Chomsky (1957, 1965, 1977*b*, 1981, 1982))
Corepresentational Grammar (Kac (1980))
Relationally Based Grammar (Johnson (1979))
Dependency Grammar (Hays (1964))
Categorial Grammar (Lambek (1961))
Cognitive Grammar (Lakoff and Thompson (1975))
Meaning-Text Models (Melčuk (1981))
The Abstract System (Harris (1968))
Configurational Grammar (Koster (1981))
Neostructural Grammar (Langendoen (1982))
Augmented Transition Networks (Woods (1970))
String Adjunct Grammar (Joshi, Kosaraju and Yamada (1972))
Equational Grammar (Sanders (1972))
Systemic Grammar (Hudson (1971))
Any *constructive* system distinct from all of the preceding frameworks.

The NL Nonconstructivity Theorem actually follows from a conclusion *infinitely weaker* than the NL Vastness Theorem, namely, just from the fact that NLs are at least of the magnitude of the continuum, which suffices to justify line (d) in the proof of the NL Nonconstructivity Theorem with no reference to megacollections. Hence the stage of the analogy in (12) of Section 2 involving just the set there called S_1 already suffices to falsify all views limiting grammars to the characterization of recursively enumerable sets. This means the conclusion follows from the existence of sentences of no greater than denumerably infinite length.

The NL Nonconstructivity Theorem states that no NL has a constructive grammar. It might be wondered to just what extent the NL Vastness Theorem is incompatible with constructivity. In particular, given the syntactic nature of the data on which the NL Vastness Theorem is based, one might assume that the result was compatible, for example, with either or both constructive phonology and/or (interpretive) semantics. But this is not the case. A grammar capable of characterizing transfinite sentences cannot contain constructive phonological or semantic components.

The implications of the NL Nonconstructivity Theorem can be summed up as follows. Since the ideas of generative grammar became dominant in the late 1950s, linguistics has in general assumed that the task of grammatical theory involves answering the question: what is the right form of *generative* grammar for NLs? The many disputes which have divided linguists over the past quarter century are then reducible by and large to disputes over claims about 'right form'. Some linguists have believed that NL grammars contain transformational rules; others have denied this. Some linguists have believed that transformational rules are parochially ordered; others have denied this. Some linguists have believed that there are interpretive semantic rules; others have denied this. And so on. Underlying all such disputes has been the assumption that it is possible through appeal to some combination of proof-theoretical devices to construct *some* generative grammar for each NL. But this assumption is falsified by the NL Nonconstructivity Theorem.

There is another way to characterize the consequences summed up in (1) and in the NL Nonconstructivity Theorem. The false finiteness limitation on sentence size determined the claim that NLs fall somewhere in the domain of objects characterizable by what one might call *theoretical computer science*. Their grammars would be some sort of Turing machine, their sentence aggregates recursively enumerable sets. Since NLs are subject to no length law, they do not lie within this limited class of mathematical objects. While this conclusion may, for various socio-historical reasons, be displeasing to some, it involves no unsurmountable theoretical or methodological difficulties. Logic and the foundations of mathematics faced similar problems at the beginning of this century but did not cease to thrive; quite the contrary. Hence the results in (1) are not at all to be seen as negative or unhappy consequences for grammatical study. They can be interpreted quite positively, as showing that NLs have a grandeur not previously recognized.

The NL Nonconstructivity Theorem shows that NLs do not have generative grammars. This is quite distinct from the claim, which we totally reject, that NLs do not have explicit grammars. This is important to recognize in view of the widespread confounding of the notions 'generative grammar' and 'explicit grammar', a confounding seen in such remarks as those by Harman in (6) and Chomsky in (7).

(6) Harman (1982: vii):

The term 'generative' derives from mathematics, not psychology. It connotes explicitness of rules, not a psychological process of sentence production. A generative grammar would therefore be a precise and explicit statement of the rules of grammar of a particular natural language like English.

(7) Chomsky (1965: 4):

A grammar of a language purports to be a description of the ideal speaker-hearer's intrinsic competence. If the grammar is, furthermore, perfectly explicit—we may (somewhat redundantly) call it a *generative grammar*.

Contrary to the implications of such remarks, explicitness and generativeness are distinct notions. A grammar *per se* merely states necessary and sufficient conditions for membership in an NL. A *generative* grammar is, as indicated by Chomsky himself many times, not only an explicit statement of such conditions, but a procedure for enumerating the members of an NL, hence a type of Turing machine. What the NL Nonconstructivity Theorem shows, then, is that NLs have no generative grammars; but this says nothing about the possibility of nongenerative (nonconstructive) grammars of NLs. Only the confounding of the notions 'explicit grammar' and 'generative grammar' could yield the illegitimate conclusion that the NL Nonconstructivity Theorem implies that NLs do not have grammars.

Moreover, not only are nongenerative grammars a logical possibility, a substantive proposal for such exists in the literature, the nonconstructive conception of grammars in Johnson and Postal (1980) and Postal (1982). To our knowledge, this is the only *extant* view of grammar and grammatical rule which survives the NL Nonconstructivity Theorem. In this view, each grammatical rule is a statement, a formula to which truth values can be assigned and a grammar is equivalently either a set of such rules or a single logical conjunction of such rules.

3.3 *Philosophical Consequences*

The chief philosophical consequence of the preceding discussion concerns the ontological status of NLs. As in other areas, one can distinguish three basic ontological positions potentially relevant to an account of NLs: the nominalist position identifies sentences with physical manifestations and thus cannot countenance the existence of more sentences than there are, for example, subatomic particles in the universe; the conceptualist position identifies sentences with some sort of psychological reality, for example, a mentally instantiated grammar that generates them and the realist/Platonist position takes sentences to be abstract objects, whose existence is independent of both the physical and the psychological realm.

The now standard observation that NLs are not smaller than countably infinite already drives the nominalist to the extreme view that the physical universe is infinite. But the proof that NLs are megacollections leaves the nominalist devoid of any interpretation for sentencehood. The conceptualist viewpoint tries to adapt to the infinitude of sentences by postulating an internalized, mentally real, algorithm (called a generative grammar) for constructing, in principle, each of the countably infinite number of finite sentences. This position is already problematic in that it does not assign any clear ontological status to most sentences, namely, those which are too big to be mentally constructed or to have actual mental representations. The question to be faced here is whether the conceptualist position claims that the latter sentences are real. If they are not real, what is the point of having a device which characterizes them? And if they are real, how does their reality differ from that of the realist's abstract objects? As far as we can tell, it does not, since these putatively mental objects have no physical, temporal, or psychological locus. The conclusion that NLs are megacollections simply worsens the already problematic status of the conceptualist position, by showing that the number of sentences lacking any psychological locus is unimaginably vast and that this collection includes sentences, equal in size to *every* transfinite cardinal. For such sentences, the notion of an actual psychological locus, even under the loosest of idealizations, makes no sense.

On the other hand, recognition of a realm of sentences equinumerous with the realm of sets raises absolutely no ontological problems not already implicit in standard set theory, problems which have to be faced by any viable ontological position. We conclude, therefore, that the demonstration that NLs are megacollections lends credibility to the realist position by showing, in another domain, the apparently insuperable problems facing any attempt to identify objects in the domain with aspects of the physical or psychological universe.

REFERENCES

Bartsch, R., and Vennemann, T., (1972) *Semantic Structures*, Athenaum Verlag, Frankfurt, W. Germany.

Brame, M. (1979) *Essays Toward Realistic Syntax*, Noit Amrofer, Seattle, Wash.

Bresnan, J. (1982) *The Mental Representation of Grammatical Relations*, MIT Press, Cambridge, Mass.

Chafe, W. (1970*a*) *A Semantically Based Sketch of Onondaga*, Indiana University Publications in Anthropology and Linguistics, Vol. 36, No. 2, P. II, Bloomington, Ind.

— (1970*b*) *Meaning and the Structure of Language*. The University of Chicago Press, Chicago.

Chomsky, N. (1957) *Syntactic Structures* Mouton & Co., The Hague, Holland.

— (1965) *Aspects of the Theory of Syntax*, MIT Press, Cambridge, Mass.

— (1977*a*) *Reflections on Language*, Pantheon Books, New York.

— (1977*b*) *Essays on Form and Interpretation*, North-Holland Publishing Co., Amsterdam, Holland.

— (1981) *Lectures on Government and Binding*, Foris Publications, Dordrecht, Holland.

— (1982) *Some Concepts and Consequences of the Theory of Government and Binding*, MIT Press, Cambridge, Mass.

Dik, S. (1968) *Co-ordination*, North-Holland Publishing Co., Amsterdam, Holland.

— (1978) *Functional Grammar*, North-Holland Publishing Co., Amsterdam, Holland.

— (1980) *Studies in Functional Grammar*, Academic Press, New York.

Dowty, D. (1978) 'Governed Transformations as Lexical Rules in a Montague Grammar', *Linguistic Inquiry*, 9, pp. 393-426.

— (1982) 'Grammatical Relations and Montague Grammar', in P. Jacobson and G. Pullum (eds.), *The Nature of Syntactic Representation*, Reidel & Co., Dordrecht, Holland.

Eisenberg, M. (1971) *Axiomatic Theory of Sets and Classes*, Holt, Rinehart & Winston, New York.

Gazdar, G. (1981) 'Unbounded Dependencies and Coordinate Structure', *Linguistic Inquiry*, 12, pp. 155-84.

— (1982) 'Phrase Structure Grammar', in P. Jacobson and G. Pullum (eds.), *The Nature of Syntactic Representation*, Reidel & Co., Dordrecht, Holland.

Harman, G. (1963) 'Generative Grammars Without Transformational Rules: A Defense of Phrase Structure', *Language*, 39, pp. 597-616.

— (1982) *On Noam Chomsky*, 2nd edn., University of Massachusetts Press, Amherst, Mass.

Harris, Z. (1968) *Mathematical Structures of Language*, Interscience Publishers, John Wiley & Sons, New York.

Hays, D. (1964) 'Dependency Theory: A Formalism and Some Observations', *Language*, 40, pp. 511-25.

Hockett, C. (1966) *Language, Mathematics and Linguistics*, Mouton & Co., The Hague, Holland.

— (1968) *The State of the Art*, Mouton & Co., The Hague, Holland.

Hudson, R. (1971) *English Complex Sentences*, North-Holland Publishing Co., Amsterdam, Holland.

— (1976) *Arguments for a Non-transformational Grammar*, The University of Chicago Press, Chicago.

Johnson, D. (1979) *Toward a Theory of Relationally-Based Grammar*, Garland Publishing Inc., New York.

— and Postal P. (1980) *Arc Pair Grammar*, Princeton University Press, Princeton, NJ.

Joshi, A., Kosaraju, S., and Yamada, H. (1972) 'String Adjunct Grammars: I', *Information and Control*, 21, pp. 93-116.

Kac, M. (1980) 'Corepresentational Grammar', in E. Moravcsik and J. Wirth (eds.), *Syntax and Semantics, Volume 13: Current Approaches to Syntax*, Academic Press, New York.

Keenan, E. (1980a) 'Passive is Phrasal (Not Sentential or Lexical)' in T. Hoekstra, H. Van derHulst and M. Moortgat (eds.), *Lexical Grammar*, Foris Publications, Dordrecht, Holland.

— (1980b) 'A Conception of Core Grammar', unpublished manuscript.

Koster, J. (1981) 'Configurational Grammar', in R. May and J. Koster (eds.), *Levels of Syntactic Representation*, Foris Publications, Dordrecht, Holland.

Lakoff, G. and Thompson, H. (1975) 'Introducing Cognitive Grammar', in C. Cogen *et al.* (eds.), *Proceedings of the First Annual Meeting of the Berkeley Linguistics Society*, Berkeley Linguistics Society, Berkeley, Calif.

Lamb, S. (1966) *Outline of Stratificational Grammar*, Georgetown University Press, Washington, DC.

Lambek, J. (1961) 'On the Calculus of Syntactic Types', in R. Jakobson (ed.), *Structure of Language and Its Mathematical Aspects*, American Mathematical Society, Providence, RI.

Langendoen, T. (1982) 'The Grammatical Analysis of Texts', in S. Allen (ed.), *Proceedings of the Nobel Symposium on Text Processing*, Almqvist and Wiksell, Stockholm, Sweden.

— and Postal, P. (1984) *The Vastness of Natural Languages*, Basil Blackwell, Oxford, England.

Lockwood, D. (1972) *Introduction to Stratificational Linguistics*, Harcourt Brace Jovanovich, Inc., New York.

Longacre, R. (1964) *Grammar Discovery Procedures*, Mouton & Co., The Hague, Holland.

Melčuk, I. (1981) 'Meaning-Text Models: a Recent Trend in Soviet Linguistics', *Annual Review of Anthropology: 1981*, 10, pp. 27-62.

Partee, B. (1975) 'Montague Grammar and Transformational Grammar', *Linguistic Inquiry*, 6, pp. 203-300.

— (1976) *Montague Grammar*, Academic Press, New York.

Postal, P. (1982) 'Some Arc Pair Grammar Descriptions', in P. Jacobson and G. Pullum (eds.), *The Nature of Syntactic Representation*, Reidel & Co., Dordrecht, Holland.

Reich, P. (1969) 'The Finiteness of Natural Language', *Language*, 45, pp. 831-43.

Sanders, G. (1972) *Equational Grammar*, Mouton & Co., The Hague, Holland.

Schachter, P. (1978) Review of R. Hudson, *Arguments for a Transformational Grammar*, *Language*, 54, pp. 348-76.

Woods, W. (1970) 'Transition Network Grammars for Natural Language Analysis', *Communications of the ACM*, 13, pp. 10-38.

NOTES ON CONTRIBUTORS

LEONARD BLOOMFIELD, a co-founder of the American Structuralist movement in linguistics, was Professor of Germanic Philology at the University of Chicago. He is the author of *Language* and many other influential works, including *Linguistic Aspects of Science* in the *International Encyclopedia of Unified Science*.

ZELLIG HARRIS was Benjamin Franklin Professor of Linguistics at the University of Pennsylvania. He is the author of *Methods of Structural Linguistics*, *Mathematical Structures of Language*, and *Papers in Structural and Transformational Linguistics*.

WILLARD VAN ORMAN QUINE was Edgar Pierce Professor of Philosophy at Harvard University. He is the author of a number of widely discussed works in philosophy including *From a Logical Point of View*, *Word and Object*, *Ontological Relativity and Other Essays*, *The Philosophy of Logic*, and *The Ways of Paradox*, as well as important texts such as *Mathematical Logic*, *Methods of Logic*, and *Set Theory and Its Logic*.

EDWARD SAPIR, a co-founder of the American Structuralist movement, was Sterling Professor of Anthropology and Linguistics at Yale University. He is the author of *Language: An Introduction to the Study of Speech* and many influential papers (some collected in *Selected Writings of Edward Sapir*).

NOAM CHOMSKY, founder of the Generative Grammar Movement in Linguistics, is Institute Professor at the Massachusetts Institute of Technology. He is the author of numerous influential works including *Syntactic Structures*, *Cartesian Linguistics*, *Aspects of the Theory of Syntax*, *Studies on Semantics in Generative Grammar*, *Essays on Form and Interpretation*, *Rules and Representations*, and *Lectures on Government and Binding*.

STEPHEN STICH teaches philosophy at the University of Maryland. He is the author of *From Folk Psychology to Cognitive Psychology: The Case Against Belief*, as well as numerous papers.

JERRY A. FODOR teaches philosophy and psychology at the Massachusetts Institute of Technology. He is the author of *Psychological Explanation*, *The Language of Thought*, *Representations*, and *The Modularity of Mind*. He is co-author of *The Psychology of Language: An Introduction to Psycholinguistics* (with T. G. Bever and M. F. Garrett).

LOUIS HJELMSLEV held the Chair of Linguistics at the University of Copenhagen. He is the author of *Principes de grammaire générale*, *Prolegomena to a Theory of Language*, and *Essais linguistiques*.

JERROLD J. KATZ teaches philosophy and linguistics at the Graduate Center of The City University of New York. He is co-author of *An Integrated Theory of Linguistic Descriptions* (with P. Postal), author of *The Philosophy of Language, Semantic Theory, Propositional Structure and Illocutionary Force*, and *Language and Other Abstract Objects*.

SCOTT SOAMES teaches philosophy at Princeton University. He is co-author of *Syntactic Argumentation and the Structure of English* (with D. Perlmutter) and author of papers on truth, semantics, and presupposition.

D. TERENCE LANGENDOEN teaches linguistics at Brookly College and at the Graduate Center of The City University of New York. He is the author of *The London School of Linguistics, Essentials of English*, and co-author of *The Vastness of Natural Languages* (with P. Postal).

PAUL POSTAL is a Research Staff Member at the IBM Thomas J. Watson Research Center. He is the author of *Constituent Structure, Aspects of Phonological Theory, On Raising: One Rule of English and Its Theoretical Implications*, co-author of *An Integrated Theory of Linguistic Descriptions*, (with J. J. Katz), co-author of *Arc Pair Grammar* (with D. Johnson), and co-author of *The Vastness of Natural Languages* (with D. T. Langendoen).

BIBLIOGRAPHY

The following is a bibliography of philosophy and linguistics. It is divided into three sections: anthologies, books, and articles.

ANTHOLOGIES

ANDERSON, S.* and KIPARSKY, P., eds. *A Festschrift for Morris Halle*, Rinehart & Winston, New York, 1973.

AUSTERLITZ, R., ed. *The Scope of American Linguistics*, Humanities Press, Lisse (The Netherlands), 1977.

BENACERRAF, P., and PUTNAM, H., eds. *Philosophy of Mathematics: Selected Readings*, Prentice-Hall, Inc., Englewood Cliffs, 1964.

BLOCK, N., ed. *Readings in Philosophy of Psychology*, Harvard University Press, Cambridge, Mass., 1980.

BORGER, R., and CIOFFI, F., eds. *Explanation in the Behavioural Sciences*, Cambridge University Press, Cambridge, 1970.

Cohen, D., ed. *Explaining Linguistic Phenomena*, Hemisphere, Washington, DC, 1974.

COHEN, D., and WIRTH, J. R., eds. *Testing Linguistic Hypotheses*, Halsted Press, New York, 1975.

Cooper, W. E., and Walker, E., eds. *Sentence Processing*, Halsted Press, Hillsdale, NY, 1979.

Coulas, F., ed. *A Festschrift for the Native Speaker*, Mouton & Co., The Hague, 1981.

DINGWALL, W., ed. *A Survey of Linguistic Science*, Greylock Publishers, College Park, Md., 1971.

Fodor, J. A., and Katz, J. J., eds. *The Structure of Language: Readings in the Philosophy of Language*, Prentice-Hall Inc., Englewood Cliffs, NJ, 1964.

French, Peter, A., *et al. Contemporary Perspectives in the Philosophy of Language*, University of Minnesota Press, Minneapolis, 1978.

GLEITMAN, L., and WANNAR, E., eds. *Language Acquisition State of the Art*, Academic Press, New York, n.d.

HALLE, M., *et al. Linguistic Theory and Psychological Reality*, MIT Press, Cambridge, Mass., 1978.

HARMAN, G., ed. *On Noam Chomsky*, Doubleday, Garden City, NY, 1974.

Hook, S., ed. *Language and Philosophy*, New York University Press, New York, 1969.

Joss, M., ed. *Readings in Linguistics*, American Council of Learned Societies, New York, 1958.

*Capitalized author headings refer to anthologies cited in the Articles section of the bibliography.

Klemke, E., ed. *Essays on Frege*, University of Illinois Press, Urbana, Ill., 1968.

KOERNER, E., ed. *The TG Paradigm and Modern Linguistic Theory*, Humanities Press, Amsterdam, 1975.

LEHMANN, W., and MALKIEL, Y., eds. *Directions for Historical Linguistics*, University of Texas Press, Austin, Tex. 1968.

LINSKY, L., ed. *Semantics and the Philosophy of Language*, University of Illinois Press, Urbana, Ill., 1970.

LYAS, C., ed. *Philosophy and Linguistics*, Macmillan, London, 1971.

Lyons, J., ed. *New Horizons in Linguistics*, Penguin Books, Harmondsworth, England, 1970.

LYONS, J., and WALES, R. J., eds. *Psycholinguistics Papers*, Edinburgh University Press, Edinburgh, 1966.

NAGEL, E., *et al. Logic, Methodology and Philosophy of Science*, Stanford University Press, Stanford, Calif., 1960.

Neurath, O., *et al. International Encyclopedia of Unified Science*, University of Chicago Press, Chicago, 1955.

PERRY, T. A., ed. *Evidence and Argumentation in Linguistics*, Walter de Gruyter, Berlin, 1980.

PIATTELLI-PALMARINI, M., ed. *Language and Learning: The Debate Between Jean Piaget and Noam Chomsky*, Harvard University Press, Cambridge, Mass., 1981.

STEINBERG, D., and JAKOBVITS, L., eds. *Semantics*, Cambridge University Press, Cambridge, 1971.

BOOKS

Black, E. *Syntactic Theory*, Holt, Rinehart & Winston, New York, 1974.

Bloomfield, L. *Language*, Holt, New York, 1933.

— *Linguistics Aspects of Science*, University of Chicago Press, Chicago (*International Encyclopedia of Unified Science*), 1939.

Botha, R. *The Methodological Status of Grammatical Argumentation*, Mouton & Co., The Hague, 1971.

— and Winckler, W. *The Justification of Linguistic Hypotheses*, Mouton & Co., The Hague, 1973.

Chomsky, Noam, *Syntactic Structures*, Mouton & Co., The Hague, 1957.

— *Aspects of a Theory of Syntax*, MIT Press, Cambridge, Mass., 1965.

— *Language and Mind* (enlarged edition), Harcourt Brace Javanovich, New York, 1972.

— *The Logical Structure of Linguistic Theory*, Plenum Press, New York, 1975. (Especially Introduction.)

— *Reflections on Language*, Pantheon, New York, 1975.

— *Essays on Form and Interpretation*, North-Holland, New York, 1977.

— *Rules and Representations*, Columbia University Press, New York, 1980.

Copper, W. S. *Foundations of Logico-Linguistics*, Reidel, Dordrecht, 1978.

Field, H. *Science Without Numbers*, Oxford University Press, Oxford, 1981.

Fodor, J. A. *The Language of Thought*, Crowell, New York, 1975.

Fodor, J. D., *Semantics: Theories of Meaning in Generative Grammar*, Harper and Row, New York, 1977.

Frege, G. *The Basic Laws of Arithmetic*, University of California Press, Berkeley, Calif., 1967.

Harris, Z. S. *Methods in Structural Linguistics*, University of Chicago Press, Chicago, 1951.

Husserl, E. *Logical Investigations 1*, Humanities Press, New York, 1970.
Itkonen, E. *Linguistics and Metascience*, Societas Philosophica et Phaenomenologica Finlandiae, Kokemaki, 1974. (Studia Philosophica Turkuensia.)
— *Grammatical Theory and Metascience*, John Benjamens, Amsterdam, 1978.
Johnston, D. E., and Postal, P. *Arc-Pair Grammar*, Princeton University Press, Princeton, 1980.
Kasher, A., and Lappin, S. *Philosophical Linguistics*, Scripto-Verlag, Kronberg. 1977.
Katz, J. J. *Language and Other Abstract Objects*, Rowman & Littlefield, Totowa, NJ, 1981.
Langendoen, D. T., and Postal, P. *The Vastness of Language*, Blackwell, Oxford, 1984.
Lenneberg, Eric H. *Biological Foundations of Language*, Wiley, New York, 1967.
Montague, R. *Formal Philosophy*, Yale University Press, New Haven, 1974.
Quine, W. V. O. *From a Logical Point of View*, Harper & Row, New York, 1953.
— *Word and Object*, MIT Press, Cambridge, Mass., and Wiley, New York, 1960.
Russell, Bertrand. *An Inquiry into Meaning and Truth*, Allen and Unwin, London and Norton, New York, 1940.
Saussure, F. de. *Course in General Linguistics*, trans. W. Baskin, Philosophical Library, New York, 1959. (McGraw-Hill paperback, 1966.)
Vendler, Z. *Linguistics in Philosophy*, Cornell University Press, Ithaca, 1967.
Wittgenstein, L. *Philosophical Investigations*, Basil Blackwell, Oxford, 1953.

ARTICLES

Benacerraf, P. 'Mathematical Truth', *Journal of Philosophy*, 70 (1973), 661-79.
Black, M. 'Comment on Noam Chomsky's "Problems of Explanation in Linguistics" ' (1970). In BORGER and CIOFFI*, pp. 124-88.
Bever, T. G. 'Some Implications of the Non-Specific Basis of Languages' (1982). In GLEITMAN and WANNAR.
Bloomfield, L. 'Language or Ideas', *Language*, 12 (1936), 89-95.
Botha, R. P. 'Protecting General-Linguistic Hypotheses from Refutation', *Stellenbosch Papers in Linguistics*, 1 (1978), 1-31.
— 'Methodological Bases of a Progressive Mentalism', *Stellenbosch Papers in Linguistics*, 3 (1979).
Bresnan, J. 'Toward a Realistic Model of Transformational Grammar' (1978). In HALLE, *et al.*
Brouwer, L. E. J. 'Intuitionism and Formalism' (1913). In BENACERRAF and PUTNAM, pp. 66-77.
Carnap, R. 'Empiricism, Semantics and Ontology' (1952). In LINSKY, pp. 208-30.
Chomsky, Noam, 'A Transformational Approach to Syntax' (1962). In Hill, A. A., ed., *Proceedings of the 1958 Conference on Problems of Linguistic Analysis of English*, University of Texas Press, Austin, 1958.
— 'Explanatory Models in Linguistics' (1962). In NAGEL.
— 'Deep Structure, Surface Structure, and Semantic Interpretation'. In STEINBERG and JAKOBVITS, pp. 183-216.
— 'A Theory of Core Grammar', *Glot*, 1 (1978), 7-26.
— 'Discussion of Putnam's Comments' (1980). In PIATTELLI-PALMARINI, pp. 310-24.

*For full citation see capitalized author entries in Anthology section.

Chomsky, Noam and Katz, J. J. 'What the Linguist is Talking About', *The Journal of Philosophy*, 71 (1974), 347–67.
— — 'On Innateness: a Reply to Cooper', *Philosophical Review*, 84 (1975), 70–87.
Copper, D. E. 'Innateness Old and New', *Philosophical Review*, 81 (1972), 465–83.
Fodor, J. A., and Garrett, M. 'Some Reflections on Competence and Performance' (1966). In L YONS and WALES, pp. 135–82.
Fodor, J. A., *et al.* 'The Psychological Unreality of Semantic Representations', *Linguistic Inquiry*, 6 (1975), 515–32.
Gödel, K. 'What is Cantor's Continuum Problem' (1964). In BENACERRAF and PUTNAM, pp. 258–73.
Goodman, N. and Quine, W. V. O. 'Steps Toward a Constructive Nominalism', *The Journal of Symbolic Logic*, 12 (1947), 1–25.
Harman, G. 'Psychological Aspects of the Theory of Syntax', *Journal of Philosophy*, 64 (1967), 75–87.
Harris, Z. S. 'Discourse Analysis', *Language*, 28 (1952), 18–23.
— 'Distributional Structure', *Word*, 10 (1954), 146–62.
— 'Co-occurrence and Transformation in Linguistic Structure', *Language*, 33 (1957), 293–340.
— 'Transformational Theory', *Language*, 41 (1965), 363–401.
Higgenbotham, J. 'Is Grammar Psychological?' In Cauman, L. S., Levi, I., Parsons, C., and Schwartz, R., eds. *How Many Questions?*, Hackett Publishing Co., Indianapolis, 1983, pp. 170–179.
Itkonen, E. 'Transformational Grammar and the Philosophy of Science'. In KOERNER, pp. 381–445.
— 'Concerning the Relationship Between Linguistics and Logic', Indiana Linguistics Club, 1975.
— 'Linguistics and Empiricalness: Answers to Criticisms', *Publications of the General Linguistics Department of the University of Helsinki*, 4 (1976).
— 'The Relation Between Grammar and Sociolinguistics', *Forum Linguisticum*, 1 (1977), 238–54.
— 'Qualitative vs. Quantitative Analysis in Linguistics'. In Perry.
— 'Rationality as an Explanatory Principle in Linguistics', *Festschrift für Eugenio Ooseriu*, eds. H. Geckeler, *et al.* Gunter Narr, Tübingen, 1981.
Katz, J. J. 'Mentalism in Linguistics', *Language*, 40 (1964), 124–37.
— 'The Real Status of Semantic Representations', *Linguistic Inquiry*, 8 (1977), 559–84.
Kiparsky, P. 'Historical Linguistics'. In L YONS, pp. 302–15.
Labov, W. 'Empirical Foundations of Linguistic Theory'. In AUSTERLITZ, pp. 77–133.
Lees, R. B. 'Review of Chomsky', *Language*, 33 (1957), 375–407.
Parsons, C. 'Foundations of Mathematics' (1967), *The Encyclopedia of Philosophy*, ed. P. Edwards, Vol. 5, pp. 188–213.
Partee, B. 'Linguistic Metatheory'. In DINGWALL, pp. 650–80, and HARMAN, pp. 303–16.
— 'Montague Grammar, Mental Representations and Reality' (1979), in FRENCH, *et al.*, pp. 195–208.
Postal, P. 'The Best Theory', In *The Goals of Linguistic Theory*, Prentice-Hall, Inc., Englewood Cliffs, NJ, pp. 131–70.
Putnam, H. 'What is Innate and Why: Comments on the Debate', In PIATTELLI-PALMARINI, pp. 287–309.

Quine, W. V. O. 'Carnap and Logical Truth' (1954), *The Ways of Paradox*, Random House, New York, 1966, pp. 100–26.
— 'Two Dogmas of Empiricism', *From a Logical Point of View*, Harvard University Press, Cambridge, Mass., 1961.
— 'Methodological Reflections on Current Linguistic Theory', *Synthese*, 21 (1970), 386–98.
Ringen, J. 'Linguistic Facts: a Study of the Empirical Scientific Status of Transformational Generative Grammars'. In COHEN and WIRTH, pp. 1–41.
— Review of *Linguistics and Metascience*, by E. Itkonen, *Language*, 53 (1977), 411–17.
Vendler, Z. 'Linguistics and the a-priori'. In *Linguistics in Philosophy*, Cornell University Press, Ithaca, pp. 1–32. Reprinted in LYAS, pp. 245–68.
Weinreich, U., *et al.*, 'Empirical Foundations for a Theory of Language Change', In LEHMANN and MALKEIL, pp. 95–195.
Zwicky, A. 'Linguistics as Chemistry: the Substance Theory of Semantic Primes', In ANDERSON and KIPARSKY, pp. 467–85.

INDEX OF NAMES